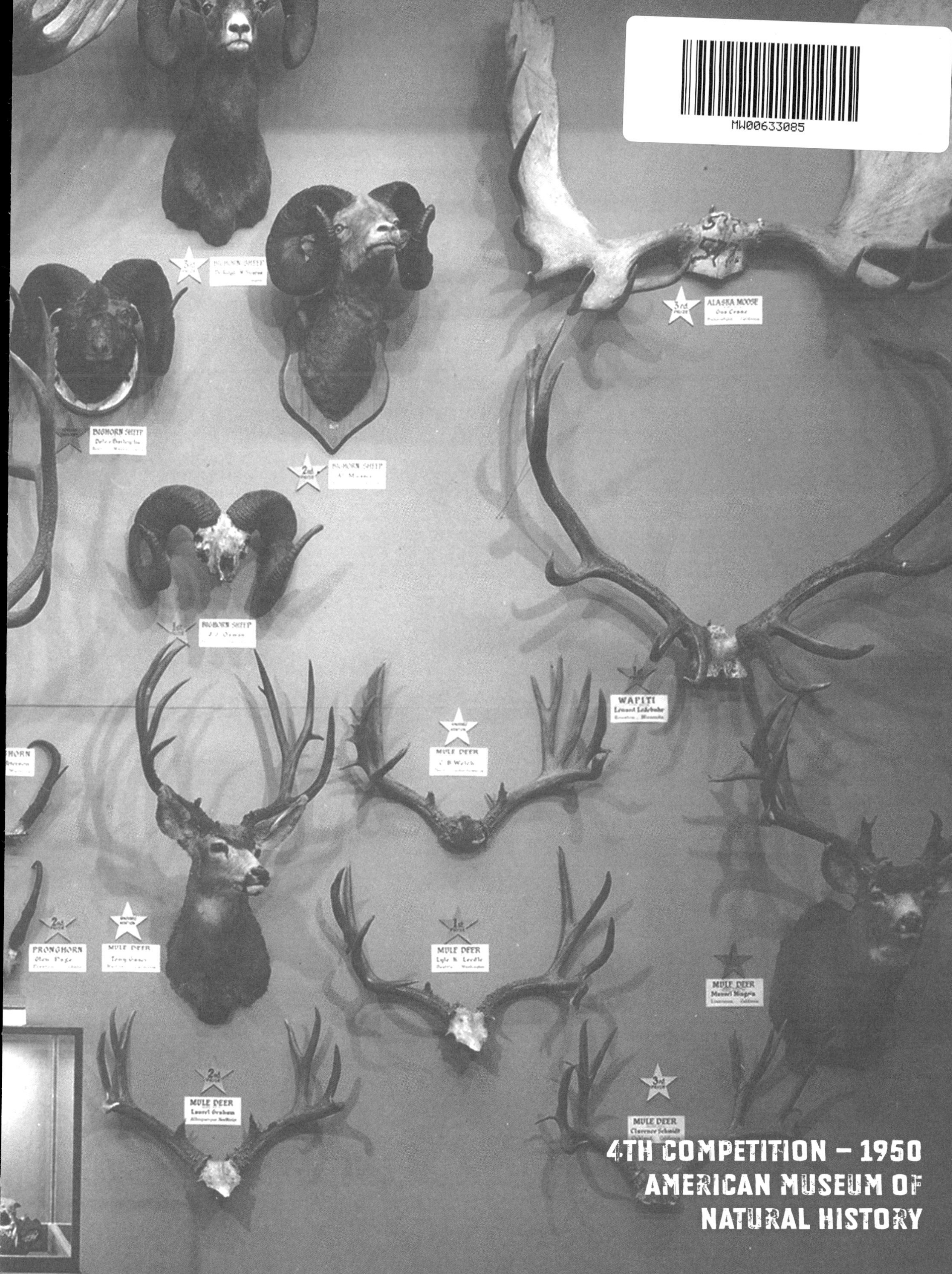

BIGHORN SHEEP
ALASKA MOOSE
3rd PRIZE
BIGHORN SHEEP
2nd PRIZE
BIGHORN SHEEP
1st
BIGHORN SHEEP
WAPITI
MULE DEER
PRONGHORN
MULE DEER
MULE DEER
MULE DEER
MULE DEER
MULE DEER
4TH COMPETITION – 1950
AMERICAN MUSEUM OF
NATURAL HISTORY

OFFICIAL.

AN AMERICAN ELK RETROSPECTIVE:

Vintage Photos and Memorabilia from the Boone and Crockett Club Archives

BOONE & CROCKETT CLUB N.A.B.G. COMPETITION - 1961 - 10TH N. 4301

AN AMERICAN ELK RETROSPECTIVE:
Vintage Photos and Memorabilia from the Boone and Crockett Club Archives

First Edition 2010

Library of Congress Catalog Card Number: 2010941332
ISBN Number: 978-0-940864-70-2
Published December 2010

Published in the United States of America
by the
Boone and Crockett Club
250 Station Drive
Missoula, MT 59801
406/542-1888
406/542-0784 (fax)
www.booneandcrockettclub.com

OFFICIAL.

AN AMERICAN ELK RETROSPECTIVE:

BOONE & CROCKETT CLUB N.A.B.G. COMPETITION - 10th - 1961

Vintage Photos and Memorabilia from the Boone and Crockett Club Archives

Published by the Boone and Crockett Club

Missoula, Montana

2010

Nº 730-
Date
6/13/46
Classifications and Tariffs in Effect on Date of Issue
Weight
of Contents)
City
Street
FREMONT CO.
SERIES (TOPOGRAPHIC)
Green
7500
7600
7700
7000
7300
30
WAPITI
X KILL
OCT 6, 196
NTY hunters had what could be called a mediocre de
k season has been relatively good. In the top photo, B
t and Don King right display three racks from elk bagged
Range of Northwest Oregon. The third set belongs to M
Wirth. The carcasses weighed between 400 and 600 pour
29, 1964
he News-Register, McMinnville, Orego

PREFACE

"MY Dear Nimrods..." So starts the letter in 1888 by Dall DeWeese about his elk hunting trip in Colorado. Most of us have no idea that our words, our clothes, our cars, and — as hunters — our guns, stamp our existence in time.

Once we look back in retrospect, it is obvious. We love to look back. Ask any hunter and he or she will be happy to tell you how it was in "the good ole days." We are all fascinated with times past. Somehow, we think the days of our grandparents were better. We long for them. We feel we somehow missed out. Yet, with a photograph we can go back. We can immerse ourselves into the photo, studying the person, the animal, the surroundings. I can, or at least I think I can, get an idea about what that person was like in the photo. In this retrospective, it is more than just the animal, the "trophy," that attracts our attention, it is the person who can tell its story.

E.A. Savage traveled from his home in Minnesota to Park County, Montana, where he and his hunting partner collected two fine wapiti and a couple mule deer bucks. Savage's bull was entered in the 1956 Competition with a score of 372-7/8 points.

This book, with its hundreds of pictures, also tells a story. Yes, it is the story of the success of the North American Model of Wildlife Conservation, but more important, it tells the story of individuals through pictures. Their characters come through to us in these still shots in time. They are proud and happy to display their elk, even if the times dictated they not smile or even look into the camera — actions that also date them.

The founding principle for the Boone and Crockett Club's measurement of heads and horns was to preserve them in posterity. When the Club started to keep records, it must be remembered that they were trying to document animals thought to be headed toward extinction. The dedicated founders of the Boone and Crockett Club had no idea that the North American Model of Wildlife Conservation would succeed and so many more trophies would be recorded. Record we did and we did it well. In this book of pictures, we bring to you a legacy of elk hunters, men and women of all walks of life — rich, poor, city and country. It tells the story of their success – and our hunting heritage — in all respects.

Enjoy,

Howard P. Monsour, Jr.
Chairman, Publications Committee
Boone and Crockett Club

TABLE OF CONTENTS
AN AMERICAN ELK RETROSPECTIVE

PREFACE................ V
By Howard P. Monsour, Jr.

INTRODUCTION IX
By Eldon L. "Buck" Buckner

CHAPTER ONE 1

Scoring Wapiti
Boone and Crockett Club's long-time Director of Big Game Records discusses the history of the wapiti category for records keeping and the changes in scoring, as well as the addition of non-typical trophies, Roosevelt's elk, and tule elk.

By Jack Reneau

CHAPTER TWO . . . 12

Distribution
Near the turn of the century, when the Boone and Crockett Club was being formed, elk had been nearly extirpated throughout most of their range. From this tragic low, modern-day, hunter-conservationists brought them back from the brink. A significant portion of current populations were reintroduced from a few remaining elk that were found in Yellowstone, thanks to the protection afforded them by its designation as the first National Park and the enforcement of its regulations by Boone and Crockett Club members. This chapter demonstrates the gradual return of elk to their historic range by tracking the entries and using these numbers as the indicators of elk populations from around North America.

By Justin Spring

CHAPTER THREE.....28

Vintage Photographs and Memorabilia
Since the dawn of time, man the hunter has kept for posterity symbols of the hunt. Cave paintings tell the story of a respect for the hunted and the hunter. Antlers and horns were kept as tools and mementos. Later, antlers, horns, and head skins were used to decorate European castles representing man's dominion over the land and the value of the landowner's holdings, including wildlife. With the advent of a camera small enough and affordable for public use, hunting photography slowing came into being in the late 1800s as the latest in a progression of keeping hunting memories alive. Along with this new technology the field photo was born.

By Keith Balfourd

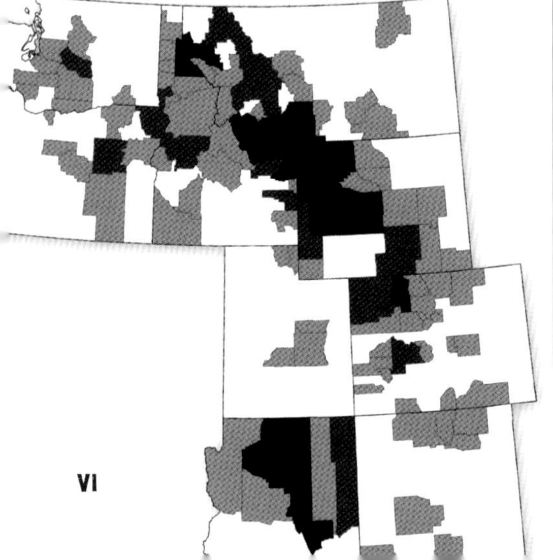

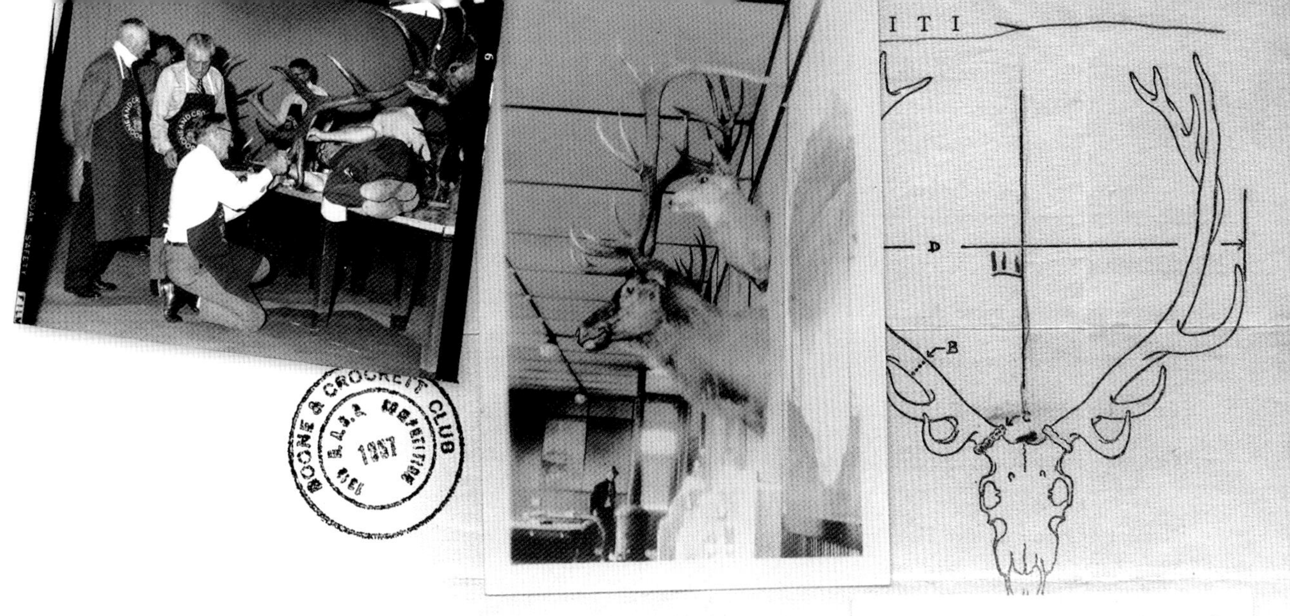

Award-Winning Elk

The Boone and Crockett Club has a history in records-keeping dating back over a hundred years. However, the first competition wasn't held by the Club until 1947. Since that first competition, a new scoring system was adopted, which quickly became the universally accepted standard for measuring native North American big game in 1950. This chapter highlights numerous prize-winning elk from the first competition through the 16th Awards Program.

By Richard T. Hale

Special Trophies

All Boone and Crockett trophies are special. Some are bigger and rank higher than others. Some are more significant for the place and time they were taken, by whom and how. The stories behind how some trophies made their way to national recognition are fascinating, and therefore make these trophies extra special. There are trophies so odd or unusual the fact that nature created them makes these rare specimens special. And there are trophies that held the distinction of being the largest on record or the recipient of B&C's highest honor. This chapter is dedicated to the standouts from the Boone and Crockett elk archives.

By Keith Balfourd

Grancel Fitz

Although he was never a member of the Boone and Crockett Club, Grancel Fitz had a profound effect on Club activities as one of the fathers of the Club's unique scoring system. A long-time advocate of an improved way to judge North American trophies, he wrote an extensive chapter on his views for the 1939 Boone and Crockett book, *North American Big Game*, the second book to rank big game trophies. The 1952 *Records of North American Big Game* was the first to incorporate all previous and new entries under the newly adopted system. Grancel and his wife, Betty, are credited with tireless work in re-evaluating previous records and were heavily involved in the North American Big Game Competitions.

By Theodore J. Holsten, Jr.

WONDERFUL WORLD OF SPORT

THE BIGGEST AND BEST

THIS SILENTLY ELOQUENT gallery in New York's Museum of Natural History drew outdoorsmen from across the continent last week—86 trophies in 25 North American categories representing the best of the big-game bag of the last two years. The occasion was the biennial awards dinner of the Boone and Crockett Club, official scorekeepers of North American game records.

Three of the prizes set new world records: a polar bear taken off Point Hope, Alaska by Tom F. Bolack of New Mexico; a white-tail deer shot in his home state by John A. Breen of Minnesota; and a mule deer with a mysterious past—it was discovered in a saloon by a Wyoming taxidermist, history and hunter forgotten. But the top excitement and the top award, the Sagamore Hill Medal, were for an elk shot by Fred C. Mercer of Montana. With right and left antler lengths totaling 10 feet, it was judged "the elk of the century." After a month's display in New York, the trophies will be taken off museum walls and shipped to their proud owners. Boone and Crockett experts find trophy hunting increasing, believe that even better trophies still await the hunter.

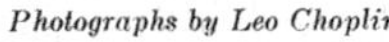

Photographs by Leo Choplin

"ELK OF CENTURY" (*above*) won top award among trophies (*opposite*) in Boone and Crockett Club competition.

INTRODUCTION

BY ELDON L. "BUCK" BUCKNER

My introduction to both elk and elk hunting occurred in 1966 when I was assigned range and wildlife management duties for the Apache National Forest in the White Mountains of Arizona. Modern-day trophy elk hunters will recognize this area and the adjacent White Mountain Apache Reservation as the Shangri-La for big bulls. I shot my first elk that November on a horseback hunt beneath the Mogollon Rim. To someone living on a young ranger's salary, the meat from that cow was more valued than any trophy antlers.

Since then, my experience with elk has been rather narrow, geographically — consisting of Arizona, Oregon, Idaho, Utah — but deep in its variety. As a ranger, I observed elk, photographed them, studied their grazing habits, helped the game department with classification counts, and conducted exams for parasites at hunter check stations. When, in 1968, I was appointed a Boone and Crockett Official Measurer, I measured more elk than any other species and witnessed first-hand the evolution of wapiti scoring systems and categories described by Jack Reneau in Chapter One. Later, as an Oregon rancher, I cussed elk for devouring my hay stacks and destroying fences, but as a game department advisory board member, I also recommended elk habitat improvement projects. I've worked as an elk guide and outfitter partner, experiencing all the hard work and frustration of that business, too. And, lastly, as an elk hunter who often uses a traditional muzzle-loader or iron-sighted vintage rifle, I've learned the difficulty of stalking close while a six-pointer approaches within ten feet as I stand, motionless, in open timber.

LEFT: The Club's 9th Competition was featured in the March 28, 1960, issue of Sports Illustrated. Fred C. Mercer of Montana received the Sagamore Hill Medal for taking what many claimed was "the elk of the century."

Since the 1960s, elk numbers in Arizona have greatly increased, as has distribution within that state. Chapter Two of this book shows a similar, phenomenal distribution increase throughout the Rocky Mountain region. With the help of such organizations as the Rocky Mountain Elk Foundation, elk have been reestablished east to Pennsylvania and south to Kentucky in huntable numbers.

The evolution of field photos is well-covered in Chapter Three by Keith Balfourd. Vintage photos predated political correctness and high-tech equipment, providing a glimpse for a younger generation of an era many of us remember with nostalgia.

The first Boone and Crockett Big Game Competition of 1947, which later morphed into the present Big Game Awards, was the spark that ignited the current interest in trophy hunting. The chapter introduced by B&C Judge Richard Hale highlights trophy elk of these events, through the 16th Awards of 1974 to 1976. Several of these award-winning elk are worthy of mentioning.

Outdoor Life *First Choice of Discriminating Sportsmen*

353 FOURTH AVENUE · NEW YORK 10, N.Y.

January 18, 1955

Mrs. Betty Fitz
c/o "Records of North American
Big Game"
5 Tudor City Place
New York 17, N.Y.

Dear Betty:

That terrific elk head shot by Bacus is at a store called "The Western Outfitters" at Grangeville, Idaho. It's in the custody of George Pfeffer. I am quite sure that you could get the head. Bacus is not interested in it. He is a meat hunter, not a head hunter; but George and I will send it in if you want it. By that time it probably will have shrunk a bit and it can be measured in New York.

I certainly hope Grancel gets his jaguar. I have never shot one of the darned things. How was the Texas deer hunt?

That elk head is the most impressive thing that I have ever seen in the way of an elk head.

Regards to Grancel,

My best wishes,

Jack

Jack O'Connor
Box 382
Lewiston, Idaho

JO'C:DC

File

I've had a letter from Bacus. See attached.

Note chart

I sent Jack a card & asked him if he scored the head. He does not answer my question.

This letter not ack.

B.1

The first place winner for the 1946 Competition was a winter-killed bull that sported 62-inch main beams, picked up by Elmer Keith in Idaho. (This single measurement determined trophy rank until the system changed in 1950.) Keith was a colorful Idaho rancher and prolific gun writer of the big-bore persuasion. His ongoing jousting in print with smaller-bore .270 fan, Jack O'Connor entertained two generations of readers, myself included, until it ended in 1982 with a stroke.

Ray Holes' saddle shop has been well-known to ranchers and outfitters in northeastern Oregon and Idaho for more than 50 years. It was interesting to me to learn that Ray's Idaho bull shot in 1945 in the Selway won the 1948 prize with beam length of 59-1/4 inches.

A letter from my old friend, Jack O'Connor, to B&C Records Secretary Betty Fitz alerted her to a huge bull shot by Elmer Bacus in the fall of 1954. Jack, then an Official Measurer for B&C, said the bull was the largest he'd ever seen. It won the 7th Competition with a score of 412-5/8. It also was from Idaho.

Dr. Phil Wright, former B&C Records Chairman, was obviously delighted when he wrote of measuring a 386-7/8 bull shot by Mildred Eder in 1969 with a .30-30 carbine. Eder, who ran a Montana ranch with her husband, grew up hunting and had learned bullet placement was much more important than the rifle caliber used.

Special elk trophies are featured in Chapter Five. They include the oldest elk trophy now in the record book, taken in 1850, as well as an even older head from the 1803 Lewis and Clark Expedition. Two Sagamore Hill Award winners are found in this section: Dr. Bentzen's trophy, found in a barn and believed taken in 1890, was the 1950 recipient, while Fred Mercer's Montana bull won the elite award in 1958. Mercer's big elk can be seen at Rocky Mountain Elk Foundation headquarters in Missoula.

LEFT: Jack O'Connor, then an Official Measurer for B&C, alerted B&C Records Secretary Betty Fitz about a bull which he claimed was the largest he'd ever seen. It won the 7th Competition with a score of 412-5/8.

Another story in the Chapter Five highlights the tale of a Roosevelt's elk, shot in 1949, lost, re-discovered in 1984, declared the World's Record in 1986, and finally restored to its original owner in 1990, is a fascinating saga in the book.

This book concludes with a biography of Grancel Fitz by B&C historian and noted book collector Theodore J. Holsten. Fitz was the man most closely associated with the B&C scoring system adopted in 1950 and authored chapters in early records books and the first scoring manuals. He was also the first hunter to collect all legal species of North American big game animals. Guided by the legendary Ned Frost, Fitz collected his bull elk in Wyoming in 1930. The bull had an inside spread of 52-3/8 inches and scored 331-6/8 years later, when the B&C minimum score was first set at 330.

Any elk hunter, veteran or novice, will find this book about as boring as having a grunting, rut-crazed bull charge through the jack pines to your call at rock-throwing distance. Enjoy!

OFFICIAL.

AN AMERICAN ELK RETROSPECTIVE:

BOONE & CROCKETT CLUB
N.A.B.G. COMPETITION
- 1961 -

Vintage Photos and Memorabilia from the Boone and Crockett Club Archives

Head-Measurements of the Trophies at the Madison Square Garden Sportsmen's Exhibition

During the week beginning May 14, 1895, there was held in Madison Square Garden, New York, a Sportsmen's Exhibition. There was a fair exhibit of heads, horns and skins, for which the credit largely belongs to Frederick S. Webster, the taxidermist.

At the request of the managers of the Exhibition, three of the members of the Boone and Crockett Club—Messrs. Theodore Roosevelt, George Bird Grinnell and Archibald Rogers—were appointed a Committee on Measurements. There were heads and skins of every kind of North American big game. Many of them were exhibited by amateur sportsmen, including various members of the Boone and Crockett Club, while many others were exhibited by furriers and taxidermists.

Some of the measurements are worth recording. For convenience we tabulate, in the case of each animal, the measurements of the specimens exhibited by amateur sportsmen who themselves shot the animals. For purposes of comparison we add the measurements of a few …ds exhibited by taxidermists or furriers; also for … we quote the figures given in

In Buxton's catalogue the largest measurements given were for a specimen which girthed 5⅛ inches, and was in length 15¾ inches.

In Ward's catalogue the two biggest specimens given measured respectively 15¾ inches in length by 6¼ inches in girth, and 12⅞ inches in length by 6½ inches in girth.

WAPITI OR ROUND-HORN ELK.

	Girth.	Length.	Spread.	Points.
15. A. Rogers, Northwestern Wyoming.	8	64¼	48	7+7
16. G. O. Shields, Clark's Fork, Wyo..	8¼	51⅜	50	6+7
17. T. Roosevelt, Two Ocean Pass, '91.	6⅞	56½	46⅜	6+6
18. T. Roosevelt, Two Ocean Pass, '91.	7¾	50¾	47	6+6
19. P. Liebinger, Indian Creek, Mont.	6⅛	50½	54	8+8

No. 15, as far as we know, is th…

1: WAPITI RECORDS

BY JACK RENEAU

Boone and Crockett Club members' interest in scoring and records-keeping runs deep into its history. On May 14, 1895, only eight years after the Club's founding, organizers of a Sportsmen's Exhibition at Madison Square Garden in New York City appointed Theodore Roosevelt, George Bird Grinnell, and Archibald Rogers — all of them founding Club members — to a special Committee on Measurements. An article summarizing their scoring efforts is detailed in a chapter that appeared in a B&C book in 1895, titled *Hunting in Many Lands*. The scoring system used then for elk was quite basic and critiqued as inadequate by the author of the article. Measurements included length and girth (circumference) of the larger antler, as well as the spread and number of points on each antler.

It wasn't until July 16, 1902, that Boone and Crockett Club's Executive Committee Chairman appointed Roosevelt, Rogers, and Caspar Whitney to a special subcommittee to devise a standard system by which all categories of North American big game, including American elk, would be rated. It's assumed Roosevelt enthusiastically embraced this assignment.

The reason for creating such a system might hold surprises. The Club wasn't interested in creating a scoring system to provide "bragging rights" for hunters. Rather, members pessimistically believed that most categories of North American big game, if not all, were in danger of extinction at that time. For example, American elk, which were widespread and estimated to number around 10 million prior to 1804 when Lewis and Clark explored the western frontier, were isolated in small, remote pockets in the mountains of the west and numbered fewer than 150,000 by 1887 when the Club was founded. Numbers continued to diminish further each year as the west was explored and settled.

Pages from the Club's 1895 book, *Hunting with Many Lands*, which included a special chapter about Roosevelt's involvement with the 1895 Sportsmen's Exhibition at Madison Square Garden in New York City.

Market hunting to provide meat, furs, and feathers for sale was rampant. "Hunting" was a 24/7 activity participated in by many to feed their families and clear the land of competition for domesticated livestock. There were no bag limits, sex or age restrictions, seasons, method of harvest restrictions, etc.

Bison, which once numbered an estimated 60 million, were reduced to fewer than a hundred wild animals by the late 1800s. Club members had every reason to be concerned about the future of North America's native big game. Extinction of our treasured wildlife was a distinct possibility.

The true reason Boone and Crockett Club members were interested in records-keeping at that time was to draw attention to this serious plight and to preserve viable statistical data so that future generations, such as ours, would

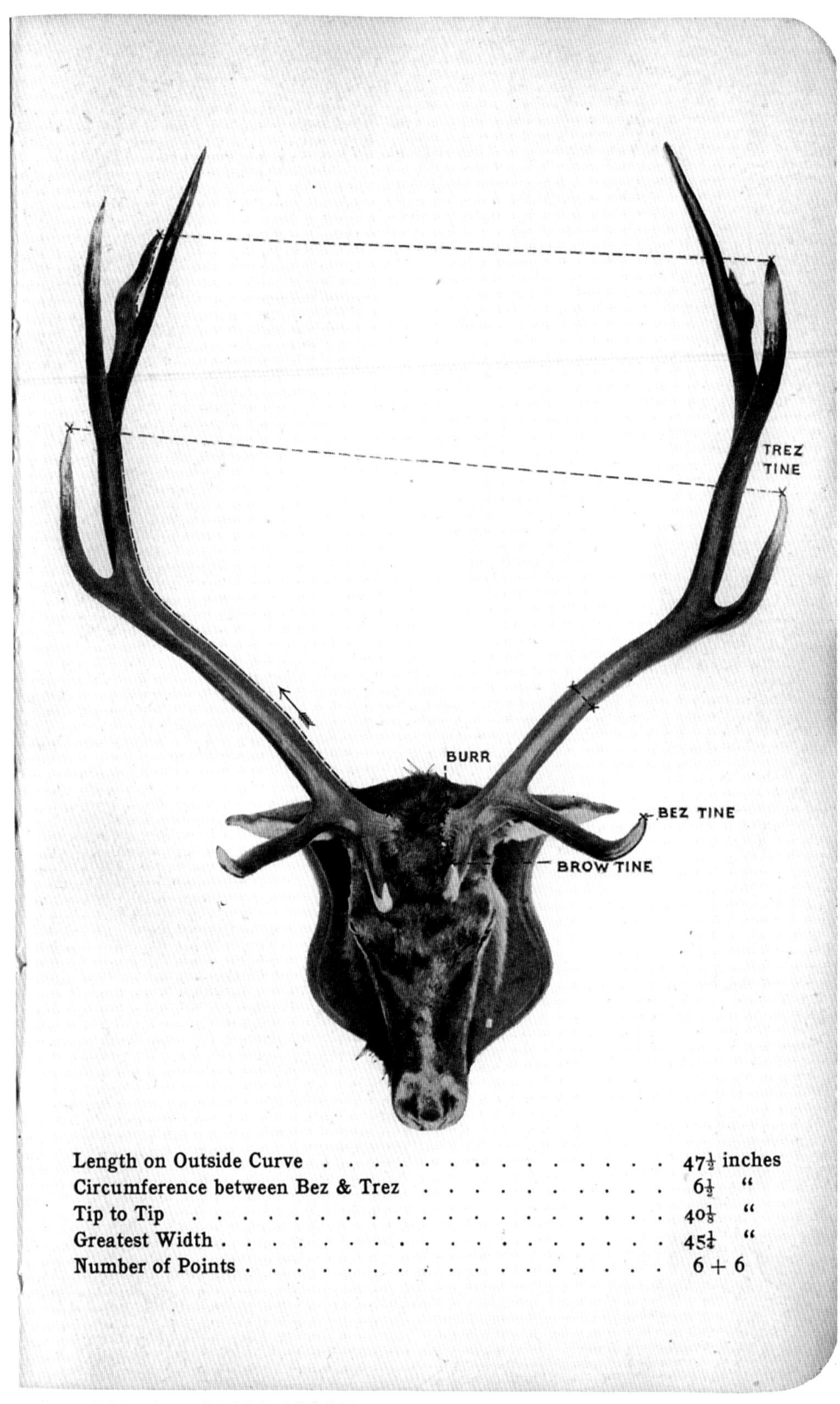

Length on Outside Curve	$47\frac{1}{2}$ inches
Circumference between Bez & Trez	$6\frac{1}{2}$ "
Tip to Tip	$40\frac{1}{8}$ "
Greatest Width	$45\frac{1}{4}$ "
Number of Points	6 + 6

know the sizes these animals attained should they go extinct.

The scoring system created for elk by Roosevelt and his fellow subcommittee members was quite primitive and published in B&C's first scoring manual, *Big Game Measurements* by James H. Kidder, in 1906. Only two copies of this rare, leather-bound, pocket-sized book are known to exist today. At that time, elk were known as wapiti, an Algonquin word meaning "white rump."

Under this system, scorers recorded the greatest spread and four measurements on each antler — namely the length of each beam, a circumference between the first and second points, the circumference of each burr, and the number of points on each antler. All elk, including non-typical elk, Roosevelt's elk, and, potentially, tule elk, were listed in one category by the length of the longer antler.

While this was a valiant attempt to create a standard scoring system by which all elk would be scored, it isn't hard to imagine how inequitable this scoring system really was. For example, I once saw a bull elk with a six-point antler on one side and a long, single spike on the other side. If that spike measured over 60 inches, it could have been ranked No. 1 and considered a World's Record at that time, but it obviously wouldn't be representative of a true trophy bull. It would be an oddity of nature.

The first two editions of B&C's All-time records book, which were published in 1932 and 1939, used this early scoring system to list and rank trophies. There were 40 elk specimens listed in the former, with main beam lengths ranging from 54-3/8 inches to 64-4/8 inches long; in the later edition, 128 were listed with beam lengths ranging in length from 55 inches to 64-6/8 inches. While it was a valiant effort to start a scoring system, it should be obvious to the average hunter how inadequate this system really was.

The Club's first ever measurer's manual was published in 1906 and included instructions on how to properly measure wapiti. Methods of changed dramatically since this publication.

The 1939 edition's significant contributions included a chapter authored by Grancel Fitz, noted hunter and outdoor writer at that time, who proposed a more comprehensive scoring system by which elk and other categories of big game could be more equitably and objectively scored and ranked. His chapter also critiqued another scoring system devised in 1935 and already in use by B&C Club member and noted New York taxidermist James L. Clark. Like Clark's system, Fitz's took into account numerous measurements, including the lengths of the main beams and points and four circumferences on both antlers; it also included deductions for lack of symmetry.

Progress on Fitz's proposed system was delayed by the outbreak of World War II. In 1949, Samuel B. Webb was appointed by the Club to chair a subcommittee consisting of Dr. Harold E. Anthony, Milford Baker, and Frederick K. Barbour, as well as Clark and Fitz, with the purpose of devising a more equitable and objective scoring system than those proposed by either Clark or Fitz. As you might guess, there was considerable friction between Clark and Fitz, but Webb was able to keep the committee on task so that a complete scoring system for native North American big game was introduced in 1950 with 15 score charts.

Prior to release of the Club's current copyrighted system, the committee's scoring system was reviewed by hundreds of outdoor writers, hunters, taxidermists, big game managers, museum curators, etc. Clark was given credit on the back of the 1950 score charts for devising the first scoring system and Fitz was given credit for creating the second. This statement apparently settled differences between these two gentlemen and gave recognition where it was really due.

The minimum entry score for elk, or wapiti as the category was called at its introduction in 1950, was set at 340 points. By 1968, the All-

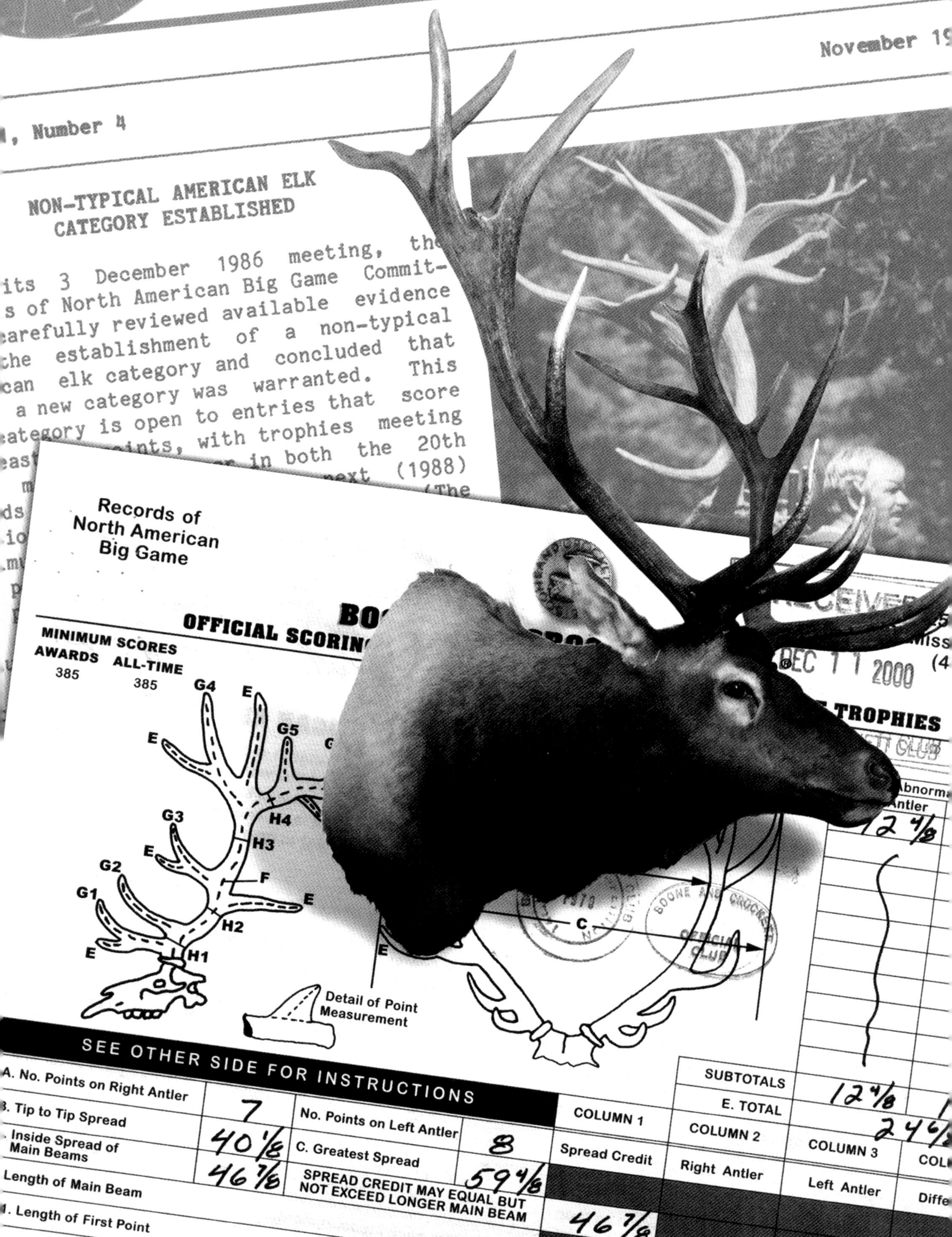

November 19
, Number 4
NON-TYPICAL AMERICAN ELK
CATEGORY ESTABLISHED
its 3 December 1986 meeting, the
s of North American Big Game Commit-
carefully reviewed available evidence
the establishment of a non-typical
can elk category and concluded that
a new category was warranted. This
category is open to entries that score
ints, with trophies meeting
in both the 20th
next (1988)
Records of
North American
Big Game
OFFICIAL SCORING
MINIMUM SCORES
AWARDS ALL-TIME
385 385
G4 E G5 E G3 H4 H3 E G2 F E G1 H2 E H1
C
E
Detail of Point Measurement
DEC 11 2000
TROPHIES
Abnorm
Antler
12 4/8
SEE OTHER SIDE FOR INSTRUCTIONS
A. No. Points on Right Antler 7
No. Points on Left Antler 8
B. Tip to Tip Spread 40 1/8
Inside Spread of Main Beams 46 7/8
C. Greatest Spread 59 4/8
Length of Main Beam
SPREAD CREDIT MAY EQUAL BUT NOT EXCEED LONGER MAIN BEAM
1. Length of First Point
46 7/8
SUBTOTALS 12 4/8
E. TOTAL 24 4/
COLUMN 1
COLUMN 2
COLUMN 3
Spread Credit
Right Antler
Left Antler

time minimum was raised to 375 points. At the close of the 18th Awards Program (1980-1982) the Records Committee created a separate Awards Program records book that listed only those trophies accepted in a specific Awards Program. Because the records book allowed for listing more trophies, an Awards Program minimum score of 360 points was set for elk. Those trophies between 360 points and 374-7/8 points are listed in one Awards book, but do not carry over into the All-time records books. They are also listed in all future editions of *Records of North American Elk*.

The final score for elk since 1950, with one minor change, has been computed by adding a spread credit. Spread credit is based on the inside spread and can equal, but never exceed, the length of the longer antler. Spread credit is added to the lengths of the main beams, the lengths of all of the normal points, and the four circumferences taken on each antler. Deductions are made for differences between the lengths of the main beams, points, and circumferences. Also, the total of the lengths of all the abnormal points, which are those points outside the typical pattern of six or more normal points per antler, are also deducted.

While Sam Webb's committee created non-typical categories for whitetail and mule deer, or "freaks" as they were called in earlier days, they did not create a separate category for non-typical wapiti in 1950. So far as is known, there is no mention in the committee proceedings as to why they didn't create a non-typical category. One can guess that the committee was not aware of a significant number of non-typical elk at the time, necessitating the creation of such a category.

The Records Committee did not create a non-typical elk category until 1986 and only after considerable discussion. Even at that time, the members debated whether or not there were enough specimens to make such a category viable. The minimum score was set at 385 points for both the Awards and the All-time minimums, only ten inches higher than the minimum All-time minimum of 375 points for typical American elk.

In 1979, the Records Committee established the Roosevelt's elk category with a specific boundary for a larger subspecies of elk inhabiting Vancouver Island; coastal Washington; Oregon; northwest California; and Afognak and Raspberry Islands in Alaska. The detailed boundary for this subspecies is described in Boone and Crockett Club's book, *Measuring and Scoring North American Big Game Trophies*.

While Roosevelt's elk are bigger-bodied than American elk, their antlers are smaller and frequently develop "crown points" in the vicinity of the fourth point (G-4) and beyond. There are no deductions for differences between the normal G-5 points and beyond. These scoring differences allow credit for the unique characteristics of this subspecies.

While there are deductions for abnormal points outside the normal point pattern below the G-4 point, there is no non-typical Roosevelt's elk category. The Awards Program and All-time minimum scores for Roosevelt's elk are 275 points and 290 points, respectively.

Tule elk, which occur in central California, were designated as a separate category in 1998 after they were taken off the Endangered Species List. These smaller elk exhibit the same antler characteristics as Roosevelt's elk and are scored using the same chart. The Awards Program and All-time minimum scores for tule elk are set at 270 points and 285 points, respectively. They represent another true conservation success story hunters can be proud of.

The Club established the non-typical elk category in 1986. Since that time, several bulls that were originally entered as typical elk have been reviewed and at the owner's request, been switched to the non-typical category. Once such example is the current Oregon state record shown at left. This bull was taken by Lawton McDaniel in 1935 and is currently owned by Doug McDaniel.

COMMITTEE
ALFRED ELY, CHAIRMAN
HAROLD E. ANTHONY
R. R. M. CARPENTER

Records of North American Big Game

IN CARE OF
AMERICAN MUSEUM OF NATURAL HISTORY
COLUMBUS AVENUE AND 77TH STREET
NEW YORK, N. Y.

UNDER THE AUSPICES OF THE NATIONAL MUSEUM OF HEADS AND HORNS OF THE NEW YORK ZOOLOGICAL SOCIETY & THE BOONE & CROCKETT CLUB

W A P I T I

SPECIES ....

MEASUREMENTS	RIGHT	LEFT
Length on outside curve **A**	....	....
Circumference between bez and trez **B**	....	....
Circumference of burr **C**	....	....
Number of points on antler	....	....

Greatest spread: **D**..........

Exact locality where killed..........

Date killed ....

By whom killed ....

Owner ....

Address ....

Remarks: ....

....

Photographs: Front view..........Profile..........
(Please place √ mark to indicate photographs furnished.)

We hereby certify that we have measured the above described trophy on..........193 , and that these measurements are correct and made in accordance with the directions overleaf.

....

By ....

Front of the 1930s score chart for wapiti

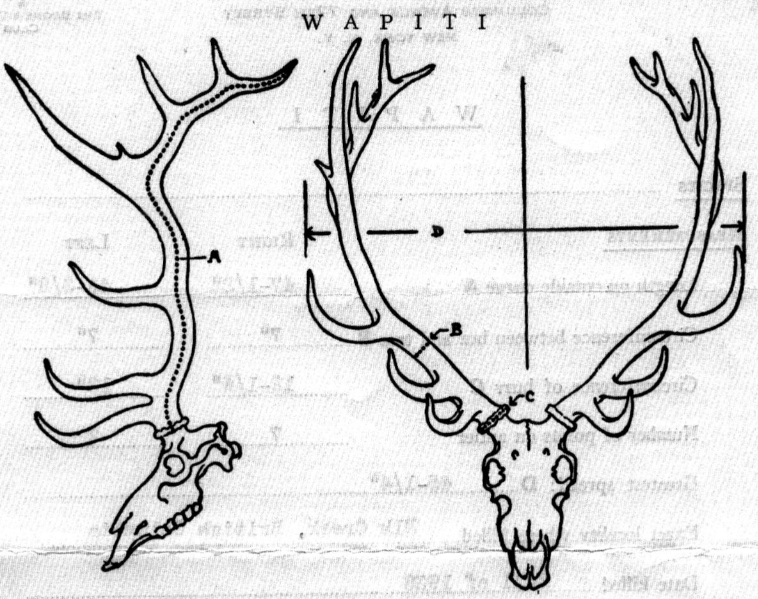

Method of Measuring

All measurements **must** be made with a steel tape.

A Length on outside curve: Measured along the main beam from the base of the burr to the tip of the most distant point on the main beam.

B Circumference midway between bez and trez.

C Circumference of burr.

D Greatest spread: Measured between perpendiculars at right angles to the center line of the skull.

Points on each side: No point shall be counted unless it protrudes at least two inches.

Remarks: State whether the trophy has any characteristics which depart from the normal for this species.

Please provide photographs showing front view and profile.

Back of the 1930s score chart for wapiti

OFFICIAL SCORING SYSTEM FOR NORTH AMERICAN BIG GAME TROPHIES

Records of North American
Big Game and North American
Big Game Competition

BOONE AND CROCKETT CLUB

% Am. Museum of Natural History
Central Park West at 79th Street
New York 24, New York

WAPITI

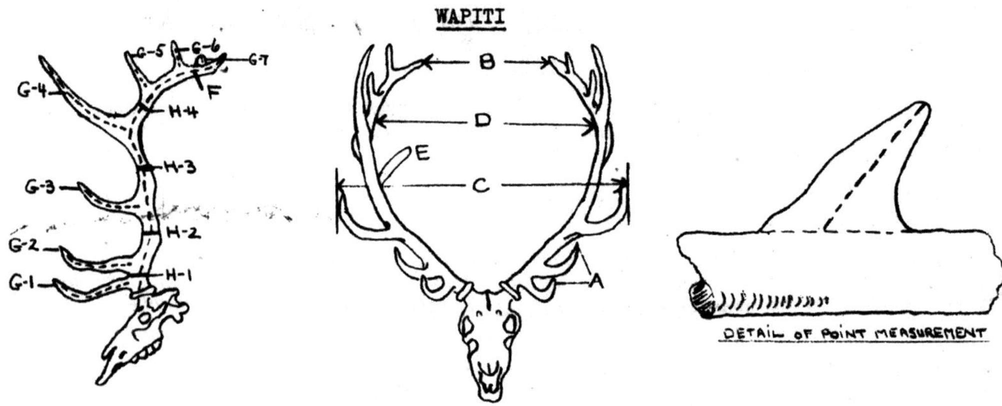

SEE OTHER SIDE FOR INSTRUCTIONS	Supplementary Data		Column 1	Column 2	Column 3	Column 4
A. Number of Points on Each Antler	R.	L.	Spread Credit	Right Antler	Left Antler	Difference
B. Tip to Tip Spread						
C. Greatest Spread						
D. Inside Spread of MAIN BEAMS | | Spread credit may equal but not exceed length of longer antler						
IF Inside Spread of Main Beams exceeds longer antler length, enter difference						
E. Total of Lengths of all Abnormal Points						
F. Length of Main Beam						
G-1. Length of First Point						
G-2. Length of Second Point						
G-3. Length of Third Point						
G-4. Length of Fourth (Royal) Point						
G-5. Length of Fifth Point						
G-6. Length of Sixth Point, if present						
G-7. Length of Seventh Point, if present						
H-1. Circumference at Smallest Place Between First and Second Points						
H-2. Circumference at Smallest Place Between Second and Third Points						
H-3. Circumference at Smallest Place Between Third and Fourth Points						
H-4. Circumference at Smallest Place Between Fourth and Fifth Points						
TOTALS						

ADD	Column 1		Exact locality where killed
	Column 2		Date killed
	Column 3		Present owner
	TOTAL		Address
SUBTRACT	Column 4		Guide's Name and Address
FINAL SCORE			Remarks: (Mention any abnormalities)

Front of the 1950 score chart for wapiti

I certify that I have measured the above trophy on 19
at (address) City State
and that these measurements and data are, to the best of my knowledge and belief, made in accordance with the instructions given.

Witness: Signature:

INSTRUCTIONS

All measurements must be made with a flexible steel tape to the nearest one-eighth of an inch. Official measurements cannot be taken for at least sixty days after the animal was killed. Please submit photographs.

Supplementary Data measurements indicate conformation of the trophy. Evaluation of conformation is a matter of personal preference.

A. Number of Points on Each Antler. To be counted a point, a projection must be at least one inch long AND its length must exceed the length of its base. All points are measured from tip of point to nearest edge of beam as illustrated. Beam tip is counted as a point but not measured as a point.

B. Tip to Tip Spread measured between tips of antlers.

C. Greatest Spread measured between perpendiculars at right angles to the center line of the skull at widest part whether across main beams or points.

D. Inside Spread of Main Beams measured at right angles to the center line of the skull at widest point between main beams. Enter this measurement again in "Spread Credit" column if it is less than or equal to the length of longer antler.

E. Total of Lengths of all Abnormal Points. Abnormal points are generally considered to be those nontypical in shape or location.

F. Length of Main Beam measured from lowest outside edge of burr over outer curve to the most distant point of what is, or appears to be, the main beam.

G-1-2-3-4-5-6-7. Length of Normal Points. Normal points project from main beam. They are measured from nearest edge of main beam over outer curve to tip.

H-1-2-3-4. Circumferences - self explanatory.

ACKNOWLEDGEMENTS

The first complete system for scoring North American big game trophies was originated and copyrighted in 1935 by Dr. James L. Clark. The second was devised by Grancel Fitz in 1939 and published in NORTH AMERICAN BIG GAME. Recognizing the need for a single, standard system of accepted authority, the Boone and Crockett Club in 1949 requested an independent committee to develop the Official Scoring System for North American Big Game Trophies. The members of this committee were Dr. Harold E. Anthony, Milford Baker, Frederick K. Barbour, Dr. James L. Clark, Grancel Fitz and Samuel B. Webb, Chairman.

This Official System is basically a consolidation of the best points in the two previously existing systems. In the process, some new points have been developed, errors corrected, and needed simplification has been achieved.

Before publication, these charts were circulated to more than 250 qualified sportsmen, guides, authors, taxidermists, game officials, and scientists for constructive criticism and approval. The Boone and Crockett Club gratefully acknowledges the contribution of this group and the work of the Committee.

2

Back of the 1950 score chart for wapiti

OFFICIAL SCORING SYSTEM FOR NORTH AMERICAN BIG GAME TROPHIES

Records of North American Big Game — BOONE AND CROCKETT CLUB — P.O. Box 547, Dumfries, VA 22026

Minimum Score: Awards 385, All-time 385

NON-TYPICAL AMERICAN ELK (WAPITI)

E G5 G6 G7 G4 H4 E E H3 G3 E E H2 G2 G1 H1 E — B D C E E E E

DETAIL OF POINT MEASUREMENT

Abnormal Points Right Antler	Abnormal Points Left Antler
E. Total of Lengths of Abnormal Points	

SEE OTHER SIDE FOR INSTRUCTIONS				Column 1	Column 2	Column 3	Column 4
A. No. Points on Right Antler		No. Points on Left Antler		Spread Credit	Right Antler	Left Antler	Difference
B. Tip to Tip Spread		C. Greatest Spread					
D. Inside Spread of Main Beams		(Credit May Equal But Not Exceed Longer Antler)					
F. Length of Main Beam							
G-1. Length of First Point							
G-2. Length of Second Point							
G-3. Length of Third Point							
G-4. Length of Fourth (Royal) Point							
G-5. Length of Fifth Point							
G-6. Length of Sixth Point, If Present							
G-7. Length of Seventh Point, If Present							
H-1. Circumference at Smallest Place Between First and Second Points							
H-2. Circumference at Smallest Place Between Second and Third Points							
H-3. Circumference at Smallest Place Between Third and Fourth Points							
H-4. Circumference at Smallest Place Between Fourth and Fifth Points							
TOTALS							

Enter Total of Columns 1, 2, and 3		Exact Locality Where Killed:	
Subtract Column 4		Date Killed:	By Whom Killed:
Subtotal		Present Owner:	
Add (E) Total of Lengths of Abnormal Points		Guide Name and Address:	
FINAL SCORE		Remarks:	

Front of the 1988 score chart for non-typical American elk

I certify that I have measured the above trophy on ______________________________ 19____

at (address) ______________________________ City __________ State ______
and that these measurements and data are, to the best of my knowledge and belief, made in accordance with the instructions given.

Witness: ______________________________ Signature ______________________________

B&C OFFICIAL MEASURER

I.D. Number

INSTRUCTIONS FOR MEASURING NON-TYPICAL AMERICAN ELK (WAPITI)

All measurements must be made with a 1/4-inch flexible steel tape to the nearest one-eighth of an inch. Wherever it is necessary to change direction of measurement, mark a control point and swing tape at this point. (Note: a flexible steel cable can be used to measure points and main beams only.) Enter fractional figures in eighths, without reduction. Official measurements cannot be taken until the antlers have dried for at least 60 days after the animal was killed.

A. Number of Points on Each Antler: to be counted a point, the projection must be at least one inch long, with length exceeding width at one inch or more of length. All points are measured from tip of point to nearest edge of beam as illustrated. Beam tip is counted as a point but not measured as a point.

B. Tip to Tip Spread is measured between tips of main beams.

C. Greatest Spread is measured between perpendiculars at a right angle to the center line of the skull at widest part, whether across main beams or points.

D. Inside Spread of Main Beams is measured at a right angle to the center line of the skull at widest point between main beams. Enter this measurement again as the Spread Credit if it is less than or equal to the length of longer antler; if longer, enter longer antler length for Spread Credit.

E. Total of Lengths of all Abnormal Points: Abnormal Points are those non-typical in location (such as points originating from a point or from bottom or sides of main beam) or pattern (extra points, not generally paired). Measure in usual manner and record in appropriate blanks.

F. Length of Main Beam is measured from lowest outside edge of burr over outer curve to the most distant point of what is, or appears to be, the main beam. The point of beginning is that point on the burr where the center line along the outer curve of the beam intersects the burr, then following generally the line of the illustration.

G. 1-2-3-4-5-6-7 Length of Normal Points: Normal points project from the top or front of the main beam in the general pattern illustrated. They are measured from nearest edge of main beam over outer curve to tip. Lay the tape along the outer curve of the beam so that the top edge of the tape coincides with the top edge of the beam on both sides of point to determine the baseline for point measurement. Record point length in appropriate blanks.

H. 1-2-3-4 Circumferences are taken as detailed for each measurement.

* * * * * * * * * * * * * * * * * * * *

FAIR CHASE STATEMENT FOR ALL HUNTER-TAKEN TROPHIES

To make use of the following methods shall be deemed as UNFAIR CHASE and unsportsmanlike, and any trophy obtained by use of such means is disqualified from entry.

I. Spotting or herding game from the air, followed by landing in its vicinity for pursuit;
II. Herding or pursuing game with motor-powered vehicles;
III. Use of electronic communications for attracting, locating or observing game, or guiding the hunter to such game;
IV. Hunting game confined by artificial barriers, including escape-proof fencing; or hunting game transplanted solely for the purpose of commercial shooting.

* * * * * * * * * * * * * * * * * * * *

I certify that the trophy scored on this chart was not taken in UNFAIR CHASE as defined above by the Boone and Crockett Club. I further certify that it was taken in full compliance with local game laws of the state, province, or territory.

Date ______________________________ Signature of Hunter ______________________________

(Have signature notarized by a Notary Public)

Back of the 1988 score chart for non-typical American elk

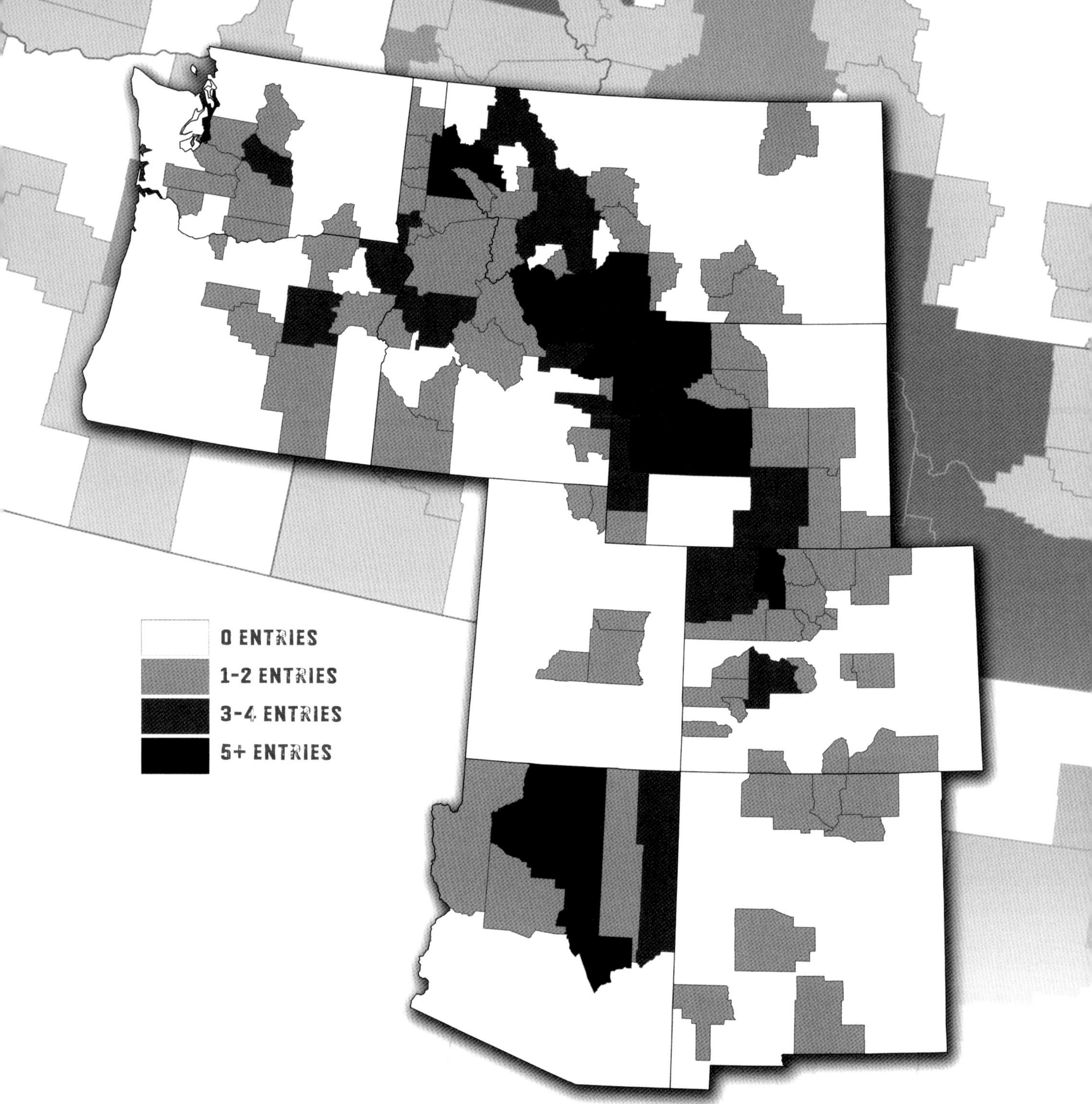

DISTRIBUTION MAP FOR AMERICAN ELK ENTRIES
1830 UP THROUGH 1980

The map shown above includes trophy entries from 1830 through 1980. Several key areas for outstanding trophy entries are evident — Idaho, Montana, and Wyoming, especially near Yellowstone National Park. You will see on the maps that follow how these different areas developed throughout the years.

OFFICIAL.

2: DISTRIBUTION

BY JUSTIN SPRING

The date of elk emergence into North America is difficult to firmly establish from the fossil record. Known specimens only date back to 40,000 years ago. Although there is a remote possibility that the species originated in the new world and then dispersed to the old world, it's extremely unlikely. The most plausible explanation for their arrival is that the red deer of Asia crossed a land bridge, making their way onto the North American continent. Relevance of the exact date elk appeared is, however, immaterial in terms of records and the present-day status of the species, save for, perhaps, a study of possible subspecies designations. What we know is that elk are a native species of North America and are an important part of both our history and present-day experience.

Elk were utilized by Native Americans at least 10,000 years before modern times, which we know through preserved remains of civilizations of that period found in archeological sites. When Europeans made their way across the Atlantic, elk nearly spanned North America from coast to coast. There were six subspecies assigned to North American *Cervus elphus*; Roosevelt's, tule, Merriam's, Eastern, Rocky Mountain or American, and Manitoba or plains elk. The idea that interbreeding could have taken place between these subspecies is possible, especially during times of glaciation, though direct genetic relationships are still being investigated. A radio-collared elk has been recorded traveling more than 1,700 miles from Wyoming to Missouri. Natural barriers created the six subspecies, three of which are still found today: Roosevelt's elk, tule elk, and Rocky Mountain or American elk. The Eastern, Manitoba, and Merriam's subspecies are extinct and tissue samples are limited. In recent times, the validity of the Merriam's subspecies has been questioned. Experts question whether Merriam's is instead a local variation of Rocky Mountain elk. They argue these elk looked slightly different, though genetically were not separated enough to be considered a subspecies. This may also hold true for some of the other classifications, though genetic investigations do not seem possible with current available tissue samples. As for the extinct subspecies, Eastern elk were found in the Eastern portion of North America; Merriam's elk were found in isolated mountain ranges of southwestern states that include Arizona, New Mexico, and Texas with populations extending down into Chihuahua, Mexico; and the Manitoba elk ranged from Manitoba through the Great Plains of the United States.

Elk populations began a near species-ending decline at the time when white settlers began arriving in the West in large numbers and were utilizing the resources. It correlated with a switch in many Native American societies from a subsistence-based existence to one driven by market demands. While the historic elk populations cannot be ascertained other than from the writings of early explorers and Native American oral records, neither reveals much beyond localized numbers. There has been some inquiry into whether Native American hunting practices, combined with the selective pressures of natural predators, put excessive stress on populations, though it has been given little credence by those well-versed in early-population dynamics.

The settlers' need for meat and animal hides created a new market and new pressures on the species. Historian Dan Flores estimates the number of buffalo consumed per native person had doubled by the 1850s and that the majority of the buffalo being taken were mature breeding cows, since their hides were preferred for robes. Although buffalo were the focus of market hunters, elk were not far behind in terms of harvest and value. Roosevelt noted that elk in the prairies were easily run down by horses because of a lack of cover.

The overwhelming slaughter became apparent and concerning to a few hunter conservationists. In 1887, Theodore Roosevelt gathered his like-minded friends, including George Grinnell, who was the editor of *Forest and Stream* magazine and one of the most public and vocal critics regarding the decimation of big game out west. During this time, the Boone and Crockett Club was formed. While Roosevelt embarked on the mission that is still carried on today by the members of the oldest conservation organization in North America, elk were being massacred. The need for food fueled by the influx of settlers landed another blow to a dying species. The destruction of market hunting was first observed in the mid- to late-1800s in the upper Midwest states. Residents there watched their elk and moose disappear. Roosevelt and Boone and Crockett Club members jumped to the conservation forefront.

The Yellowstone Protection Act of 1894 passed largely due to the efforts of Grinnell via his *Forest and Stream*. Club member John Lacey introduced the bill that outlawed the killing of any animal in Yellowstone unless it was in defense of human life. It also banned the defacing of mineral deposits and timber theft. With this bill, the first wildlife refuge in the United States was created. While the park had been created years earlier, there was no jurisdiction to prosecute those guilty of stealing game, fish, timber, minerals, or any other natural resource owned by the United States government. The Yellowstone Protection Act outlined penalties for poaching and mandated the confiscation of all items used in the offense. While the membership of the Boone and Crockett Club was limited to just 100 regular members and about 50 associate members (now referred to as professional members), two of these gentlemen were military men in charge of protecting the park prior to the act. This gave the Boone and Crockett Club the necessary insight to deal with the problems the military had encountered in enforcing park regulations. The act also banned taking fish by any means other than hook and line and established seasons and quantity limits.

The turn of the century also saw the creation of forest reserves. At the time they were created, their intended purpose was exactly that: a reserve. This meant no hunting, trapping, fishing, logging, etc. Hunting today would most likely be a far different endeavor had the reserve's original purpose been enforced. It was Gifford Pinchot, a Club member and one of a seven members of the Club's forestry committee, who convinced the Club and academic forestry circles that the best management of these forests was multiple-use. The military closure and

Appearing rather pensive, George Custer poses during the Yellowstone Expedition with his trophy elk and his .50-caliber Remington No. 1 sporting rifle. "The elk," said Custer, "looked as natural as if enjoying a gentle slumber."

William R. Pywell, photographer, Albumen print, 1873.
Chicago Historical Society, Chicago, Illinois, (ICHI-09936)

enforcement that had occurred in Yellowstone created major backlash and would not do. Finally, after years of battling, Roosevelt signed into law a bill transferring management of the forest reserves to the Department of Agriculture. Pinchot's idea of multiple-use was signed into law. This was a major milestone in wildlife conservation and hunting as we know it today. The professional foresters took care to ensure the National Forests provided habitat to all species of concern, which at the time were mostly game. Current policies are based on these original guidelines, which laid the platform for elk reintroduction.

Club member John Lacey, the Iowa Congressman so instrumental in the Yellowstone Protection Act, fought for the transfer of the forest reserves to the Department of Agriculture. He added yet another feather to his cap of wildlife conservation leadership by introducing the Lacey Act to help enforce states' individual game laws. The act, which outlawed transport or sale across state lines of any fish, animal, or plant taken in violation of any game law, was bitterly contested by market hunting lobbyists who saw it as effectively ending their trade. President William McKinley signed the act into law on May 25, 1900.

1830-1910

Estimates at this time put the national population of elk, which had once numbered in the millions, at around 50,000, the majority of which were living in the Yellowstone area. Arizona elk are thought to have been extirpated by around 1900 and New Mexico had its last reported sighting around 1909. In this 10-year period, the last elk were documented in Nevada, Utah, and Kansas. The Black Hills of South Dakota had abundant wildlife documented by Colonel Custer and, in fact, a photo exists of an elk bull he took there. But this population was quickly wiped out when miners rushed in for the gold discovered there. Most know of Custer's fate at the hand of the Sioux and Cheyenne after his intrusion into the Black Hills. The fate of elk in South Dakota would parallel his. The last documented North Dakota elk was taken by a Mr. Hart in 1913. Elk were already extirpated from all of eastern North America. Oregon, Washington, and California elk were limited to isolated coastal populations of Roosevelt's and tule subspecies. American elk remained in Idaho, Montana, and Wyoming, though very limited in numbers. Colorado had an estimated population of fewer than 1,000 animals, possibly even as low as 500. The first ten years of the 20th century was an all-time low for elk in North America. Only 17 Boone and Crockett entries record a kill date prior to 1910. Eight are from Colorado, four from Wyoming, and one each in Montana, British Columbia, Iowa, and either Arizona or New Mexico (kill location listed as the border between the two). The Iowa trophy is the only elk in the book that may have been considered part of the Eastern elk subspecies. The bull taken on the Arizona/New Mexico border is the only one that may have been a Merriam's elk. The Boone and Crockett Club hunter-conservationists had stopped the complete eradication of North American elk with little time to spare. By 1905, the groundwork had been laid for public lands and parks in which the elk had a place to recover. Oregon was one of the first western states to close elk hunting in 1900. The hunting ban continued through 1903 and was reopened in 1904 due to public pressure caused by the need for elk meat. Hunting was closed again in 1909 all the way through 1932 because struggling elk populations could not support any significant harvest.

1911-1920

The period of 1911 to 1920 does not appear important in terms of trophies entered into the Club's records, though this was the period when elk restoration began in earnest. The first relocation of elk from Yellowstone was occurred in

DISTRIBUTION MAP FOR AMERICAN ELK ENTRIES
1830 UP THROUGH 1940

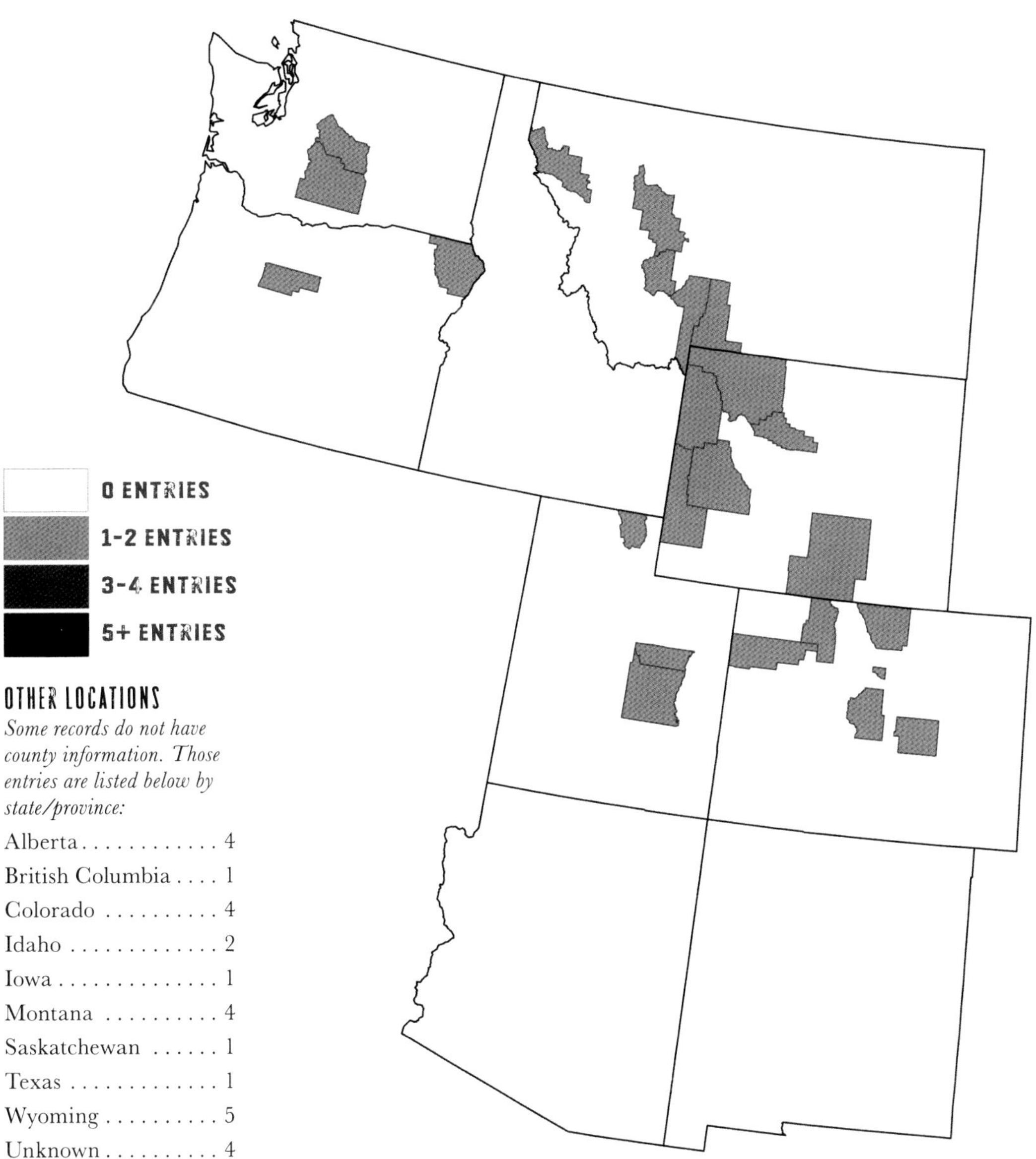

The elk herd in Yellowstone National Park grew due to the efforts put in place by the Yellowstone Protection Act of 1894 and subsequent enforcement of new game laws and closed seasons. This allowed the first relocation of elk from Yellowstone to occur in 1910. Elk restoration was in full swing from 1911 to 1930 and with the eradication of wolves in Yellowstone by 1926, Yellowstone's elk population continued to grow.

Montana in 1910. In 1913, Montana closed the entire state to elk hunting and through multiple translocations of elk from Yellowstone, the population gradually returned to the habitats they previously occupied. The process took 12 years. In 1911, J.B. Dawson of Routt County, Colorado, sold 12 elk to the state of New Mexico and Yellowstone Park donated another 50 in 1914 to help with its reintroduction effort. While Washington still had some remnant populations, these mostly consisted of Roosevelt's elk found on the Olympic Peninsula. In 1912, the state tried its first reintroductions of elk from Montana, presumably from the Yellowstone area. The first attempts failed due to issues with elk causing damage to farming operations. Over the next few years, the elk and the offspring of this original move were subsequently eliminated. Eighty-four additional elk from Montana were released near Enumclaw and North Bend. This introduction resulted in a fine, huntable herd that still exists today. From 1913 through 1930, around 240 elk were moved from Montana to Washington.

The state of Utah began reintroductions in 1912. Elk were brought by crate from Yellowstone and the recently created Jackson Hole Elk Refuge, designated by Roosevelt's successor, President Howard Taft. While Colorado still had a few small populations of elk in extremely isolated areas, relocations to the Centennial State began from Yellowstone also began in 1912. A look at the records book shows that Colorado has consistently been home to trophy elk since then. In 1913, the Winslow Elks Lodge of Arizona transplanted 86 elk from Yellowstone to Sitgroves National Forest on the north slope of the Mogollon Rim. Over the next 15 years, 217 additional elk were acquired. These elk are the forefathers of the world-class herds of elk that roam Arizona today.

While Yellowstone National Park was created before Roosevelt gained national prominence, it was the formation of the Boone and Crockett Club in 1887 that can be credited with playing a significant part in the preservation of our first national park. When the Club was formed on that December night of 1887, the purposes of the organization outlined then were obviously fueled by the atrocities being committed in the Yellowstone valley. One of the key objectives was "*to work for the preservation of the large game of this country, and, so far as possible, further legislation for that purpose, and to assist in enforcing the existing laws.*" It was the arrival of the United States Army that slowed the illegal poaching taking place, though it would take the legislation pressed by Boone and Crockett to stop it all together. Roosevelt was most vocal about the importance of making Yellowstone a safe haven for these elk, to which a majority of American herds can trace their ancestry today.

While Roosevelt had created the Teton National Forest years earlier, the area just outside in the Teton valley was historic wintering grounds for elk. The animals wintering there were extremely vulnerable and were being harvested only for their residual fangs, or "ivories," as they are most commonly called. While the state of Wyoming had created game laws to prevent the slaughter in 1910, public outcry pressured the government into also allocating $10,000 worth of hay for the elk. In 1911, 2,500 elk starved to death and Congress appointed another $20,000 to investigate and pay for feed for the wintering elk. D.C. Nowlin was assigned to this detail and in 1912, he was appointed the first refuge manager and given a $45,000 allocation to purchase elk winter range. The National Elk Refuge was born.

1921-1930

From 1921 through 1930, elk were still struggling to gain firm footing, although gains had been made. Reintroductions continued even though federal funding was not available in the amounts necessary to pay for large-scale projects. Many introductions were still being funded by private conservationists. The 1920s

DISTRIBUTION MAP FOR AMERICAN ELK ENTRIES
1941 THROUGH 1950

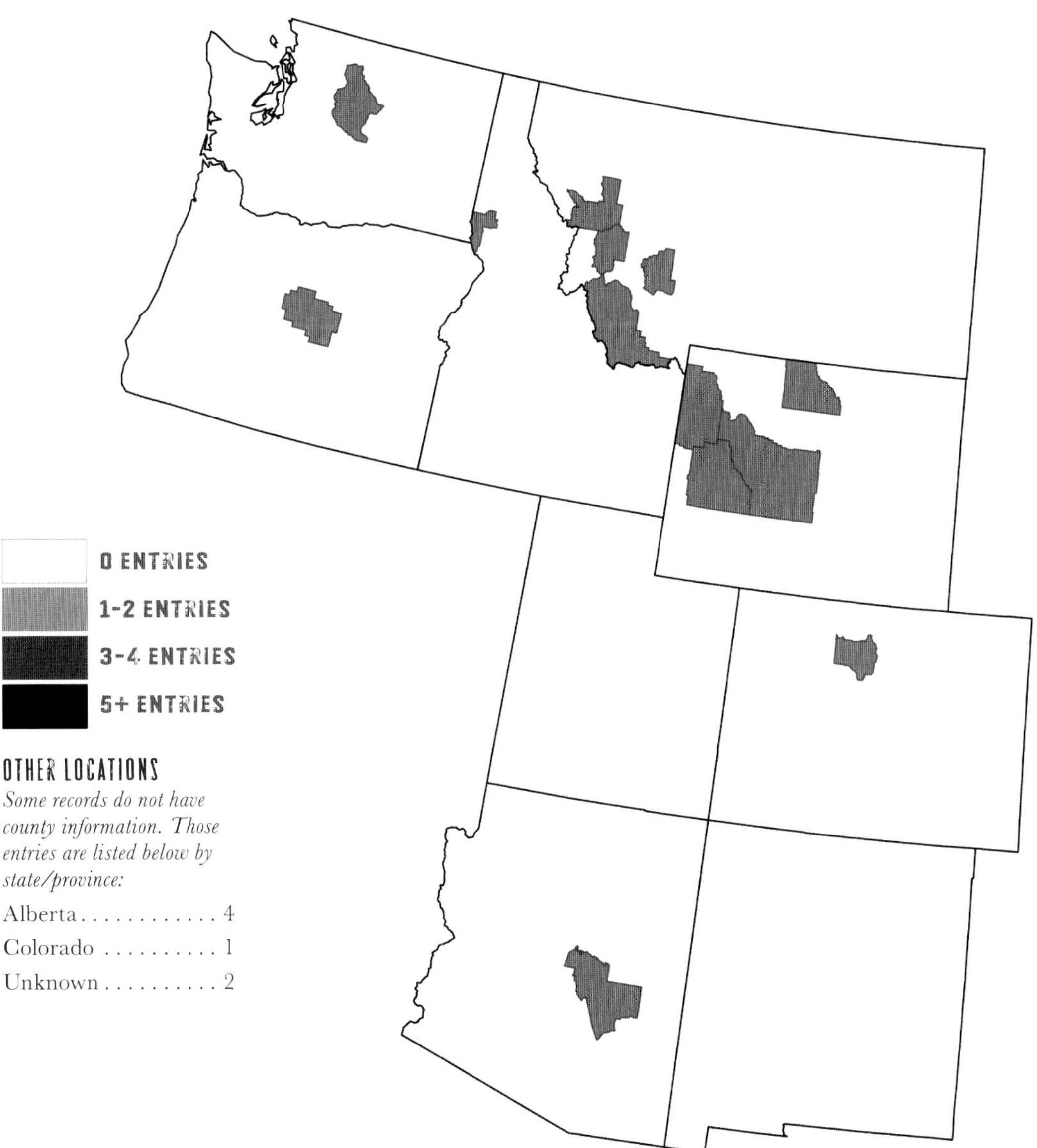

This time period saw newly formed herds grow solid roots and take off. From 1939 to 1948, more than 1,000 elk were transplanted to their historic ranges. The majority of entries still came from Montana and Wyoming. However, additional trophies were harvested in Alberta, Idaho, Oregon, Colorado, and Arizona.

were a time of destruction by the newly created National Biological Survey, which had undertaken outright eradication of grizzlies, wolves, rodents, and birds. In 1926, the last wolf was killed within Yellowstone National Park. With the removal of the elks' natural predators from the ecosystem, the land was ripe for a major elk recovery. This decade records only 11 trophies taken, most of which come from states around Yellowstone; Montana with five, Wyoming with three and Idaho with one. A single entry from Saskatchewan was recorded and the first B&C bull from Washington was taken.

1931-1940

The 1930s didn't start out impressively, though as the decade was closing down, one of the greatest examples of wildlife legislation passed. In 1937, the Pittman-Robertson act became law. It imposed an 11 percent tax on all hunting rifles and ammunition and a 10 percent tax on pistols. These funds went to the Department of the Interior, where they were earmarked for wildlife restoration projects. These projects included the selection, restoration, rehabilitation, and improvement of areas of land adaptable as feeding, resting, or breeding places for wildlife. This includes acquisition, condemnation, lease or gift of such areas, as well as research of wildlife management. There are a few requirements to qualify for these tax dollars, such as the state must put up 25 percent of the total cost and their license fees must go directly to wildlife management and not to a general state fund. This was an attempt to improve funding for state game agencies and to prevent hunters from paying the state's everyday bills. It didn't take long for states to start utilizing this program. New Mexico lists July 1, 1938, as the date funds became available there. This was a major milestone in that state's reintroduction history as officials attest these funds are still used to improve elk habitat to this day. With its Pittman-Robertson funds, Montana was able to purchase in 1938 its first wildlife management area and hire its first wildlife biologist. In 1933, B&C club member Aldo Leupold, the father of wildlife management, published his famed text on the subject. His publication was used in universities across the country to develop wildlife management programs yielding educated biologists to fill newly created positions, made possible thanks to Pitman-Robertson.

Everything was coming together: Elk populations were on the rise and states started authorizing limited hunting seasons. The prevalence of 360-point bulls started its exponential rise that continues today. Twenty-one trophies taken during this period are still found in pages of the Boone and Crockett Club's records book. The first entries of this period appear from Texas, which reintroduced elk in 1927, and Oregon, which re-opened its season in 1932. Utah started its rise to the top with three B&C bulls taken during the 1930s. The first elk seasons were authorized in 1925 in the Beehive State and the hunting of elk continued on a very limited basis until the mid 1970s, when general units were made available to hunters for the first time every year.

1941-1950

The early 1940s saw a decrease in hunting pressure as many able-bodied men were fighting in WWII. With their habitat protected and with management procedures in place, this time period saw the newly formed herds grow solid roots and take off. The 1940s produced 20 entries for the B&C records book. The entries continued to come from Montana, Wyoming, and Idaho. Oregon and Washington were still in the mix and the Canadian province of Alberta contributed a few records, as well. In 1947, the first B&C bull was recorded from Arizona. In 1935, that state's elk population was deemed sufficient to support a limited hunt. Officials issued 266 bull permits and 145 elk were harvested. The hunts continued every year through 1943. The elk seasons

DISTRIBUTION MAP FOR AMERICAN ELK ENTRIES
1951 THROUGH 1960

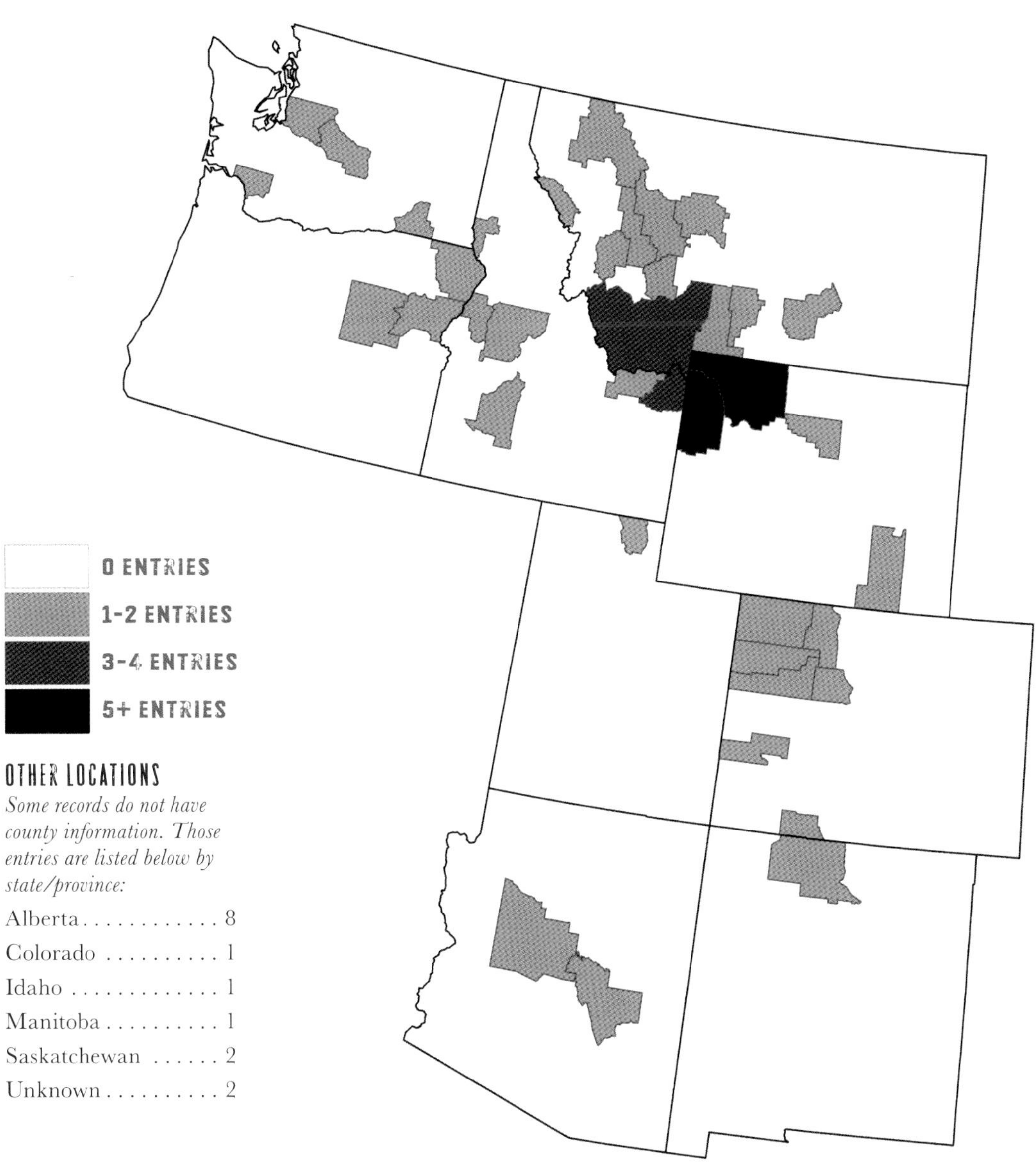

0 ENTRIES
1-2 ENTRIES
3-4 ENTRIES
5+ ENTRIES

OTHER LOCATIONS

Some records do not have county information. Those entries are listed below by state/province:

Alberta 8
Colorado 1
Idaho 1
Manitoba 1
Saskatchewan 2
Unknown 2

In the 1950s, changes in hunting seasons and increased opportunities resulted in a dramatic rise in hunters taking to the field. It was during this time period that Montana hunter Fred Mercer harvested an impressive bull scoring 419-4/8 points, which received the Sagamore Hill Medal. The elk still stands as the Montana state record.

in 1944 and 1945 were canceled due to the war and, in 1946, a hunt resumed. Twelve years after its first season, Arizona produced its first recorded B&C elk. In the 1940s, hunter participation vastly increase; it was a major milestone. In addition, young, eager biologists were in place to research and work on habitat acquisition and quality enhancement. Fresh out of school and funded by a surplus of Pittman-Robertson funds that had accumulated through the war, wildlife conservation made leaps and bounds across the country. From 1939 through 1948, more than 17,000 deer, 7,000 pronghorns, and 1,000 elk were transplanted to their historic ranges.

1951-1960

The 1950s, however, were not a great time for conservation as the Bureau of Reclamation shifted some refuges and lands to different purposes. On a positive note, this was a time that many additional conservation organizations got their feet under them. Increases in elk numbers resulted in private landowner conflicts. Teton National Park had an overabundance of elk and population reductions began on the north side of the park. An initial goal of 20,000 elk on the refuge was continually reduced and, in the mid-1970s, 7,500 animals were deemed the appropriate population for the area. Wyoming wasn't the only state having problems with increasing elk numbers. Washington experienced complaints with its Yakima herd, the first successfully reintroduced herd in the state. From 1950 to 1952, there were approximately 212 antlerless elk taken for every 100 antlered bulls. Washington had authorized cow hunts in 1938, 1943, and from 1949 to 1951 to try and alleviate complaints from landowners. Beginning in 1939 and into the 1940s, the state undertook the process of building an elk fence 10 miles long. Then, from the period of 1943 to 1979, a 27-mile long elk fence was built in the Blue Mountains of Southwest Washington. The decade from 1950 to 1960 showed a shift in Montana's elk hunting opportunities and effort. Hunting seasons were becoming more liberal during this decade, culminating in 84 percent of hunting districts having open or either-sex seasons nearly two months long. The number of people hunting public land began to rise dramatically. From 1950 through 1965, the number of hunter visits to national forests for the purpose of hunting went from 1.3 million to 6 million annually. It's instructive to remember that it was roughly 60 years earlier when these areas were being considered as off-limits to hunting at all. The number of Colorado elk permits issued annually began with a meager 7,517 in 1945, jumped to 25,266 in 1950, and stayed at about that point for the first five years of the 1950s, continuing its climb to 39,495 licenses sold in 1960. Arizona issued 2,225 in 1955, Idaho was in the No. 2 spot in the amount of licenses issued at 52,257 that same year. Montana led with 62,147 licenses; Wyoming allowed 24,295; Washington had 37,701; Oregon was at 29,309; Utah only issued 1,473; New Mexico gave out 708; and Alaska issued 501 even though that state had never entered an elk into the records books. California issued 150 and Nevada rounded out the U.S. states with 60 tags. In 1955, there were nearly 235,000 licenses issued in 11 states. While these numbers reflect total licenses, including antlerless permits, the period from 1951 to 1960 yielded just 86 total trophies in the B&C records book. In 1958, Fred Mercer took the current Montana state record bull. This bull scores an impressive 419-4/8 points and was the largest elk on record since the turn of the century. Montana's expanded hunting possibilities resulted in 21 B&C entries during this time. Manitoba and New Mexico listed their first B&C elk entries during this time as well, although the trophy quality began to slide in terms of mature bulls being taken.

1961-1970

The 1960s was a time of plenty in terms of elk and elk hunting. 1965 data show that Idaho had

DISTRIBUTION MAP FOR AMERICAN ELK ENTRIES

1961 THROUGH 1970

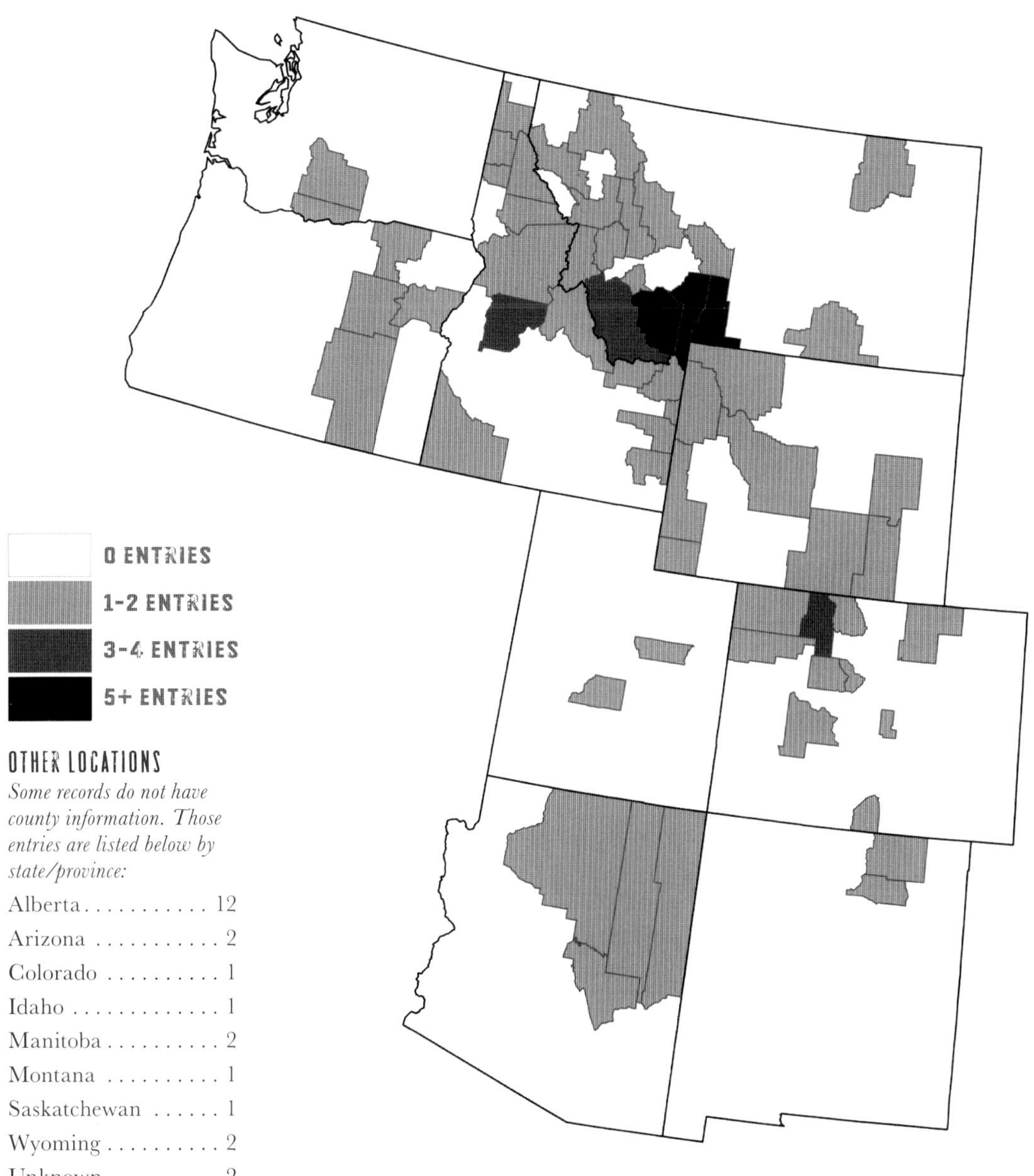

More than 125 elk were harvested during the 1960s, the greatest number of entries since the Club began keeping records. This level wasn't achieved again until the 1990s, when elk entries skyrocketed to over 200 entries. Success of the relocated elk from decades earlier is evident with the increase in entries from Colorado, Oregon, and Arizona.

the most expensive nonresident elk tag at $103 dollars. The average resident elk tag cost hunters a mere $10.12 for the 13 western states allowing hunting. The nonresident average tag price was $66.80. At this time, Nevada, Utah, and South Dakota did not even issue nonresident tags. The environmental movement, in comparison to the conservation movement of Roosevelt and Grinnell, started to take root with the passage of the Clean Water Act of 1960. On September 3, 1964, Congress created the National Wilderness Preservation System "to secure for the American people of present and future generations the benefits of an enduring resource of wilderness." The system initially contained 9.1 million acres of public lands, but by 2001, there were 90 million acres of wilderness preserved in the United States.

Alaska reported its highest elk harvest from the transplanted herds on Afognak and Raspberry islands, setting it at under 150 animals until a severe winter in the mid-60s took a heavy toll on numbers. Elk are still there today, though the difficulty of the terrain and relatively small horn size these elk exhibit keep hunting pressure low. Alaska's transplants took place in 1987 and were a pure Roosevelt's elk strain from the Olympic Peninsula in Washington. Additional transplants took place in 1987 which consisted of both Roosevelt's and American elk, though the populations remain isolated, allowing the Afognak and Raspberry herds to be considered Roosevelt's elk in terms of records listings.

The 1960s were great years for elk. Alonzo Winters killed his World's Record typical in the White Mountains of Arizona in 1968 and New Mexico produced a 434-3/8 point non-typical.

There were 126 entries taken between 1961 and 1970. This number was not obtained again until the 1990s, when elk entries skyrocketed to more than 200. The 1960s also brought the introduction of two of the most-used elk cartridges including the .300 Winchester Magnum introduced in 1963. This was Winchester's answer to the Remington 7mm Magnum introduced the year prior. During this decade, the number of elk taken increased, though many states began to see that statewide "any bull" regulations were leading to many younger bulls being taken and few specimens reaching maturity.

Oregon began trying alternative regulations to increase bull numbers, one of which required a bull to have at least three points on one side. This resulted in numerous spike bulls taken illegally. After removing the regulation, the state saw a 30 percent decrease in illegal takes. The state continued with different approaches and separated eastern hunts from western hunts in 1963. Regulations allowed for a high harvest, but trophy standards weren't being reached. This is evident in the overall lack of entries the Club has recorded from Oregon during that time period.

The original boom in wildlife management came after WWII due to increased need for biologists and the availability of funding through the GI bill. A major development in the field of wildlife biology occurred when Vietnam veterans returned home looking for jobs in the late 1960s and early 1970s. Many veterans came from small towns and communities where the outdoors and hunting were major aspects of life. This fostered a desire to pursue wildlife management as a career. As the 1970s progressed and the environmental movement accelerated, more protections were outlined for wildlife and the habitats required to survive. With more and more people involved in big game research, new regulations and regulation changes were common.

1971-1980

Oregon saw a 45-percent increase in Rocky Mountain elk during this decade, but bull-to-cow ratios were decreasing. Data from 1974 to 1975 reveal ratios of only three to six bulls per 100 cows. During this time, significant timber

DISTRIBUTION MAP FOR AMERICAN ELK ENTRIES
1971 THROUGH 1980

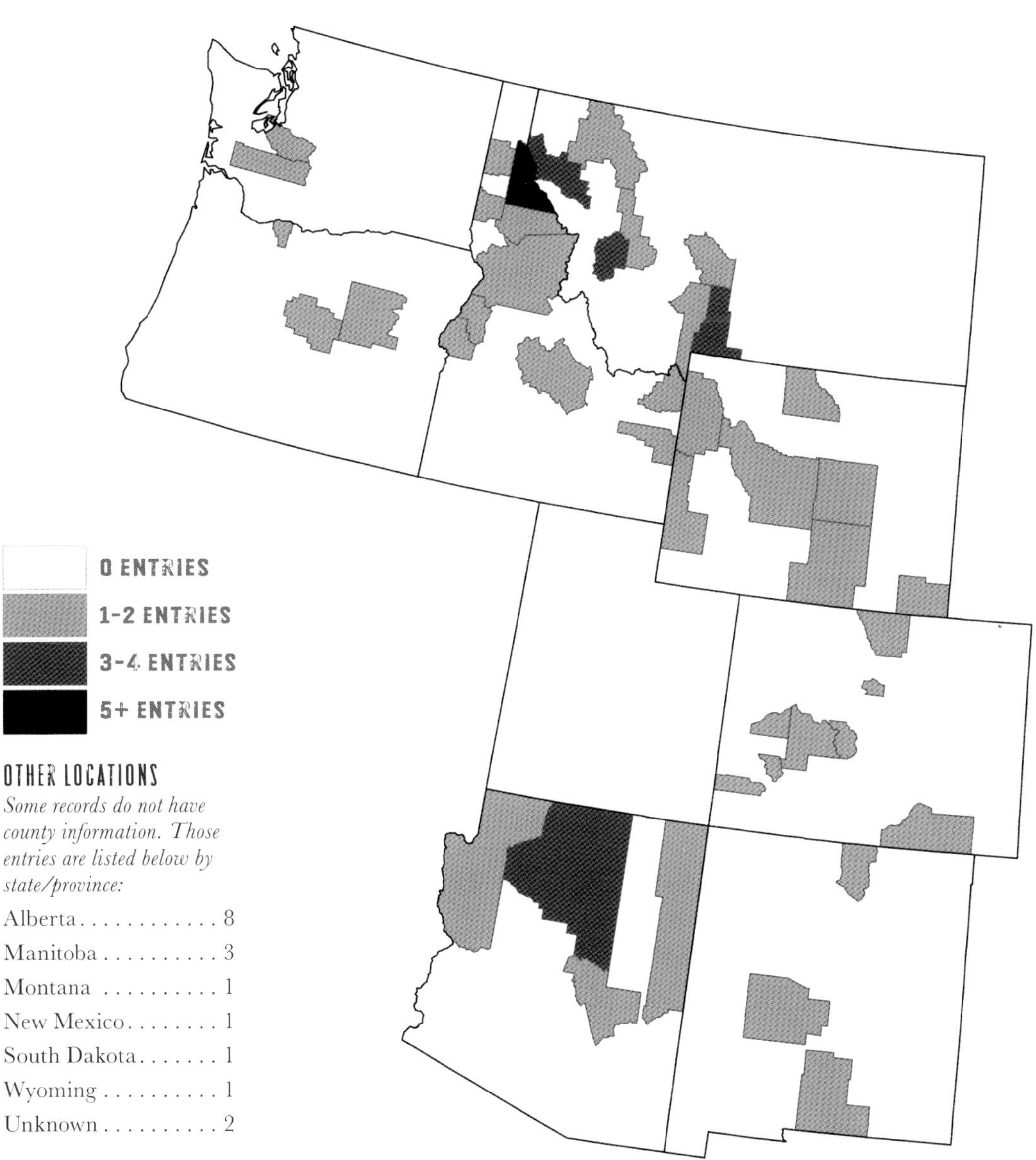

OTHER LOCATIONS

Some records do not have county information. Those entries are listed below by state/province:

Alberta 8
Manitoba 3
Montana 1
New Mexico 1
South Dakota 1
Wyoming 1
Unknown 2

The number of elk entries appearing in Arizona grew during the 1970s while most other states had fewer entries, specifically Oregon and Montana. We also saw the first elk entry from South Dakota.

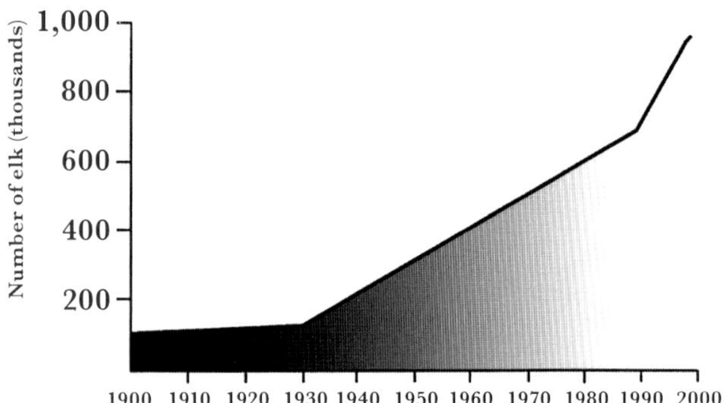

Elk Population trend in the United States, 1900 to 2000.
The recovery of elk from the unstable and low population numbers of less than a century ago attests to the success and farsightedness of professional wildlife management and the conservation movement.
***North American Elk Ecology and Management*,** pages 701-703

harvest took place. National forest lands produced millions of board feet of timber a year and, while the openings created increased elk forage, it has been shown that the roads created for log removal allowed for greater access to previously unreachable areas. Beyond anecdotal evidence, the actual effects of logging on wildlife were not known. More extensive research did not get under way until the early 1980s, though many 1970s ideas have translated into current road closures and management practices on state and federal lands. Jack Ward Thomas, former chief of the U.S. Forest Service and Boone and Crockett Endowment Professor at the University of Montana, helped create a research area known as the Starkey Experimental Forest in Oregon. This is a 40-square-mile fenced enclosure used to study the effect of cattle, land access, and hunting pressure on elk. This forest is still in operation today and allows a limited number of elk permits. Hunters and their ATVs are tracked with handheld GPS units to monitor the response of radio-collared elk.

During this decade, the hunting industry grew and, with the increase in popularity and revenue, came legal issues. In 1975, a case was brought against Montana questioning the authority of the state to "discriminate" against nonresident hunters by charging them higher license fees. After a district court upheld the practice, an appeal went all the way to the Supreme Court. There it was decided that state taxes used to enforce nonresident game laws were legal and that higher nonresident hunting fees did not violate the law. This remains important, as many landowner access programs and other beneficial wildlife programs are currently funded by nonresident fees. Today, both resident and nonresident tag fees continue their climb, perhaps approaching a point beyond the financial capabilities of the average sportsman. Montanans in November 2010 voted to increase nonresident elk and deer combination permits by over $250.

Trophy management appeared on the radar of game managers in the 1970s. Colorado implemented a ban on the taking of spike bulls with the intent of increasing trophy quality. In 1972, that state expanded the regulation to ten areas that require a legal bull to have at least four points on one side. Montana noticed trends similar to those in Oregon and Colorado with the Gravelly/Snowcrest elk herd, where the Mercer bull came from in 1958, and tried the same type of branched antler regulation in the early 1980s. This resulted in an increase in illegally taken spike elk, which were mostly left to rot. Obviously, this was not the desired effect. This was a time period of testing the effects of hunting regulations and sharpening the learning curve of wildlife managers. The 1970s produced 83 currently accepted entries, all from the same states and provinces as previously mentioned, although South Dakota made its entry into the list of states producing bulls of 360 points or better.

While many of the mechanisms affecting elk numbers can be contributed to today's game management and overall habitat protection, a great deal of thanks goes to the pioneers of wildlife conservation. This publication shows us what it was like "back in the day" and few could argue elk hunting today is as it used to be. You would be hard pressed to find someone to argue that opportunities are getting worse. Today, elk are found in much of their historic ranges, including in the East, where they had been extirpated for well over 100 years. States such as Pennsylvania, Kentucky, Wisconsin, Michigan, Virginia, Tennessee, Arkansas, and others continue reintroduction programs that work toward the end goal of bringing elk back to the landscape.

REFERENCES:

Arizona Game and Fish Department. *Elk* http://www.azgfd.gov/h_f/game_elk.shtml

Arizona Game and Fish Department. *Elk in Arizona.* Wild Kids, http://www.azgfd.gov/i_e/ee/resources/wild_kids/elk712.pdf

Boone and Crockett Club. *A Whitetail Retrospective: Vintage Photos and Memorabilia from the Boone and Crockett Club Archives* (Missoula: Boone and Crockett Club, 2006)

Brasher, Anne, Moyle, Peter. *Conservation in the USA*; legislative milestones (Marine Bio.org Sept. 2004)

Dixon, Susan L., Lyman, R. Lee. *On the Halocene History of Elk (Cervus elaphus) in Eastern Washington* (Columbia: https://research.wsulibs.wsu.edu:8443/xmlui/bitstream/handle/2376/1274/v70%20p262%20Dixon%20and%20Lyman.PDF?sequence=1)

Hamlin, Ken. *FWP 2005 Elk Management Plan* (Bozeman: Montana FWP. 2005)

Hicks, Jason F. et al. *Reintroduction and Genetic Structure: Rocky Mountain Elk in Yellowstone and the Western States* (Journal of Mammalogy, Feb. 2007 pg 129-138)

Jense, Grant. *1980 Utah Elk Status Report* (Utah Division of Wildlife (http://www.muledeerworkinggroup.com/Docs/Proceedings/1980-Western%20States%20Elk%20Workshop/1980%20Utah%20Elk%20Status%20Report.pdf)

Miller, Jim. *The Co-Evolution of Wildlife Management and The Wildlife Society* (Speech available http://joomla.wildlife.org/index.php?option=com_contenet&task=view&id=292)

Oregon Department of Fish and Wildlife. *History 1792-1990* (http://www.dfw.state.or.us/agency/history.asp)

Rattenbury, Richard C. *Hunting the American West: The Pursuit of Big Game for Life, Profit, and Sport, 1800-1900.* (Missoula: Boone and Crockett Club, 2008)

Reiger, John F. *American Sportsmen and the Origins of Conservation* (Corvallis: Oregon State University Press, 2007)

Rocky Mountain Elk Foundation. *Elk In History* (www.rmef.org/AllAboutElk/ElkInHistory/)

Swift, Lloyd W. *A Partial History of the Elk Herds of Colorado* (American Society of Mammalogists 1945 Journal of Mammalogy pp. 114-119)

Toweill, Dale E., Thomas, Jack Ward. *North American Elk: Ecology and Management* (Washington DC: Smithsonian Institution Press, 2002)

Trefethen, James B. *An American Crusade for Wildlife* (Alexandria: The Boone and Crockett Club, 1975

Louise F. Campbell harvested this wapiti near Tonto Lake, Arizona, in 1967. The bull was entered in the 13th Competition with a score of 375-1/8 points.

3: VINTAGE PHOTOS

BY KEITH BALFOURD

Long before word spread in the 19th century about a group measuring antlers and horns for a records book, the field photo was the next in a progression in big game records keeping. Its predecessors were simple drawings, paintings, and head skins preserved by being "stuffed" with rags and cotton. The cameras that were available were too large, cumbersome, and expensive to take into the field to capture the hunting experience. This is the reason why nearly all early hunting photography was staged, after the fact, back in town or in camp where the big boxes could be more easily transported.

Ironically, the year after Theodore Roosevelt and his friends formed the Boone and Crockett Club, George Eastman (later a Boone and Crockett member) offered the first camera fit for widespread public use. He called his fixed-focal lens, single-shutter box the Kodak. The year was 1888. Personal photography began to boom and, along with it, the real opportunity to take a camera hunting.

Some of the earliest examples of hunting and field photography, including those received by the Boone and Crockett Club for records-keeping purposes, were what one would expect from an era of both new-fangled technology and our hunting culture at the time.

In the photos, the animal itself was less important than the man and his rifle. The family rifle, shotgun, or both were prized possessions, much more than tools. They represented freedom, survival, household security, male authority, and family heirlooms to be passed to the eldest male when the time came. Naturally, it was rare, then, to see early hunting photography—in the field or otherwise—without the prominence of "Old Bess." Later, the man, his rifle, and his horse or vehicle seemed to take precedence.

In the early days of portable cameras, there were still few of them making it into the field. Consequently, much of the historical photos in B&C archives are of just the hunter or a family member standing with a lopped-off head or antlers on a skull plate. It also stands to reason that some trophy-entry photography consisted of posed shots of a mounted head taken outside for the photo or simply a mounted head on a wall. It's not what we would consider field photography today, but it was as good as anyone thought to get back in the day.

We must also keep in mind that it took some time for hunters to become aware of Boone and Crockett records keeping and for that option to gain acceptance. Early hunting photography was taken with the purpose of preserving a memory for the family, not book-publishing, and it remained an option available only to those who could afford a camera and thought about taking one with them hunting. Most early hunting excursions were either on foot or on horseback, which allowed deeper access to the wilderness. If you couldn't eat it or drink it, it didn't get packed with the necessities for the hunt.

Regardless of the limitations, early photography is a cherished piece of our hunting heritage. It shows a drastic change from the sophistications of today, both in equipment and culture, and remains a treasure of man, animal, and sport.

T I

B

C

Meth

All measurements r

A Length on outside curve: M
of the burr to the tip of th

B Circumference midway betw

C Circumference of burr.

D Greatest spread: Measured
center line of the skull.

Points on each side: No point
two inches.

Remarks: State whether the
from the normal for this sp

Please provide photographs sho

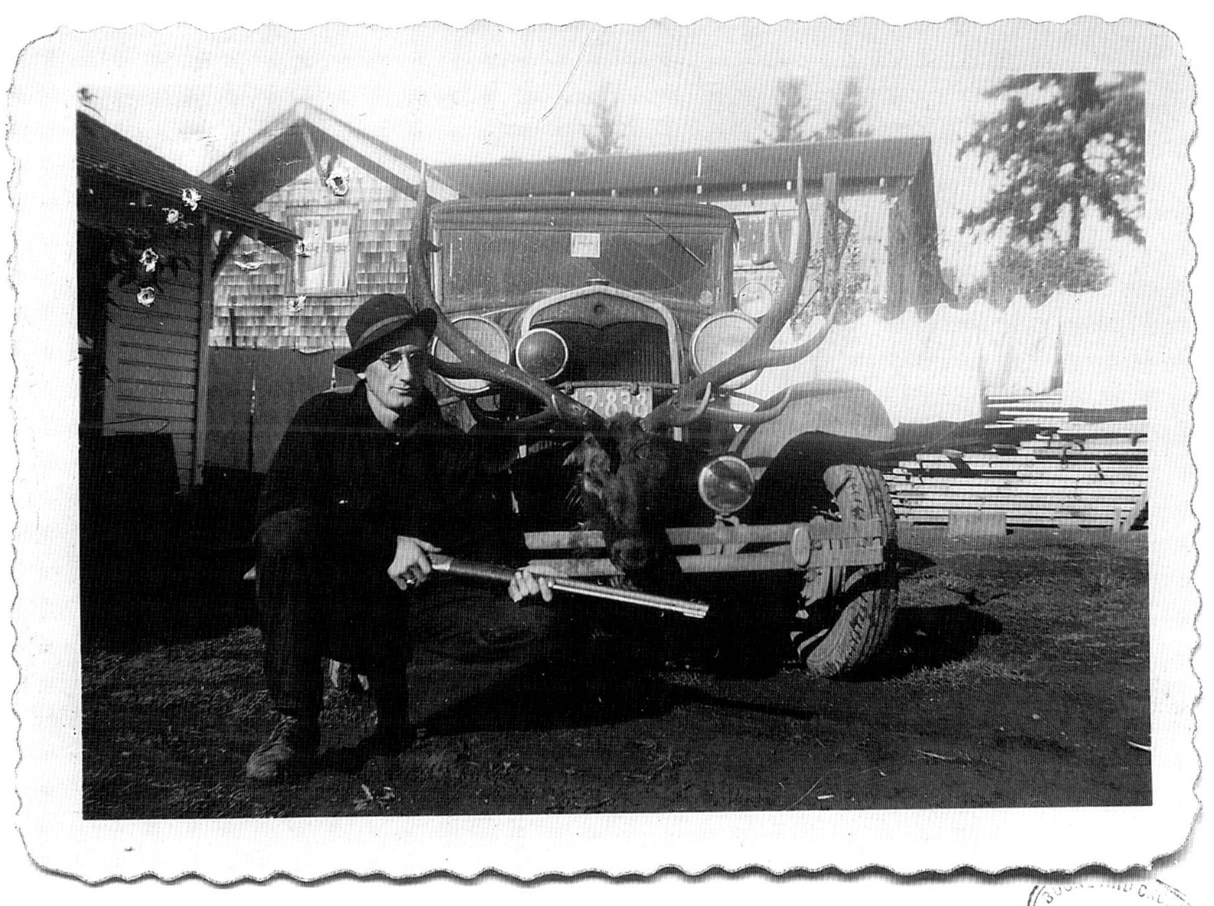

ABOVE: This Lincoln County, Oregon Roosevelt's elk was taken in November 1944 by Verlin "Dusty" Rhoades. This bull, which has a score of 316-5/8 points, wasn't entered in the Club's Records Program until the 22nd Awards Period in the mid-1990s. The rifle and automobile were typical in hunting photographs from this era.

LEFT: August Jordan took this wapiti in September 1946 at the head of the Yellowstone River in Wyoming. It was entered in the Club's first big game competition held in 1947 and was scored using the original system. Unfortunately, this bull was never re-scored under the Club's current scoring system and is therefore not listed in our records books. No matter, it's still a fine specimen.

NOTE: Many of the following photos are as stated, "vintage." The Boone and Crockett Club has carefully ushered in a new era with the advancement and availability of photographic equipment. Today, our expectations consist of presenting a blood-free trophy and hunter in an uncluttered, natural environment. These guidelines were born out of respect for the animal and its habitat.

ABOVE: Art Wright stopped to pose for a quick snapshot of his trophy elk taken in 1953. Wright harvested the bull scoring 387-2/8 points while hunting near Colorado's White River.

RIGHT: Hunter John Caputo, Sr., is pictured with his guide Buck Sanford and the elk they brought down in Park County, Wyoming, during the 1968 season. The bull has a final score of 380-6/8 points and was entered in the Club's 14th Competition.

LEFT: This is a typical vintage photograph from our records-keeping archives. Alan Foster harvested this prized wapiti scoring 393-2/8 points. He was hunting near Waterton National Park in Alberta, Canada, in 1952.

Sporting Goods

"Sporting Goods of Selected Quality"

M. F. SMITH, Owner

Phone 259-M   Buhl, Idaho   ~~119 S. Broadway~~ 1008 West Main

December 29, 1954

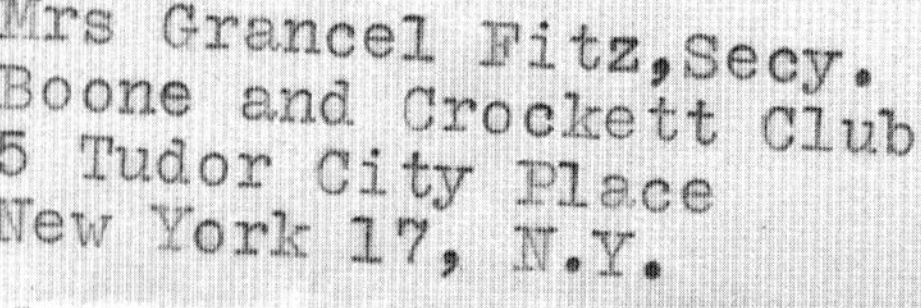

Mrs Grancel Fitz, Secy.
Boone and Crockett Club
5 Tudor City Place
New York 17, N.Y.

Wapiti

Dear Madam:

Inclosed are the measurements of and Elk, (Wapiti) killed in Idaho Nov. 1 of this year. The measurements taken are accurate to the best o our ability. Would like information as to where we can get it measured officially and how to enter it into the records if it is a record.

Number of points on each antler R. 6, L. 6.
Tip to tip Spread 40 5/8"
Greatest Spread 50 .4/8"
Inside Spread of Main Beams 46 5/8"
Total lengths of all abnormal points (None)
Length of Main Beam
" " First Point
" " Second
" " Third
" " Fourth
" " Fifth
No sixth or seven
Circumference at
" "
" "
" "

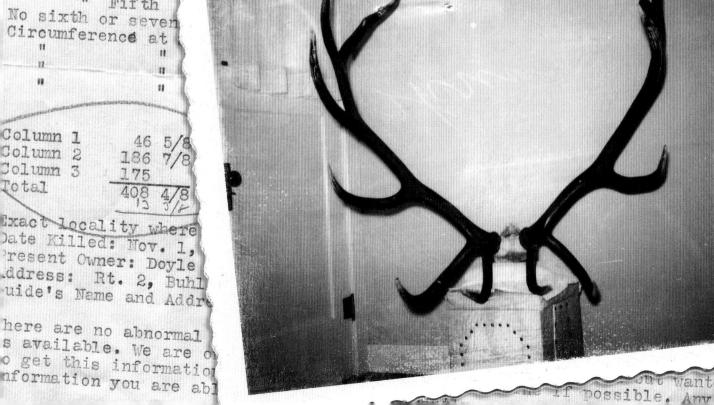

Column 1 46 5/8
Column 2 186 7/8
Column 3 175
Total 408 4/8
13 5/8

Exact locality where
Date Killed: Nov. 1,
Present Owner: Doyle
Address: Rt. 2, Buhl
Guide's Name and Addre

here are no abnormal
s available. We are o
o get this informatio
nformation you are abl ... wante
... if possible. Any

TEMPLE BAGS HUGE ELK.

Butte Miner Bureau.

DILLON, Nov. 18.—The hunting party composed of Paul Temple, W. E. Talent, Sam Freeman and Jack Keenan arrived in Dillon last night from the Boulder elk reserve, where they hunted from the 12th to the 15th. Temple was the only successful elk hunter, bringing back a 600-pound bull with a huge spread of antlers. It took an entire day to move the animal from the spot where it was killed to the camp, as it was necessary to build a sled to haul it out on and in many places they had to hew a road through the timbers. Talent brought back a fine buck deer.

ABOVE: Paul H. Temple used a Savage Model 99 to harvest this record-book bull elk sporting a 53-2/8 inch greatest spread. As noted in the newspaper clipping at right, Temple was joined by W.E. Talent and Jack Keenan on the November 1927 hunt in Jefferson County, Montana. Decades after the hunt Temple's son, Gary, had the bull officially scored and entered the animal the Club's 25th Awards Program with a final score of 377-4/8 inches.

LEFT: Shown in the background is the original correspondence from Idaho hunter Doyle Shriver regarding the bull he harvested on November 1, 1954. The wapiti was entered in the 7th Competition with a final score of 393-2/8 points after being scored by a Boone and Crockett official measurer.

VINTAGE PHOTOS & MEMORABILIA

ABOVE: P.L. Jones took this fine bull in November of 1934 near Oregon's Granite Meadows. Unfortunately it was never re-scored under the current system. Whether it was taken in Umatilla or Wallowa County is unknown, as there is a location known as Granite Meadows in both counties.

RIGHT: This bull was presumably taken by a native near Riding Mountain, Manitoba, in 1907. It is currently owned by the Banff Museum and scores 364-3/8 as a typical. Clearly, it would score much higher if entered as a non-typical.

LEFT: The photo to the left did not have any information attached to it, although the excessive crowning leads to suspicions it may be a red deer from another continent. Unfortunately, the details are likely lost with time.

ess:

Signature: [signature]

INSTRUCTIONS

easurements must be made with a flexible steel tape to the nearest one-eighth of
ial measurements cannot be taken for at least sixty days after the animal was ki
e submit photographs.

ementary Data mea
rmation is a matt   Evaluation of

nber of Points on
ch long AND its
ip of point to n   on must be at l
t measured as a   points are measu
                                                              counted as a po

to Tip Spread m

atest Spread mea
ll at widest pa

de Spread of Ma   the center line
st point betwee
if it is less th   line of the skul
                                                              Spread Credit"

l of Lengths of
ntypical in sha

h of Main Beam   ally considered t
tant point of w

4-5-6-7. Length   outer curve to th
from nearest e

                                                              main beam. They a
4. Circumferenc

complete syst
ed in 1935 by
shed in NORTH   was originated an
accepted auth   rancel Fitz in 19
to develop th   ingle, standard
f this committ   sted an independen
L. Clark, Gra   Game Trophies. T
                                                              ederick K. Barbour

ial System is basically a consolidation of the best points in the two previously
ystems: In the process, some new points have been developed, errors corrected,
simplification has been achieved.

lication, these charts were circulated to more than 250 qualified sportsmen,
thors, taxidermists, game officials, and scientists for constructive criticism
l. The Boone and Crockett Club gratefully acknowledges the cont...
and the work of the Committee

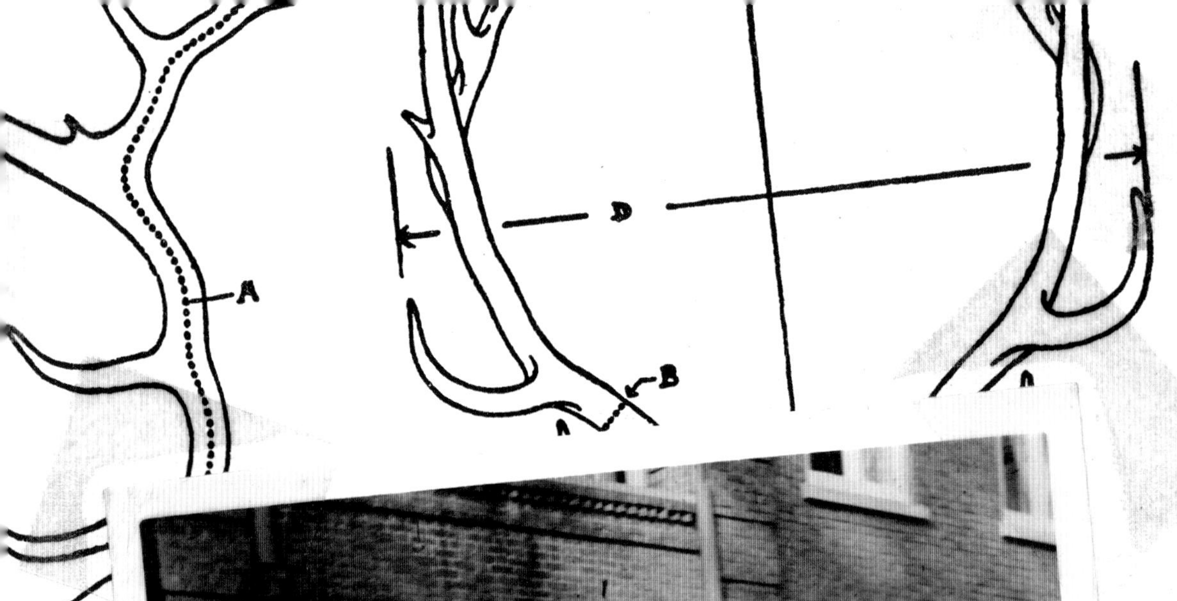

neasurem

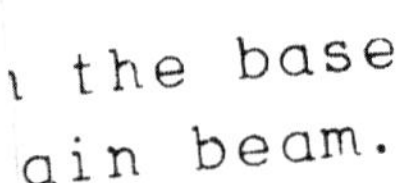

th on ou
he burr

cumferenc

cumferenc angles to

eatest spr protrudes
e center l

ints on e ch depart

marks: Sto
fro

VINTAGE PHOTOS & MEMORABILIA

G. J. VAN HEEK JR.
„DE WIGWAM"
BODDENKAMP No. 40
ENSCHEDE
POSTBUS 47

ENSCHEDE, 4th July 1949.

Boone and Crockett Club,
American Museum of Natural History,
Central Park West at 79th Street,

N e w   Y o r k 24, N.Y.

Dear Sirs,

In receipt of your esteemed circular, in which you put the request to me to enter any of the trofees in my possession for registration, I beg to reply that I am pleased to give you the measurements of a wapiti and two mountain goats.

The three animals were bagged by myself during my hunting trip in the Rockey Mountains, Canada, in the fall of 1939.

The measurements are given on a separate sheet. It may be of interest to you to know that these trofees ...nted by Messrs. Rowland Ward in London. They were ... my house and of same I have much ... to as a present.

...ures given by me are not complete, ...lled up.

..., I remain,

Yours truly,

G.J. van Heek

OPPOSITE & ABOVE: G.J. van Heek traveled to the Canadian Rockies in 1939 where he was fortunate enough to take a wapiti and two goats, one billy and one nanny. The elk was entered around 1949 and a follow-up score chart was never received when the new scoring method was devised.

VINTAGE PHOTOS & MEMORABILIA

ABOVE: George Agars 372-2/8 typical American elk was officially entered and accepted in 2006, though Boone and Crockett still had correspondence on file between Mr. Agar and Mrs. Grancel Fitz (the records secretary at the time) from the late 1950s. We have an original letter from George, though no score chart indicating it was ever entered. The bull was taken in Bonner County, Idaho, on October 16, 1955.

RIGHT: Pictured here is Bill Mercer with his 1964 Elk Mountain, Colorado bull. His hunting partner's name is unknown, but there is no doubt the bull fell to the Savage 99 he is proudly holding.

LEFT: Pictured is John S. Maxson with his Fremont County Wyoming bull. It was taken September 13, 1954, and has a final score of 381-4/8.

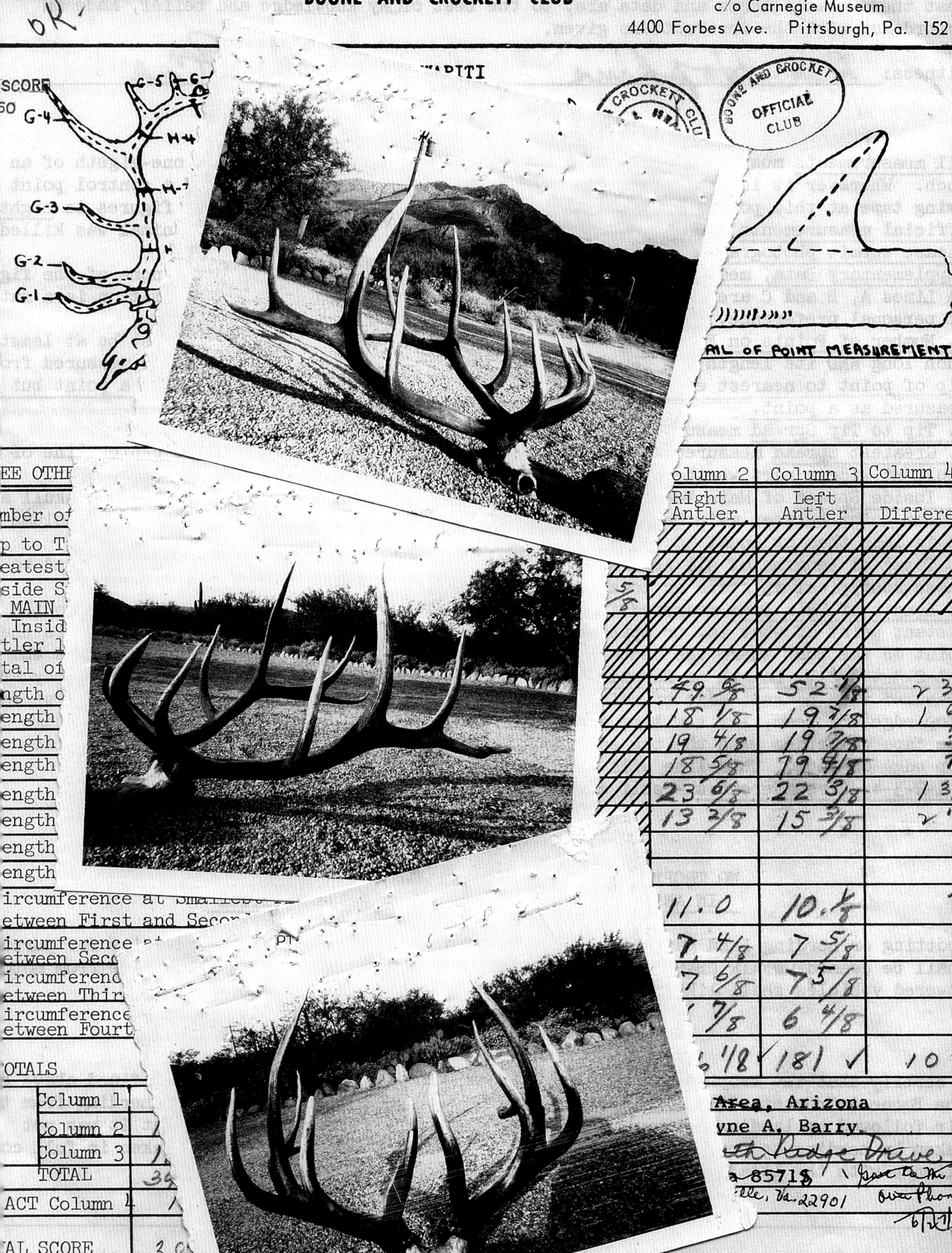

GAME COMMITTEE — BOONE AND CROCKETT CLUB

c/o Carnegie Museum
4400 Forbes Ave. Pittsburgh, Pa. 152

WAPITI

BOONE AND CROCKETT OFFICIAL CLUB

	Column 2	Column 3	Column 4
	Right Antler	Left Antler	Difference
...mber of...			
...p to T...			
...eatest...			
...side S... 5/8			
MAIN ... Insid...			
...tal of...			
...ngth o...	49 6/8	52 1/8	2 3
...ength	18 1/8	19 7/8	1 6
...ength	19 4/8	19 7/8	
...ength	18 5/8	19 4/8	
...ength	23 6/8	22 3/8	1 3
...ength	13 2/8	15 3/8	2
...ength			
...ength			
...ircumference at Smallest ... etween First and Second ...	11.0	10 1/8	
...ircumference at ... etween Seco...	7 4/8	7 5/8	
...ircumferenc... etween Thir...	7 6/8	7 5/8	
...ircumference ... etween Fourt...	7/8	6 4/8	
...OTALS	1/8	181	10

Column 1	
Column 2	
Column 3	
TOTAL	3...
...ACT Column 4	
...AL SCORE	38...

...Area, Arizona
...yne A. Barry
...th Ridge Drive
...a 85718
...lle, Va. 22901

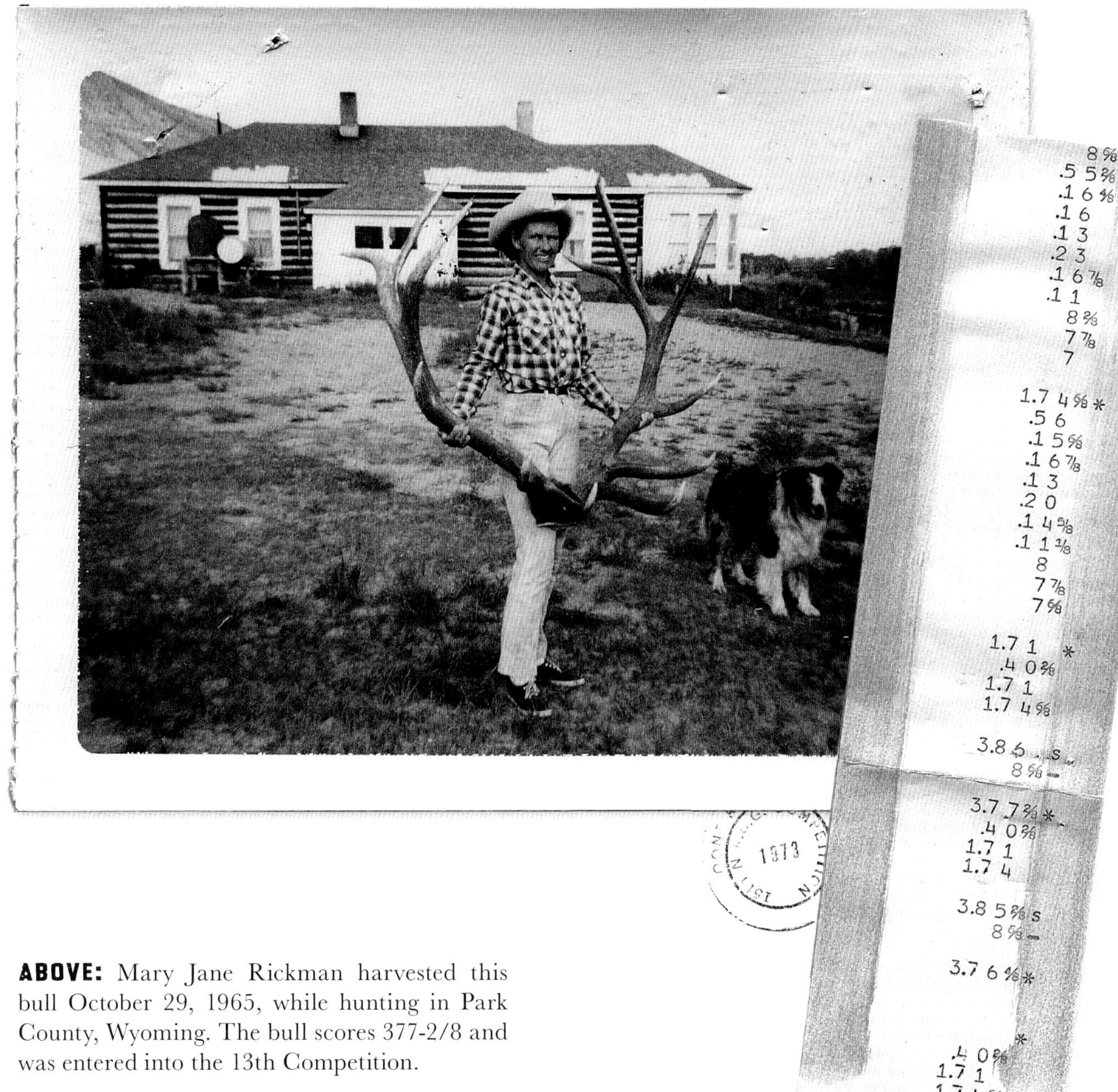

ABOVE: Mary Jane Rickman harvested this bull October 29, 1965, while hunting in Park County, Wyoming. The bull scores 377-2/8 and was entered into the 13th Competition.

LEFT: This bull was taken in November of 1965 by Wayne A. Barry. It was sent for display at the 13th Competition and was returned to the point of shipment. Mr. Barry, however, could not be contacted for years, at which point the trophy was sold to help offset the bull's storage costs paid for by the Club. The bull was taken near Mormon Lake, Arizona.

VINTAGE PHOTOS & MEMORABILIA

ABOVE: The Altadena American Legion post sent in this entry in the early 1950s, although it never appeared in any publications. At the time, a category did not exist for this type of antler configuration and, therefore, all that remain are photos in the archives.

RIGHT: This entry did not come with much information. The owner, L.M. Brownell, knew that it was taken October 1, 1956, in the Big Horn Mountains of Wyoming, although he did not know who had taken it. It was attributed to an unknown hunter in the records at a score of 379-5/8 points.

LEFT: Fain J. Little took this 340-2/8 point Roosevelt's elk three miles south of Astoria, Oregon, in 1945. The antlers hung on his wall until 1990, when he submitted it for entry into the records book.

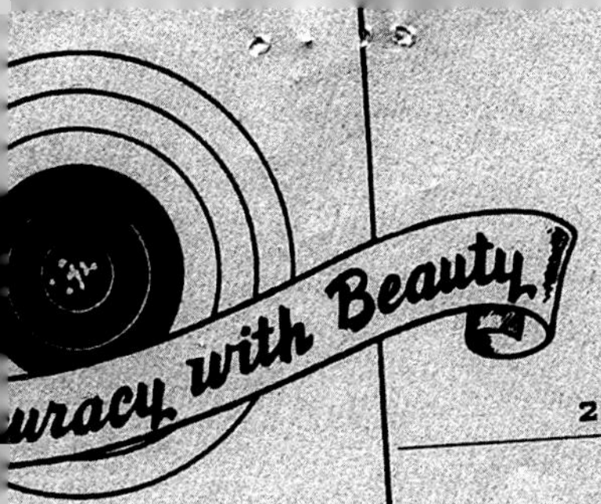

LENARD M. BROWNELL

Custom Stockmaker

237 WEST 6TH — SHERIDAN, WYO.

H QUALITY
OCKING ONLY

OMPLETE CUSTOM
ADE RIFLES

February 7, 1957

Mrs. Grancel Fitz, Secretary
Boone and Crockett Club
5 Tudor City Place
New York City 17, New York

Dear Mrs. Fitz:

I have a set of elk antlers from an elk killed this past fall. With the help of Dr. Ray Bentzen, owner of the No. 1 elk head, and Jack Adams, owner of the Big Horn Taxidermy here in Sheridan, we have carefully measured this head to total 381 3/8 points.

As I have never registered a head before, I am not familiar with the correct procedure but understand that I may enter it for the yearly awards.

At any rate, if the Club is interested in an elk head of this size being recorded, I will be pleased to hear ... you with your instructions.

... your book "Records of ... two snap shots of the

Yours very truly,

L M Brownell

L. M. Brownell

Killed on Duck Creek
RECEIVED
DEC 04 1992
BOONE & CROCKETT CLUB
Don Bull elk 1961
Halfway, Oregon
BOONE & CROCKETT CLUB
11th N.A.B.G. COMPETITION
1963

ABOVE: Pictured here is Daniel L. Smith with a tremendous Roosevelt's elk he took in November of 1960. The bull was reported to have come from the northwestern corner of Oregon just south of Astoria. Judging from the field photo included with the entry, which was received in 1996, the terrain and vegetation matches that of the region, helping to corroborate the location of kill. The bull has a final score of 333-3/8.

RIGHT: Pictured is Eva Calonge with a Fremont Count, Idaho, 6x6. The bull scores 375 points and was taken October 1, 1960, and entered a little over a year later, in January of 1962.

LEFT: This bull was taken in 1961 by Donald B. Martin in Baker County, Oregon. This tremendous trophy scores 377-7/8 points.

easurements must be rest one-eighth of an
cial measurements ca the animal was killed
se submit photograph

ementary Data measu . Evaluation of
rmation is a matter

mplify addition pl

umber of Points on ction must be at least
inch long AND its le ll points are measured
tip of point to nea is counted as a point
not measured as a po

Tip Spread measured between tips of antlers.

Circumferences - self explanatory.

e publication, these charts were
s, authors, taxidermists, game officials, and
pproval. The Boone and Crockett Club gratefully acknowledges the contribution of
group and the work of the Committee.

ABOVE: This bull was killed in Idaho sometime around 1929 by Ben Howland (pictured). It scores an impressive 372-6/8 points.

RIGHT: The original entry score on this bull was 396-2/8 and, as such, was invited to the 14th Competition. Judges found the bull had an abnormal point that had been scored as a normal and had to drop the score significantly. It came in at 371-4/8, falling short of the minimum, which was 375 at the time. When the non-typical category was created, the necessary corrections were made and the bull scored 394-4/8. It was taken by Charles R. Pennock in 1942 from Sublette County, Wyoming.

LEFT: Montana resident Harold Schulz took this 369-point bull in his home state in 1950. It was invited to the yearly competition in 1951, although Schulz was not able to attend. The bull was never re-measured for inclusion into the records and is listed as a rejected trophy that remains on file for inclusion if a confirming score is obtained.

THE WILDERNESS SOCIETY

PUBLISHERS OF *THE LIVING WILDERNESS*

1840 MINTWOOD PLACE, N.W.

~~WASHINGTON 9, D. C.~~

COLUMBIA 1588

Moose, Wyoming
April 91 1953

Mrs. Grancel Fitz, Secretary
Boone and Crockett Club,
5 Tudor City Place,
New York 17, N. Y.

Dear Mrs. Fitz:

I am very much interested in the material you sent me on Mr. Maurice's elk head from New Zealand. I have studied the photographs very carefully and it is my opinion that this animal has some red deer ancestry. I am now engaged in a study of specimens which we collected in New Zealand a few years ago on the Fiordland Expedition. Some of the skins that I have here are certainly cross-bred specimens, between elk and red deer. We have some antlers judged to be cross-bred, which have the termi tines arranged very much like those in Mr. Maurice's trophy.

I wish it were possible to obtain the canine teeth from this specimen. I wonder if by any chance Mr. Maurice kept them, or could obtain them. I would be very much interested in examining them. In this kind of stu I find the canine teeth more significant than any other part of the specimen, since for each species, elk and red deer, they hold true to s and form, and the hybrid specimens have canine teeth that are intermedi

Again, I think you for letting me see this material, and I hope these suggestions will be of some use.

Sincerely yours,

Olaus J. Murie
Olaus J. Murie

Records of
Big Game

G-4
G-3
G-2
G-1

SEE OTH

A. Numb

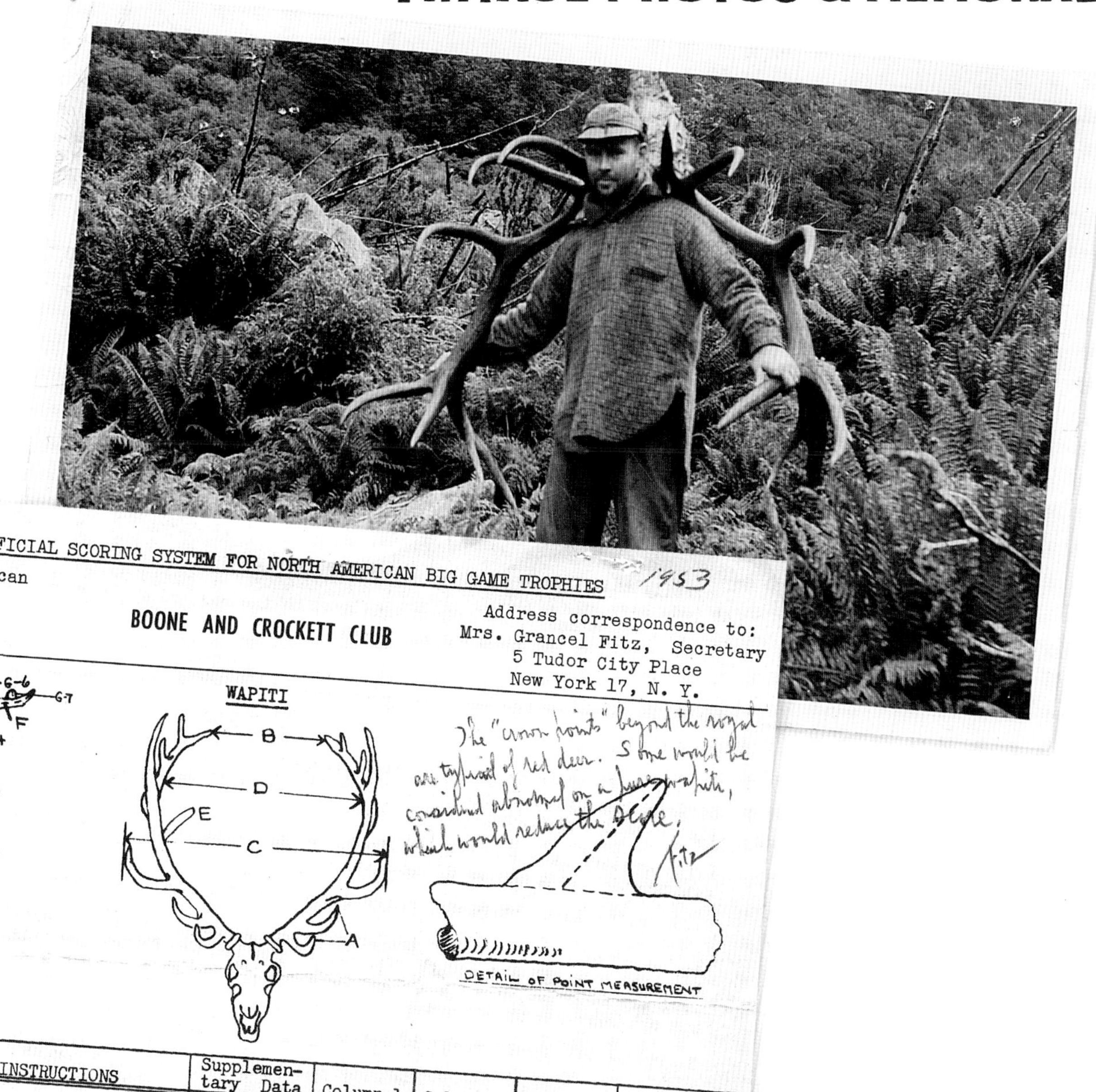

OFFICIAL SCORING SYSTEM FOR NORTH AMERICAN BIG GAME TROPHIES 1953

merican
ee

BOONE AND CROCKETT CLUB

Address correspondence to:
Mrs. Grancel Fitz, Secretary
5 Tudor City Place
New York 17, N. Y.

WAPITI

The "crown points" beyond the royal are typical of red deer. Some would be considered abnormal on a huge wapiti, which would reduce the score. Fitz

FOR INSTRUCTIONS	Supplementary Data R.	Supplementary Data L.	Column 1	Column 2	Column 3	Column 4
Each Antler			Spread Credit	Right Antler	Left Antler	Difference
	9	7				
	36					
	59					
Spread credit may equal but not exceed length of longer antler			42			
Main Beams exceeds longer difference						
ll Abnormal Points						—
t				55 3/8	54	2
nt				18 2/8	17	1 2/8
				19 2/8	19	4/8
al) Point				18	16	—
				14 6/8	14	2
if present				14	14	6/8
t, if present				7 4/8	8 4/8	—
est Place nd Points				4 4/8	—	1
est Place d Points				10 4/8	9 7/8	4 4/8
st Place n Points				7 4/8	7 4/8	5/8
st Place Points				7 5/8	7 5/8	—

LEFT: This New Zealand red deer was taken in 1952 and submitted for inclusion in the Records Program. It was obviously not eligible for entry since it was not a North American big game animal, but had been kept in the rejected section of the archives.

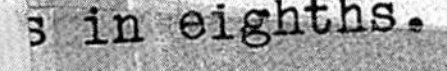

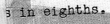

ABOVE: Mr. M.A. Gamblin took this Powell County, Montana, bull, displayed sitting below four fine mule deer, in October of 1951. The bull scores 359-1/8 points. It was dropped from the records by 1968 when the minimum score was at an all-time high of 375 points.

RIGHT: Not very much is known about this bull. It was purchased at an auction in Arkansas in 1977. The buyer put it on display in his store. He could not recall the name of the hunter who had taken this bull, but he did know it was taken sometime around 1912 in Jackson County. It has a final score of 388-/8 points.

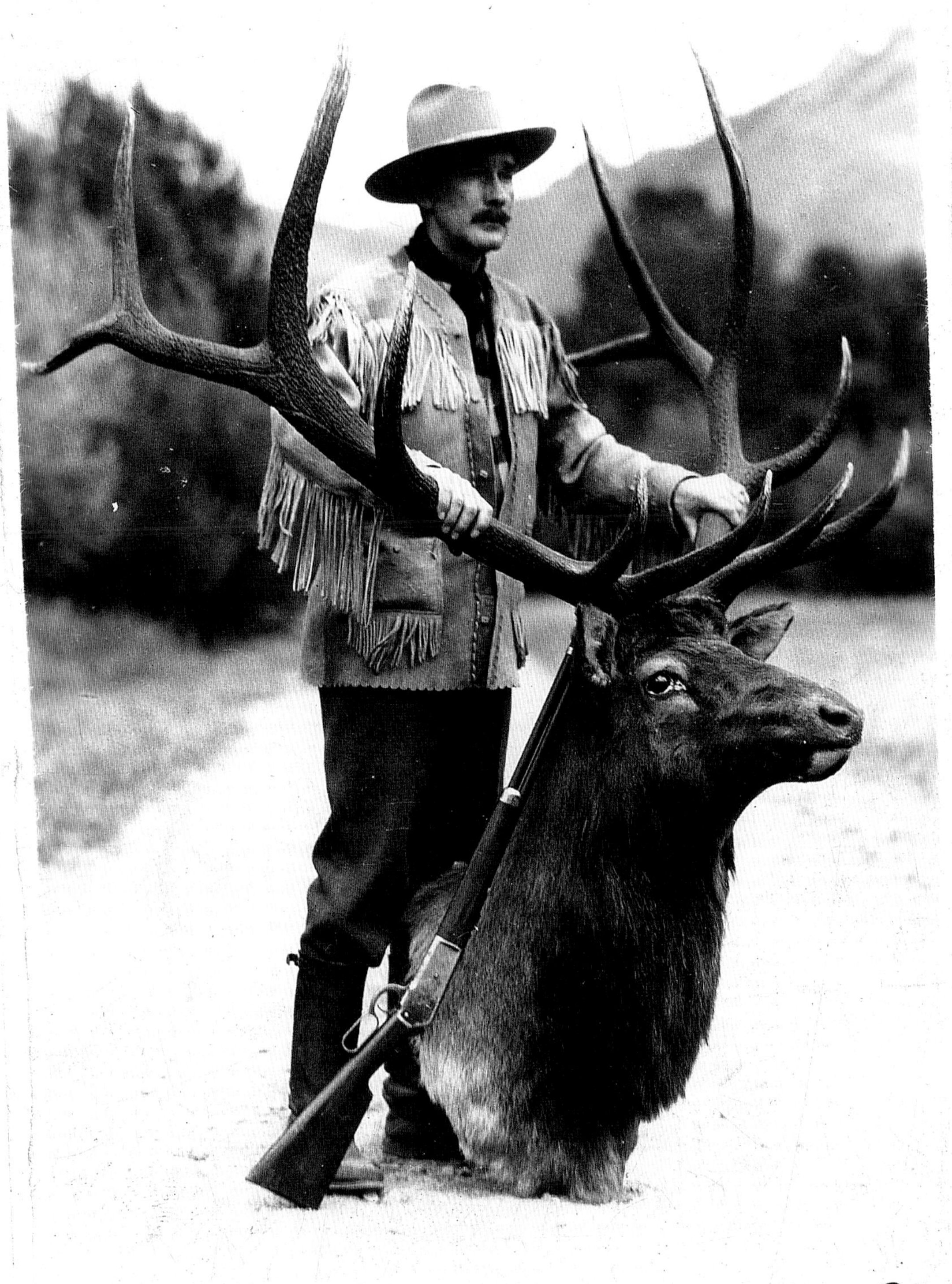

Record elk - owned by Larry Larom - Valley Ranch, Valley - Wyo -

ABOVE: This fine bull is pictured outside the Boise Fish and Game Commission office where it was scored in 1964. It was taken by an unknown hunter in 1915 and hung in the Boise Elks Lodge until John M. Anderson purchased it in the early 1960s.

RIGHT: Fred Space harvested his bull near Colorado's Muddy Creek in October of 1951. The bull scores 345-1/8 points and was dropped from the records after the minimums increased.

LEFT: Unfortunately, all we know about this bull is printed on the bottom of the photo. It is the front of a postcard found in donated materials from Grancel Fitz's family to the Club. There are no correlating score charts or entry materials.

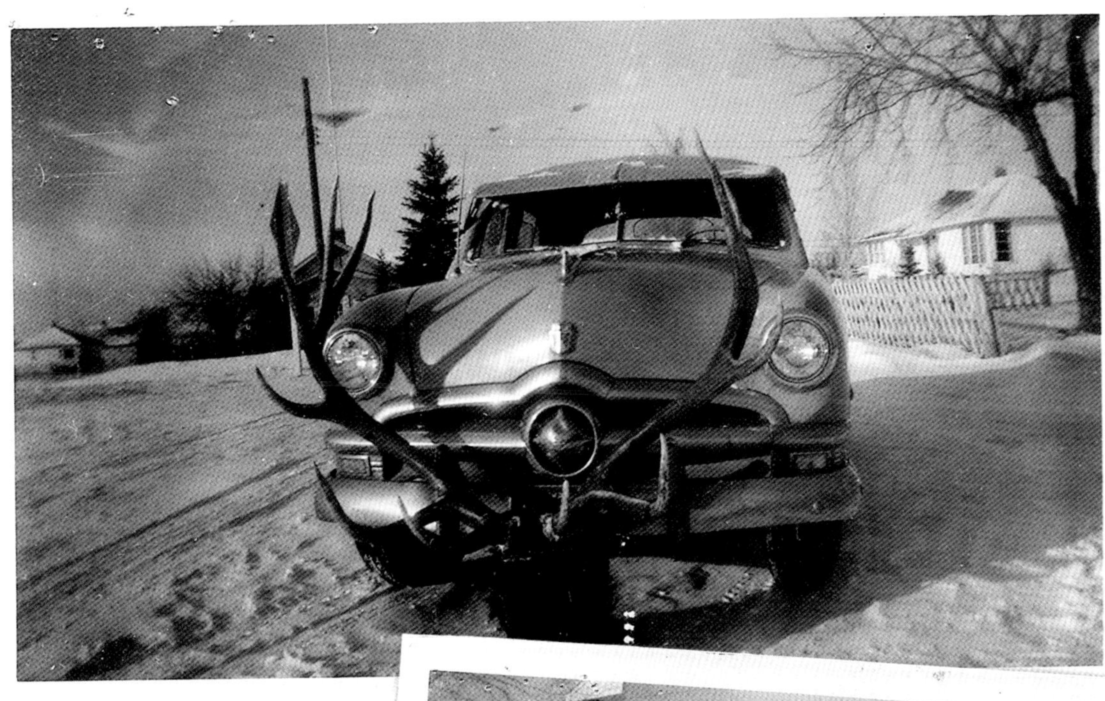

ABOVE: This tremendous 386-1/8 typical American elk was taken in December of 1962 near Forest Gate Store in Saskatchewan. The hunter, Edwin L. Roberts, was invited to send his trophy to the 1963 Competition. He replied he would like to, but the bull had been stolen shortly after being measured. As far as is known, it has never been recovered.

LEFT: This bull was entered in 1965 by Harold Mailman from Elbow River, Alberta. It has very impressive tine length, though its inside spread is a mere 32-7/8 inches. It is currently scored as a typical, though has never been re-measured as a non-typical. It would almost certainly rank very high in this fairly recently created category.

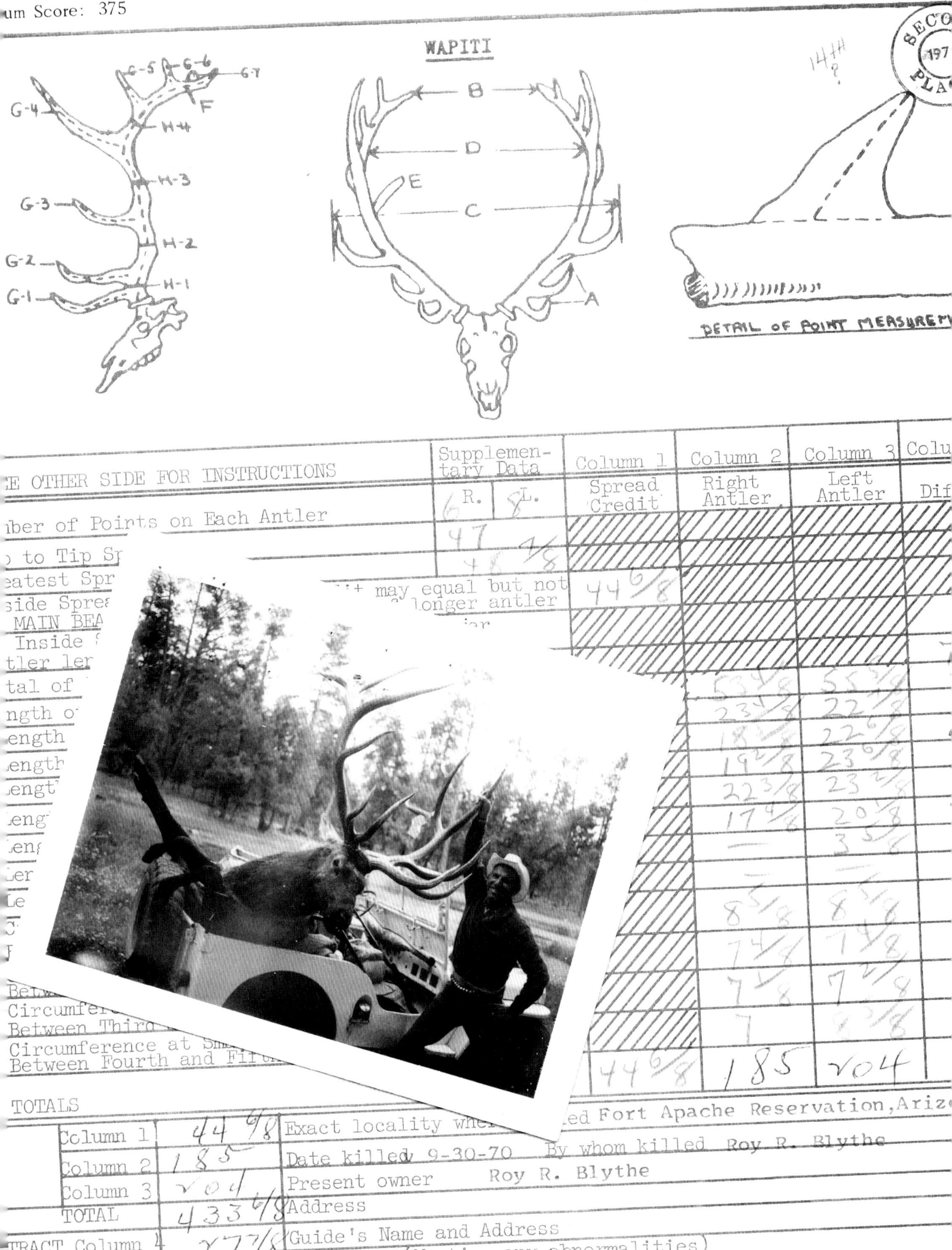

um Score: 375

WAPITI

E OTHER SIDE FOR INSTRUCTIONS	Supplementary Data R.	Supplementary Data L.	Column 1 Spread Credit	Column 2 Right Antler	Column 3 Left Antler	Colu… Dif…
ber of Points on Each Antler	6	8				
to Tip Sp	47	4/8				
eatest Spr	48	1/8				
side Sprea … may equal but not … longer antler			44 6/8			
MAIN BEA						
Inside						
tler len						
tal of						
ngth o				53 [illegible]/8	55 [illegible]/8	
ength				23 [illegible]/8	22 [illegible]/8	
ength				18 [illegible]/8	22 6/8	
ength				19 2/8	23 6/8	
engt				22 3/8	23 2/8	
eng				17 4/8	20 1/8	
en				—	3 5/8	
er						
e				8 5/8	8 5/8	
C				7 4/8	7 4/8	
Betw…				7 [illegible]/8	7 2/8	
Circumfere… Between Third				7	8 [illegible]/8	
Circumference at Sma… Between Fourth and Fift…			44 6/8	185	204	

TOTALS

Column 1	44 6/8
Column 2	185
Column 3	204
TOTAL	433 6/8
TRACT Column 4	27 7/8

Exact locality whe… …ed Fort Apache Reservation, Ariz…

Date killed 9-30-70 By whom killed Roy R. Blythe

Present owner Roy R. Blythe

Address

Guide's Name and Address

(Mention any abnormalities)

ABOVE: This great Shoshone County, Idaho, non-typical fell in October of 1974 to Hugh M. Kitzmiller's .308 Winchester. The bull was not entered until the 21st Competition and has a final score of 393-3/8.

RIGHT: This bull is listed as having an unknown hunter, and rightfully so. Neil Hinton purchased it for a nominal fee from a college student who had found the rack in an old barn and needed money. Mr. Hinton then took it to Mr. Jack O'Connor who taped it at a reported 430 points, though the score chart and records of its measurement by O'Connor could never be located. It was re-measured in 1969 at 420-5/8. At the time, it was the fourth-largest elk ever entered. After an error in spread credit was corrected, the bull was entered at 410 points, which is where it sits today.

LEFT: Roy R. Blythe took this 405-7/8 typical on the Fort Apache Reservation of Arizona in 1970. It was invited to the 14th Competition where it received the 2nd Award.

OFFICIAL.

Remarks: Because of the [illegible]
uncommon flat character I also took the following measurements which are shown on the diagram on the right below which I altered to a six point.
There is approx 1# of skull on the antlers. the entire weight is 33 lbs.

8" cir
5¼"
9¾"
8⅛
6½"
9⅛" cir

To
this
ack No

e on

Tolany Par[illegible]

ABOVE: Pictured is Charlotte Dunsmoor Wall. The six year old is proudly holding a 363-1/8 Roosevelt's elk her father, Oliver Dunsmoor, took near Astoria, Oregon, prior to 1938.

RIGHT: Oscar B. Skaggs harvested this 382-2/8 point bull close to the town of Williams, Arizona, in 1954. It was scored almost a year to the date later and remains in the book at this score today.

LEFT: October 15, 1949, found S.J. Seidensticker on Blacktail Creek in Beaverhead County, Montana, where he took this fine bull. The 6-point bull boasts 1st circumference measurements of more than 12 inches, with main beams of 52 inches on the left and 55 inches on the right.

VINTAGE PHOTOS & MEMORABILIA

Measurement at time of Shooting was 376 4/8

ABOVE: Taken near Duck Mountain, Manitoba, this bull fell to G.N. Burton on September 20, 1965. It has a final score of 380 points.

RIGHT: Washington resident Frank L. Vennum traveled to northeastern Oregon and took this fine bull in Umatilla County sometime during November of 1947. It was never re-measured when the new system was adopted in the 1950s.

LEFT: Kenneth Smith collected this 378-4/8 point bull in early November 1954. The photo shown is a newspaper clipping submitted with his entry. It was taken in Park County, Wyoming.

Records of North American Big Game

COMMITTEE
[...]ED ELY, CHAIRMAN
[...]LD E. ANTHONY
[...] M. CARPENTER

IN CARE OF
AMERICAN MUSEUM OF NATURAL HISTORY
COLUMBUS AVENUE AND 77TH STREET
NEW YORK, N. Y.

UNDER THE AUSPICES OF
THE NATIONAL MUSEUM OF HEADS AND HORNS OF THE NEW YORK ZOOLOGICAL SOCIETY
&
THE BOONE & CROCKETT CLUB

Destroyed by fire
See Vancouver
1-1-50

WAPITI

SPECIES Cervus Canadensis canadensis

MEASUREMENTS

	RIGHT	LEFT
Length on outside curve **A**	$57\frac{1}{2}$	54
Circumference between bez and trez **B**	~~$12\frac{1}{2}$~~ $8\frac{1}{2}$	~~$10\frac{1}{4}$~~ 8 5/8
Circumfe[...]	$12\frac{1}{2}$	$13\frac{1}{4}$
Number[...]		6

Greates[...]

Exact [...]

Date [...]

By w[...]

Ow[...]

R[...]

We hereby c[...]

on Dec.24 1948 ....193 ,

MER M. RUSTEN, M.D., CHAIRMAN
18420 D EIGHTH AVE. N.
WAYZATA, MINN. 55391

MILFORD BAKER
MAYWOOD ROAD
DARIEN, CONN

BOONE AND CROCKETT CLUB

ME COMMITTEE

March 17, 196

Re: Wapiti killed 10/9/66
Hiesie, Bonneville County, Idaho

Dear Mrs. Smith:

Thank you for sending in the chart for above Wapiti. Official Acknowledgment is enclosed.

Our office force is not sufficiently large to interfile all charts as they come in with previous charts. According to the Records Book published in 1964 your trophy would rank 27. New charts have been received which will change the rank somewhat but it will give you an idea as to where your trophy ranks. Also up to the time of publication of 1964 Records Book no other woman had killed a wapiti as large as yours. Congratulations!

ANNOUNCEMENT LETTER SENT
ADDING MACHING TAPE SHOWING SCORE LOWERED TO 389 6/8

ABOVE: This great Montana bull was taken in Flathead County, Montana, by Pat Roth in 1966. It has a final score of 375-7/8 points.

RIGHT: Roger Linnell took this bull, scoring 395-4/8, in Fremont County, Wyoming, during October of 1955. It was sent to the 16th Awards and received a Certificate of Merit.

LEFT: Mrs. E. LaRene Smith took this fine bull in Bonneville County, Idaho, in 1966. It was shipped to the 13th Competition. At the time, it was the largest elk to be entered by a female hunter. It scores 381 points.

ABOVE: Kenneth A. Evans is pictured here with a bull scoring 385-1/8 taken in October of 1966 near Grande Cache Lake, Alberta.

RIGHT: Harry Shaw, Jr., took yet another trophy-quality bull from Montana in 1950. With an entry score of 363-2/8 points, we can find no documentation that it was ever officially measured and is therefore not currently included in the records.

LEFT: This bull was taken in either 1923 or 1924 by Henry Lambert in Gallatin County, Montana. The handsome 6x6 scores 382-2/8 points.

must be made with a flexible steel tape to the nearest one-eighth
ments cannot be taken for at least sixty days after the animal was
otographs.

conformation of the trophy. Evaluation o

ata measureme
a matter of ... n must be a

ints on Each ... points are n
ND its lengt ... counted as
nt to neares
d as a point

pread measur ... the center

ead measure
dest part w ... line of the

ad of Main B ... Spread Cred
between ma
s less than ... rally consic

ngths of all
al in shape ... outer curv

ain Beam me
oint of wha ... main beam.

7. Length o
nearest edg

cumferences

... es was origi
plete system ... y Grancel F
n 1935 by D ... a single, s
in NORTH A ... quested an
epted autho ... Big Game Tr
develop the Official Scoring System for North American Big Game Tr
is committee were Dr. Harold E. Anthony, Milford Baker, Frederick
Clark, Grancel Fitz and Samuel B. Webb, Chairman.

System is basically a consolidation of the best points in the two
tems: In the process, some new points have been developed, errors
... has been achieved.

Signature:

INSTRUCTIONS

ements must be made with a flexible steel tape to the nearest one-eighth
easurements cannot be taken for at least sixty ... animal was
valuation o
mi
n must be a
ary oints are n
ion counted as
of
long
of p
measu he center
o Tip ine of th
est Sp pread Cre
ll at w
de Spre ly cons
est poir
if it i
al of Le outer cu
nontypic
of burr over
measured from lowest outside edge
ngth of Main Beam
distant point of what is, or appears to be, the main beam.
-3-4-5-6-7. Length of Normal Points. Normal points project from main bea
ured from nearest edge of main beam over outer curve to tip.
2-3-4. Circumferences - self explanatory.

ACKNOWLEDGEMENTS

first complete system for scoring North American big game trophies was o
yrighted in 1935 by Dr. James L. Clark. The second was devised by Grance
published in NORTH AMERICAN BIG GAME. Recognizing the need for a single
stem of accepted authority, the Boone and Crockett Club in 1949 requested
mmittee to develop the Official Scoring System for North American Big Gam
mbers of this committee were Dr. Harold E. Anthony, Milford Baker, Freder
. James L. Clark, Grancel Fitz and Samuel B. Webb, Chairman.

his Official System is basically a consolidation of the best points in th
isting systems: In the process, some new points have been developed, er
...ation has been achieved.

...re than 250 qualifi

ABOVE: This 376-5/8 point typical was taken by Melvin Van Lewen in 1961. The entry was received the following year and the owner was listed as the Colorado Division of Wildlife. It's assumed the bull was donated by Mr. Van Lewen, who signed the Fair Chase statement and is the one pictured.

LEFT: Mrs. Arvid F. Benson took this bull near Jackson Hole, Wyoming, in 1947. While women trophy hunters were not common in this day, they obviously existed. Mrs. Benson traveled from Arlington, Virginia, to take this 344-5/8 bull.

ABOVE: While Gary Beley took this fine Yellowstone migration bull near Gardiner, Montana, in 1964, it was not entered until 1990. Under the old system without non-typical category, it would have scored 349-6/8 points and would not have qualified for the records. It is currently listed at 403-2/8 points as a non-typical American elk.

RIGHT: Pictured here is Fred Huntington, Jr., the founder of RCBS, a company which today still produces reloading supplies. From the correspondence in the file, we know Fred traveled all over the world from his home in California pursuing numerous game species. This particular bull was taken near Alberta's Big Smoky River in September of 1961.

LEFT: In this photo, Christine and Chris Mullikin pose with a mounted elk taken in the fall of 1961. There were three hunters shooting at this bull and, while Chris Mullikin had possession of the mount, the bull is listed as being taken by a Mr. Terry Carlson. According to Chris, Terry made a running shot on the bull and struck the fatal blow.

iversity of Montana
issoula, Montana 59801
6) 243-0211

Mrs. Walter F. Toerge
Secretary, Records C
Boone and Crockett C
Carnegie Museum
4400 Forbes Ave.
Pittsburgh, Pa. 1521

Dear Mrs. Toerge:

Enclo ... is ... earl
fall in western Montana. Mrs. ... I think ... iat
part Indian, the wife of a rancher. I think ... hun
that an Indian woman apparently about 50 years old who has hun
big game for over 35 years should shoot such a fine animal wit
a .30-30 carbine. I hope she wins first award!

Although points G-4 and G-5 are quite close toge
on each side, there is no question in my mind that all of the
points on this head are normal. Grancel Fitz says in connectio
with scoring of elk heads, "The scoring system does not attemp
regulate spacing between antler points."

I have urged Mr. and Mrs. Eder to wait until th
competition is over in the spring of 1971 before having the h
mounted. They returned the head to their home in Helmville to
from a local taxidermy shop.

Sincerely yours,

Philip L. Wright

Philip L. Wright

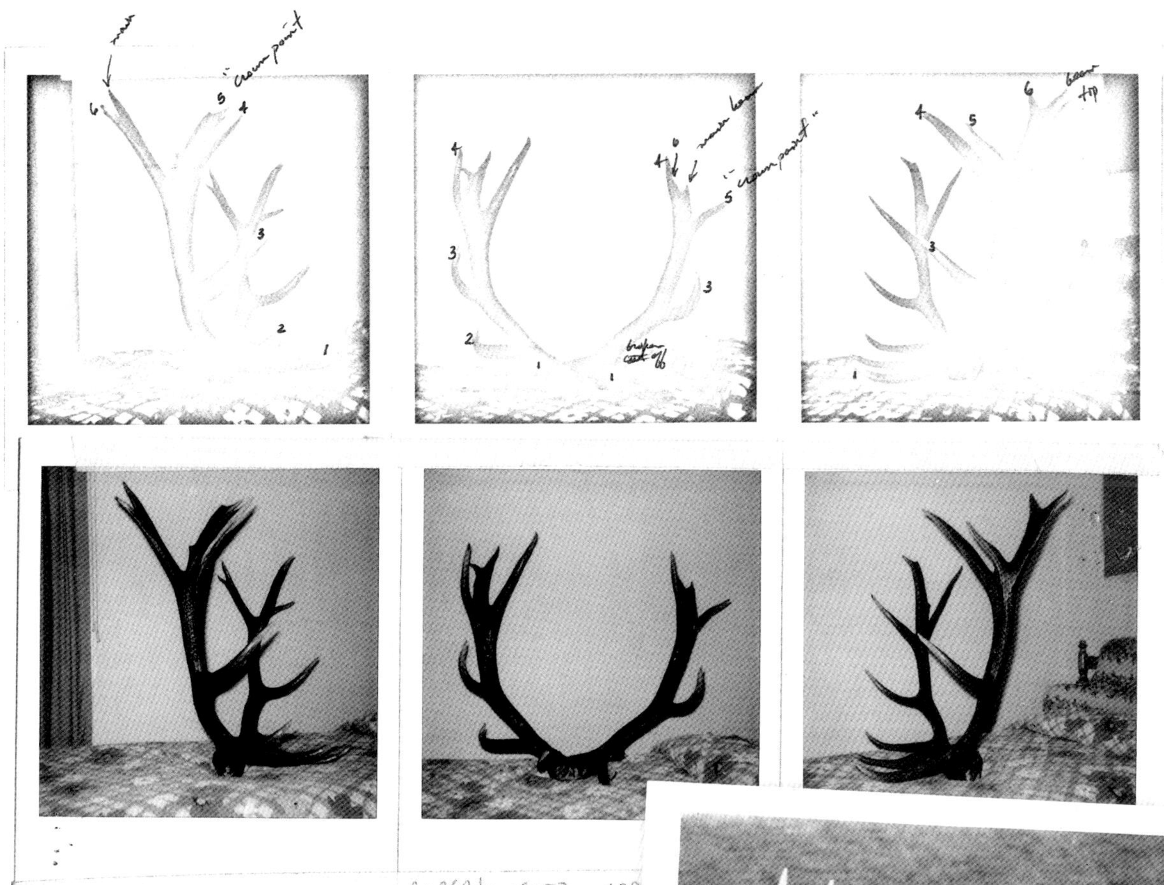

ABOVE: Robert Lenz took this mature Roosevelt's elk in 1948 while hunting Grays Harbor County of Washington state. The bull scores 299-5/8 points with 21-7/8 total inches of crown points.

RIGHT: Tom Nidey took this 377-6/8 typical in 1959 from Colorado's Routt National Forest, which was set aside by President Roosevelt in 1905.

LEFT: Mrs. Mildred Eder harvested this Powell County, Montana, bull on October 19, 1969. She was nearly 50 when she harvested the bull and had been hunting elk in Montana for 35 years. The bull fell to her Model 94 .30-30 Winchester. It received honorable mention at the 14th Competition.

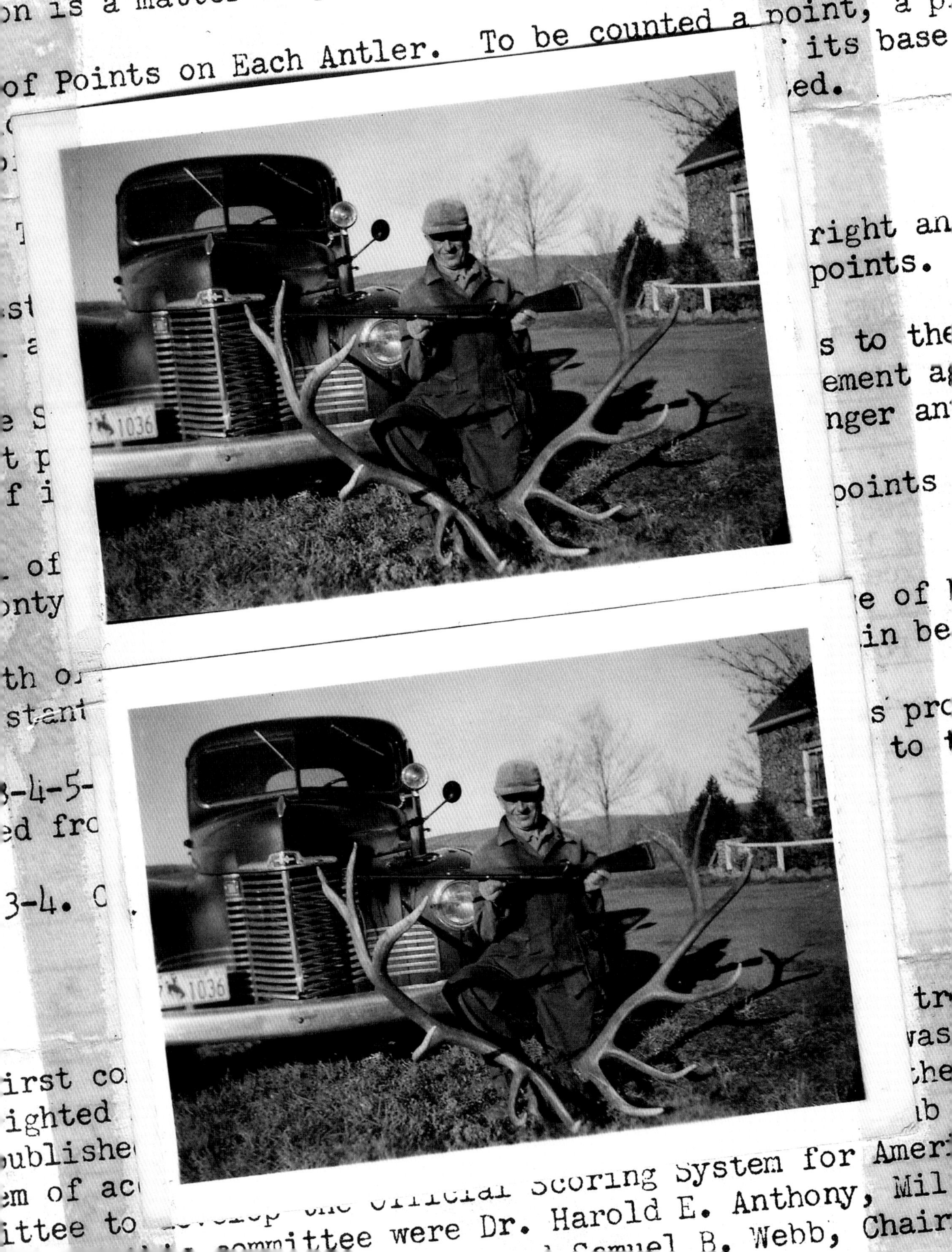

To be counted a point, a p
of Points on Each Antler.
its base
right an
points.
s to the
ement a
nger an
points
1036
Scoring System for Ameri
Dr. Harold E. Anthony, Mil
committee were
Samuel B. Webb, Chair

ABOVE: Gaylord Hagen took this bull on Fort Peck Game Reserve, currently known as the C.M. Russell Wildlife Refuge, in northeastern Montana on November 25, 1962. The bull was dropped from the records when the its score of 361 fell below minimum. It was re-entered in 1999 at the request of the hunter's son.

RIGHT: Marshall Sherman of Colorado took this fine bull in Summit County of his home state in October of 1966. The trophy scores 382-4/8 points.

LEFT: Fredrik Schnepper took this fine bull in October 1951. In his correspondence, he informed the Records Committee that the bull was taken at 553 steps with an open sight Winchester model 70. The bull scores an impressive 362-3/8 but was dropped when the minimums were increased.

VINTAGE PHOTOS & MEMORABILIA

ABOVE: Glen Daly took this bull on the Fort Apache Indian Reservation in 1957. The original entry score was 389-5/8, though it had not met the required drying period. It was measured again in February of 1958 at 384-3/8, though upon inspection by the Judge's Panel, its final score was adjusted to 385-5/8.

RIGHT: While hunting in Jefferson County, Washington, in 1965, David D. Godfrey took this Roosevelt's elk with his .308 Winchester. The bull was invited to the 18th Awards, though it was discovered that two of the crown points had been scored as normal G5s. After the necessary corrections were made, this bull had a final score of 337-1/8. It is the 12th largest Roosevelt's elk from Washington in the book today. At the time of entry it was the state record.

LEFT: Not much is known in terms of the history of this fine bull, which hangs in the Altadena, California, American Legion Post. It has a typical entry score of 365 points, although with such limited history, it was dropped when the minimum was raised; it is currently not included in the records book.

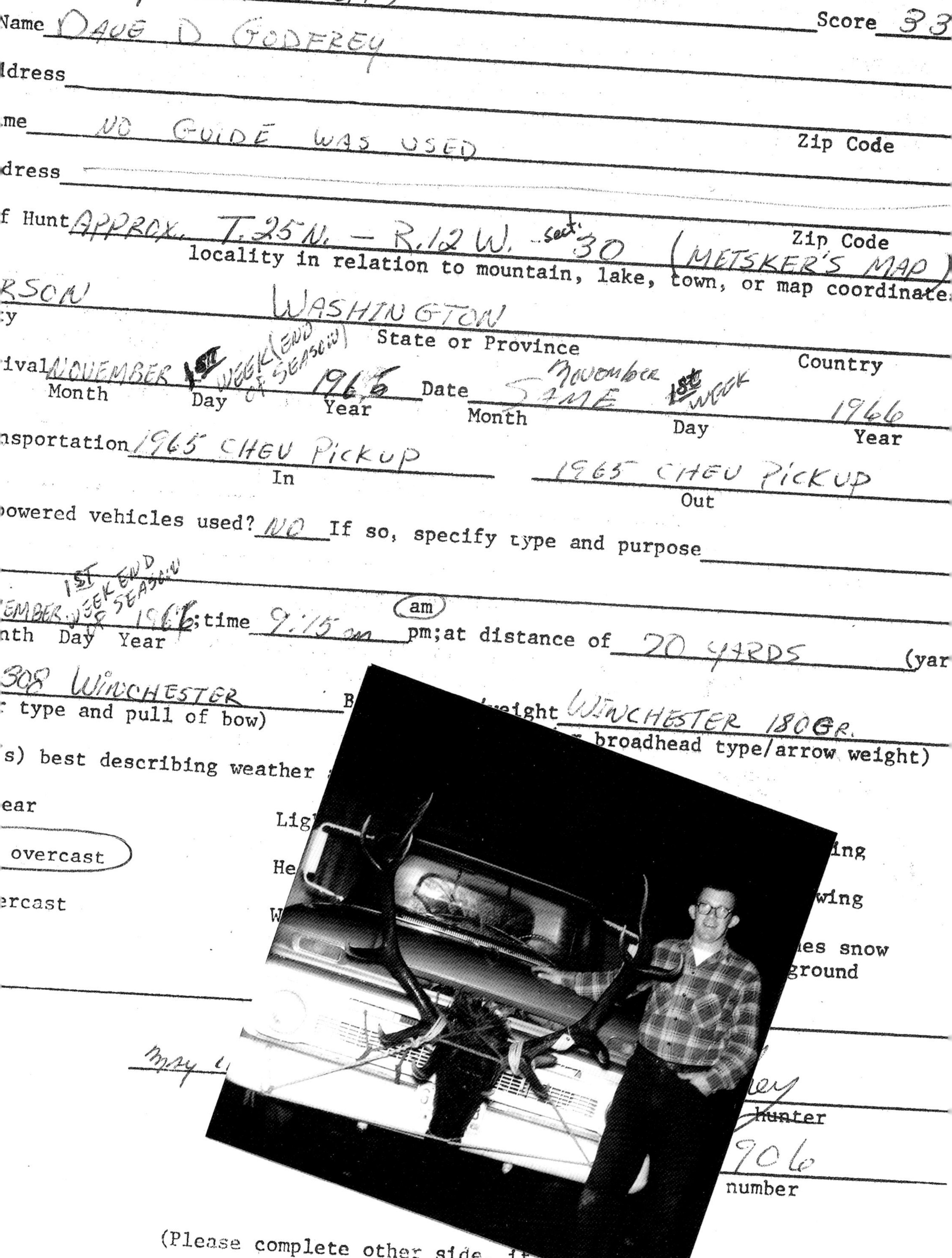

Name DAVE D GODFREY Score 33

ldress

.me NO GUIDE WAS USED Zip Code

dress

f Hunt APPROX. T.25N. – R.12W. sect. 30 (METSKER'S MAP) Zip Code
locality in relation to mountain, lake, town, or map coordinate

RSON WASHINGTON
:y State or Province Country

ival NOVEMBER 1st WEEKEND OF SEASON 1966 Date November SAME 1st WEEK 1966
Month Day Year Month Day Year

nsportation 1965 CHEV PICKUP 1965 CHEV PICKUP
In Out

powered vehicles used? NO If so, specify type and purpose

EMBER 1st WEEKEND OF SEASON 1966; time 9:15 am (am) pm; at distance of 20 YARDS (yar
nth Day Year

308 WINCHESTER B... weight WINCHESTER 180GR.
type and pull of bow) ... broadhead type/arrow weight)

s) best describing weather ...

ear Lig... ...ing

overcast He... ...wing

ercast W... ...es snow
...ground

May ... ...ey
hunter

906
number

(Please complete other side, if ...

VINTAGE PHOTOS & MEMORABILIA

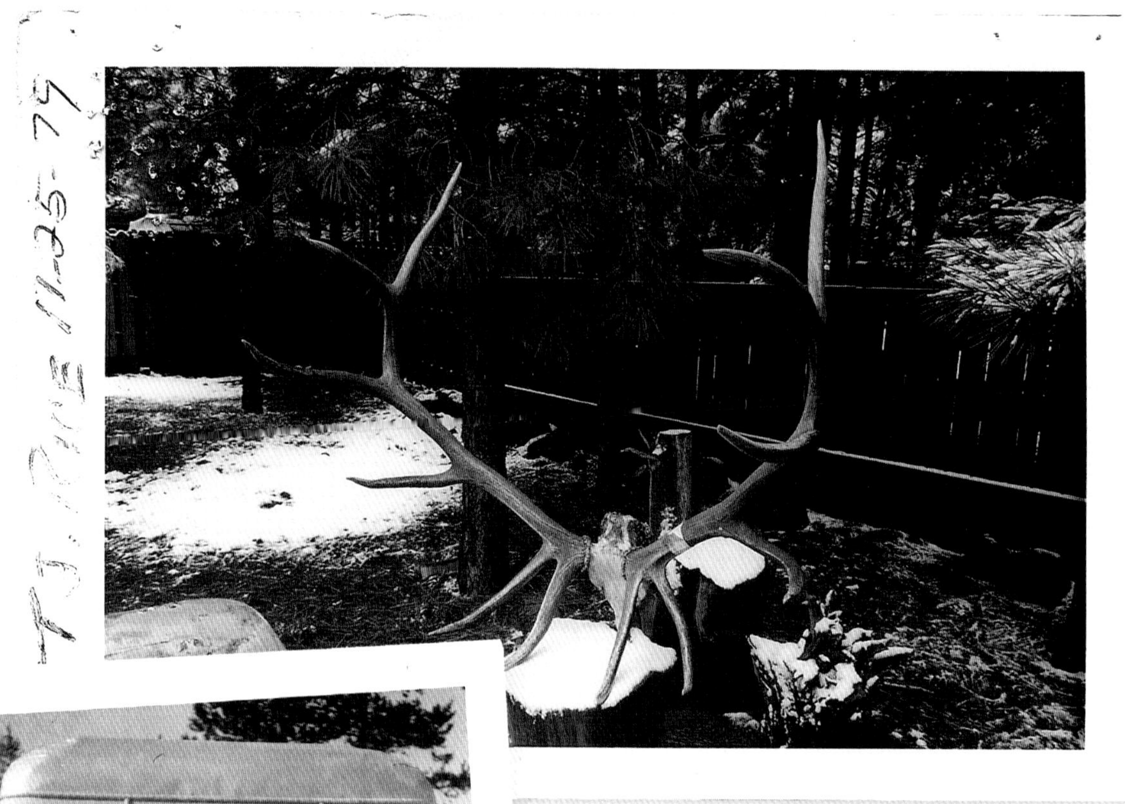

ABOVE: Terry J. Rice harvested this 399-3/8 typical American elk in November of 1979 while hunting in Coconino County, Arizona. It was invited to the 18th Awards, though Mr. Rice could not get it there. It was rescored by two additional official measurers and the asterisk was finally removed in 1989. The bull still ranks as a top 20 entry from Arizona to this day.

RIGHT: The bull proudly displayed on the grill of the Jeep was taken in 1949 near Ten Sleep, Wyoming, by Stephen Pease, Jr. It had an entry score of 366, though after the necessary corrections were made, it scored 338-4/8 and never appeared in any publications.

LEFT: Gene Riordan's son entered this bull for him in the 19th Awards. He had taken it with a .300 Weatherby near Jackson Hole, Wyoming, in 1960. The bull's final score is 385-3/8 points.

INSTRUCTIONS

...ements must be made with a flexible steel tape to the nearest one-eig...
...easurements cannot be taken for at least sixty days after the animal...
...mit photographs.

...ary Data measurements ... the animal
...on is a matter of perso...

...f Points on Each Antle... Evaluation
...ng AND its length mus...
...point to nearest edg...
...ured as a point. ...ection must be

...p Spread measured be... ...ll points are
... is counted as

...pread measured betw...
...widest part whether...

...ead of Main Beams me... to the center l...
...t between main bea...
...s less than or equ...

...ngths of all Abnorm... ...er line of the s...
...l in shape or loca... ..."Spread Credit...

...in Beam measured f... ...e generally considere...
...int of what is, or...

Length of Normal... ...over outer curve to
...arest edge of mai...

...nferences - self ... from main beam. The

...e system for sco...
...5 by Dr. James ...
...ORTH AMERICAN B...
... authority, the ... ...ophies was originated a...
...p the Official ... ...ed by Grancel Fitz in l...
...mittee were Dr. ... for a single, standard
Grancel Fitz a... ...requested an independe...
...can Big Game Trophies.
...n is basically ... ...er, Frederick K. Barbou...
...n the process, some new points have been developed, errors correct...
...ation has been achieved. ...nts in the two previousl...

...these charts were si...

4: AWARD WINNERS

BY RICHARD T. HALE

It is not generally known that Boone and Crockett's records keeping goes back more than 100 years. This statement will contradict previously published information, but the relatively recent discovery of an early Boone and Crockett scoring manual published in 1906 rewrites history for North American big game records-keeping.

The famous "first" Boone and Crockett book, *Records of North American Big Game*, published in 1932, was historically regarded as the Club's initial effort. It is a landmark book, and early printings have long been difficult to find. In modern times, it has been reprinted twice and these editions are readily available.

The first Boone and Crockett so-called "big game competitions" were held annually from 1947 to 1949.

Rankings were based on simple measurements of length of the longer horn or antler or the greatest length of the skull. There were no additions, deductions, or other complications.

For the 1950 Big Game Competition, the new Official Scoring system was in place. This system was a joint venture by James L. Clark, Grancel Fitz, Dr. Harold E. Anthony, Milford Baker, Thomas H. Barbour, and Samuel Webb; Webb served as the chairman. Its work was chiefly a reconciliation of the systems of James Clark and Grancel Fitz. Clark and Fitz had, in certain ways, debated the intricacies of a new system since at least the publication of the 1939 *North American Big Game* book.

Members of the 14th Competition's Judges Panel verified the score of numerous wapiti including a couple of non-typical bulls that were determined to be below the minimum score for wapiti. Unfortunately, at this time in records keeping history, the Club had not created a category for non-typical elk. Since the introduction of the category with the 18th Awards Program several of these older non-typical elk have taken their rightful places in the records book.

Verbal and written history indicate the early awards committees were somewhat less diplomatic in deciding issues, as compared to the modern, smoothly run events assembled by current Records Committee Chairman Buck Buckner.

Since 1952, a few minor changes have been adopted. Instructions for taking measurements have been modified and added to in the interest of clarification. Minimums have been changed; special and previously unforeseen situations have been addressed. New categories have been added.

The near universal acceptance of the Boone and Crockett Official Scoring System, as originally formulated and occasionally modified during the last 60 years, shows the wisdom and foresight of the original committee members. We owe them a debt of gratitude.

The first ten Big Game Competitions were held at the American Museum of Natural History in New York City. In 1963, they moved to the Carnegie Museum in Pittsburgh, Pennsylvania, which held the next four competitions. After this, they were conducted in widely varied

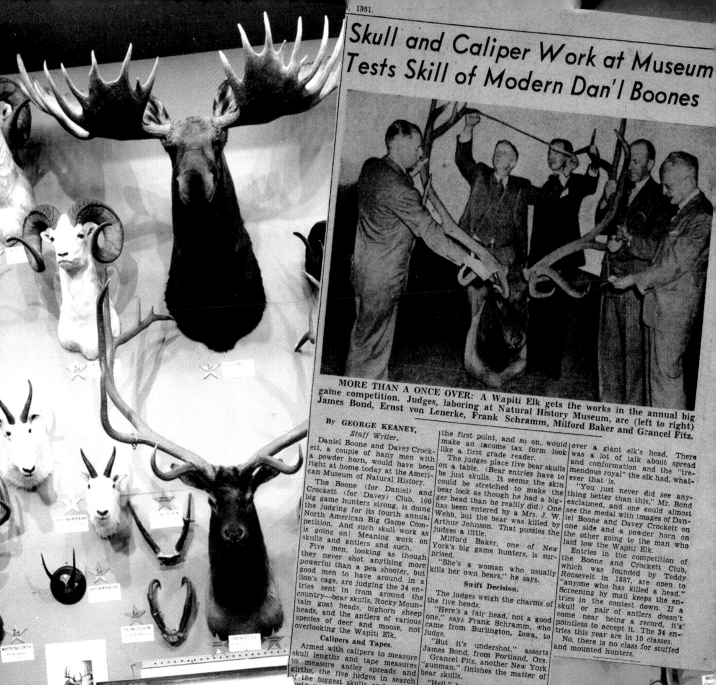

, 1951.

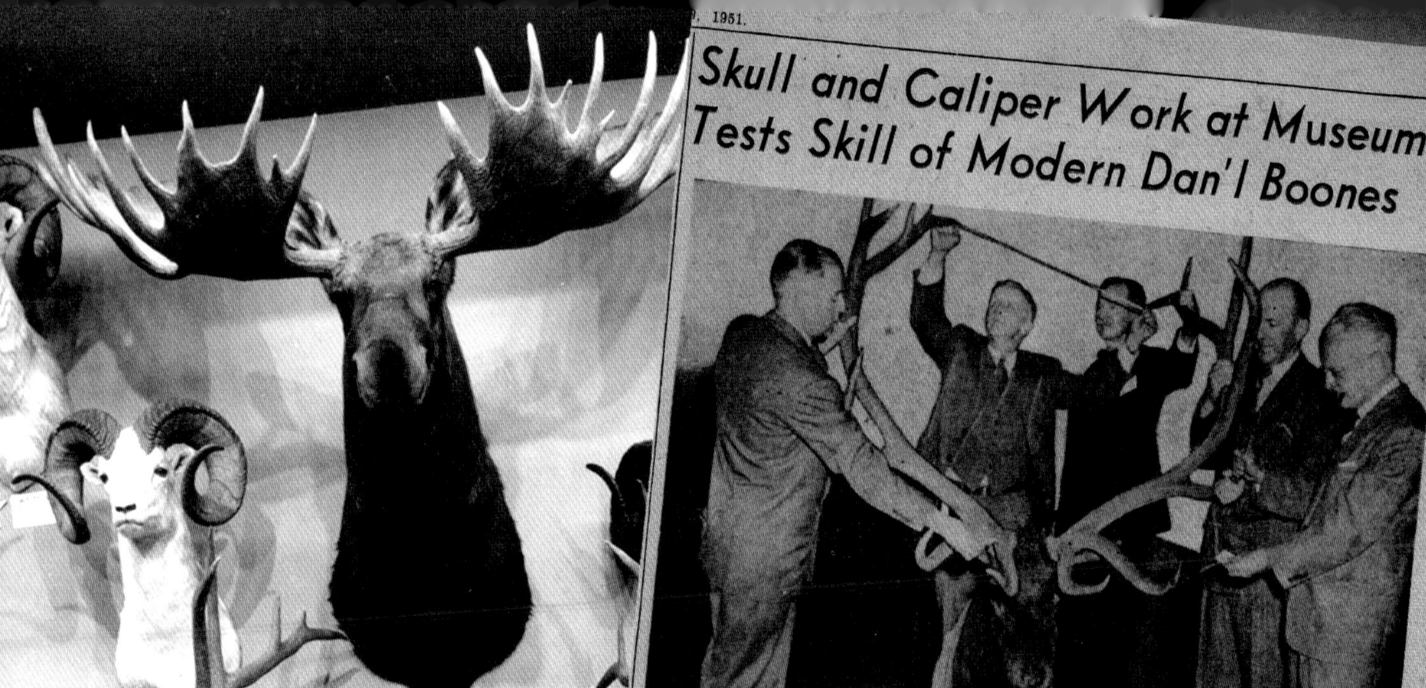

Skull and Caliper Work at Museum Tests Skill of Modern Dan'l Boones

MORE THAN A ONCE OVER: A Wapiti Elk gets the works in the annual big game competition. Judges, laboring at Natural History Museum, are (left to right) James Bond, Ernst von Lenerke, Frank Schramm, Milford Baker and Grancel Fitz.

By **GEORGE KEANEY,**
Staff Writer.

Daniel Boone and Davey Crockett, a couple of hany men with a powder horn, would have been right at home today at the American Museum of Natural History.

The Boone (for Daniel) and Crockett (for Davey) Club, 100 big game hunters strong, is doing the judging for its fourth annual North American Big Game Competition. And such skull work as is going on! Meaning work on skulls and antlers and such.

Five men, looking as though they never shot anything more powerful than a pea shooter, but good men to have around in a lion's cage, are judging the 34 entries sent in from around the country—bear skulls, Rocky Mountain goat heads, bighorn sheep heads, and the antlers of various species of deer and moose, not overlooking the Wapiti Elk.

Calipers and Tapes.

Armed with calipers to measure skull lengths and tape measures to measure antler spreads and girths, the five judges in search of the biggest skulls and antlers [illegible]uldn't be more serious if they [illegible]e five Einsteins, each with a [illegible]ry. The sco[illegible] sheet they use [illegible]ey check a de[illegible]r's antlers for [illegible] length of ma[illegible] in beam, cir[illegible]e between [illegible] the burr [illegible]d the first point, and so on, would make an income tax form look like a first grade reader.

The judges place five bear skulls on a table. (Bear entries have to be just skulls. It seems the skin could be stretched to make the bear look as though he had a bigger head than he reallly did.) One has been entered by a Mrs. J. W. Webb, but the bear was killed by Arthur Johnson. That puzzles the judges a little.

Milford Baker, one of New York's big game hunters, is surprised.

"She's a woman who usually kills her own bears," he says.

Swift Decision.

The judges weigh the charms of the five heads.

"Here's a fair head, not a good one," says Frank Schramm, who came from Burlington, Iowa, to judge.

"But it's undershot," asserts James Bond, from Portland, Ore.

Grancel Fitz, another New York "gunman," finishes the matter of bear skulls.

"Hell," he says, picking one up, "this is a better skull. That's all there's to it."

(The winners are hush-hush. Hunters will just have to wait with their pistols cocked until they're a[illegible]nounced in a month.)

The j[illegible]s moved on to drool over a giant elk's head. There was a lot of talk about spread and conformation and the "tremendous royal" the elk had, whatever that is.

"You just never did see anything better than this," Mr. Bond exclaimed, and one could almost see the medal with images of Daniel Boone and Davey Crockett on one side and a powder horn on the other going to the man who laid low the Wapiti Elk.

Entries in the competition of the Boone and Crockett Club, which was founded by Teddy Roosevelt in 1887, are open to "anyone who has killed a head." Screening by mail keeps the entries in the contest down. If a skull or pair of antlers doesn't come near being a record, it's pointless to accept it. The 34 entries this year are in 10 classes.

No, there is no class for stuffed and mounted hunters.

PRIZE WINNING TROPHIES
Submitted for the
1950 NORTH AMERICAN
BIG GAME COMPETITION
of the
BOONE AND CROCKETT CLUB

areas of the continent in an effort to involve and attract big game hunters and others interested in our native big game animals. This last change of venue has also helped spread the message of the North American model of wildlife management and conservation to the public.

The first 14 events were called North American Big Game Competitions. The 15th event was held in Atlanta, Georgia, and called the North American Big Game Awards Program. The name change came about to more accurately reflect the actual goal of the awards as a celebration of modern wildlife conservation. That name remains in use today. We have now begun planning for the 28th Big Game Awards to be held in Reno, Nevada, in the spring of 2013.

As you look through the vintage photos in the following chapters, it is apparent the North American Model of Wildlife Conservation has worked to a remarkable degree. For example, notice that the wapiti award-winners get larger over time: This continues today.

In the 1950s, conventional wisdom held the really top-end bulls were a past relic.

With the winter range settled, overgrazing by livestock, and fewer acres of undisturbed land, the common thinking was that the really huge bulls were gone. Note that the 4th Big Game Competition winner was a 366-inch bull. A nice trophy, but not even eligible for the All-time records book today. If you had asked the early committee members about the potential for a new World's Record wapiti, they would have said it was not likely unless an old trophy turned up from some long-forgotten hunt. How times have changed.

Today, one of the nicer aspects of trophy-elk hunting is its varied geography. There are increasingly more states and provinces that have produced award-winners. Some areas are more consistent producers than others, but a giant bull can come from literally anywhere it's allowed to mature. Idaho, Alberta, Montana, Wyoming, Colorado, and Arizona are all represented by award-winning bulls. We currently see winners in Nevada, New Mexico, and Utah, as well.

Early Competitions were held at the American Museum of Natural History in New York City and they received a fair amount of press from the NY papers.

As I reviewed the past Big Game Competitions, I could not help thinking of Art Popham, long-time regular member of the Boone and Crockett Club, Records Committee member, and veteran of many judging panels. Art chaired the 1960 competition. Forty years after the event, he still spoke of the lengthy discussion regarding two award-winning trophies: one, a new World's Record polar bear and the other, Fred Mercer's breathtaking elk from Madison County, Montana. In my opinion, Mercer's is the most beautiful elk of all time.

The polar bear was taken in full compliance with the game laws of the time by a very well-known and well-liked big game hunter—and future Governor of New Mexico. The elk was taken on a very difficult hunt and, as I remember the story, meat and, later, antlers were packed out in a blizzard. Art spoke with a firm voice about holding out for the Sagamore Hill Award to be presented to Mr. Mercer. He prevailed and was very proud of that victory for the rest of his life. He felt that act had set the precedent to value hardship and fair chase over small numerical advantages.

As you contemplate those long-distant hunts and admire the fruits of our predecessors' labors, I hope you take a minute to mentally thank the men and women with the determination in their souls to ensure that the opportunity to pursue these majestic animals has not only been maintained, but improved. That is the final measure of a hunter-conservationist.

To enjoy the resource and leave it in better condition than you found it: This is a success story of which I am proud to be a part. You should be as well. Enjoy the stories.

1st Prize 1947

OFFICIAL

Records of North American Big Game

IN CARE OF
AMERICAN MUSEUM OF NATURAL HISTORY
COLUMBUS AVENUE AND 77TH STREET
NEW YORK, N. Y.

UNDER THE AUSPICES OF THE NATIONAL MUSEUM OF HEADS AND HORNS OF THE NEW YORK ZOOLOGICAL SOCIETY & THE BOONE & CROCKETT CLUB

COMMITTEE
ALFRED ELY, CHAIRMAN
HAROLD E. ANTHONY
R. R. M. CARPENTER

On exhibition 1947

WAPITI

SPECIES

MEASUREMENTS	RIGHT	LEFT
Length on outside curve **A**	62	60-1/2
Circumference between bez and trez **B**	7-1/2	7-1/16
Circumference of burr **C**	12-1/2	12-1/2
Number of points on antler	6	6

Greatest spread: **D** Unknown

Exact locality where killed Salmon River, Idaho

Date killed March 1939

By whom killed Winter killed.

Owner Elmer Keith

Address North Fork, Idaho

Remarks:

Photographs: Front view ...... Profile ......
(Please place √ mark to indicate photographs furnished.)

We hereby certify that we have measured the above described trophy on April 20, 1948, and that these measurements are correct and made in accordance with the directions overleaf.

Measured by: T. Donald Carter

FIRST PRIZE | ELMER KEITH
1947 COMPETITION

The elk-shed antlers highlighted below were entered by Elmer Keith of North Fork, Idaho, in 1936. Keith was an Idaho rancher, highly influential firearms enthusiast, and prolific outdoor writer. He was instrumental in the development of the first magnum revolver cartridge, the .357 Magnum, as well as the later .44 Magnum and .41 Magnum cartridges. During the 1950s and 1960s, he was especially well-known for regular monthly columns he wrote for *Guns and Ammo* magazine.

Following is an excerpt from a 1948 letter he sent to Harold E. Anthony, Chairman of the Club's Records Program at the time:

"... At any rate I did not kill the old boy. Ran into him in deep snow when chasing a bear that had thawed out too early....At a glance I knew it was the finest elk head I had ever seen alive and have killed some good ones and guided others for even better but this head was outstanding in length. I made several trips back up there on snow shoes and was sorely tempted to bump the old bull and save his fine head and cape as he was very thin. However, I waited thinking I would at least pick up his horns. He died a natural death of starvation, and horns loosened so brought them out."

THE UNIVERSITY OF BRITISH COLUM
VANCOUVER, CANADA

MENT OF ZOOLOGY

Dear Dr Anthony,

Herewith photographs of entered by me in the big gam I hope this reaches you before date of Dec. 1.

Pressure of work has made it impossible for me to get the photographs taken sooner. I studied the possibility of sending my sheep head down but customs red tape & the very high express rates make that possibility virtually prohibitive.

I hope that some more equitable way of completing the records of bighorn can be found before another contest as the present rule makes it almost impossible for big game hunters in western Canada to compete successfully.

Sincerely yours

I. McT Cowan

AWARD WINNER

2ND COMPETITION - 1948

FIRST PRIZE | UNIVERSITY OF BRITISH COLUMBIA, MUSEUM OF ZOOLOGY 1948 COMPETITION

The First Prize winner from the Club's 2nd Competition was entered by Dr. Ian McTaggart Cowan, professor of zoology at the University of British Columbia. Nearly 20 years later, Dr. Cowan became a Boone and Crockett Club Member. He maintained his membership with the Club until his death in 2010.

Before the Club's official scoring system was implemented in 1950, it was not mandatory for trophy owners to ship their heads in for verification. Unfortunately, this bull was never remeasured under the new system so it's not listed in our current records.

1st Prize
1948 Com
Official
acc. by judges

Committee
Alfred Ely, Chairman

Records of North American Big Game

In care of
American Museum of Natural History
Columbus Avenue and 77th Street
New York, N. Y.

Under the … of The National … of Heads and … of the New York Zoo… Society & The Boone & C… Club

WAPITI

Species Cervus canadensis nelsoni

Measurements

	Right	Left
Length on outside curve A	59	59
Circumference between bez and trez B	7¼	7½
Circumference of burr C	13	13¼
Number of points on antler	6	6
Greatest spread: D	47¾	

Exact locality where killed Believed to be Kootenay dist, British Colum

Date killed not known exactly but about 1900

By whom killed not known

Owner Museum of Zoology, University of B.C.

Address Vancouver, B.C.

Remarks:

Photographs: Front view .... Profile ....
(Please place √ mark to indicate photographs furnished.)

We hereby certify that we have measured the above described trophy on Dec. 10, 1947 .... 193 , and that these measurements are correct and made in accordance with the directions overleaf.

the ...
and certificat...
of 1948. Ther...
for the inspec...
the American ...

Invi...
the Boone and...
trophies, to ...
and to others...
to meet many ...
exchange idea...
scope has bee...
have many pl...

The...
from sportsm...
conditions s...
its thanks a...
January 19th...

Wi...
will be pre...

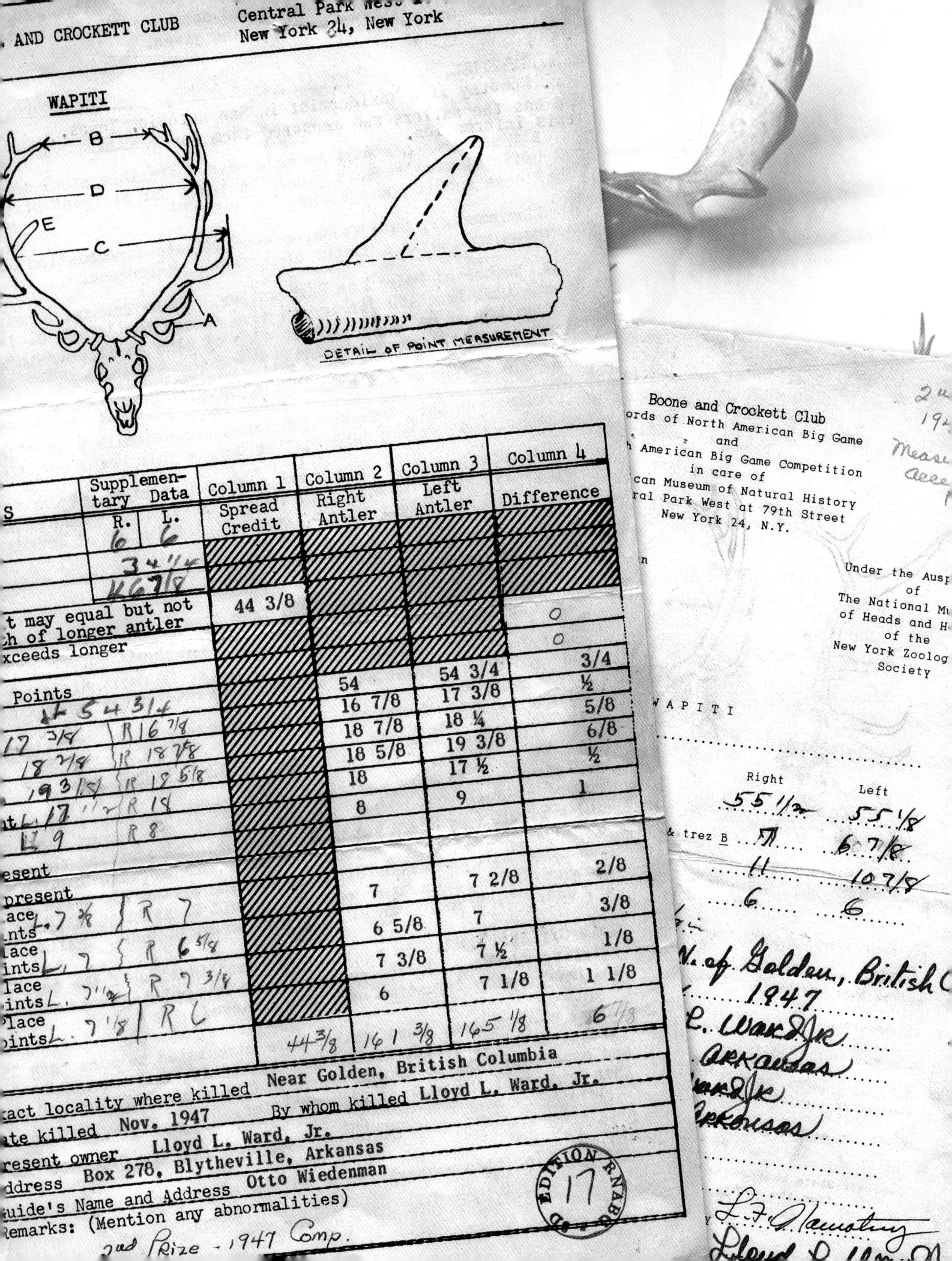

AND CROCKETT CLUB

Central Park West
New York 24, New York

WAPITI

S	Supplementary Data R.	Supplementary Data L.	Column 1 Spread Credit	Column 2 Right Antler	Column 3 Left Antler	Column 4 Difference
	6	6				
	34 1/4					
	46 7/8					
t may equal but not h of longer antler			44 3/8			0
xceeds longer						0
					54 3/4	3/4
Points				54		½
L 54 3/4				16 7/8	17 3/8	5/8
17 3/8	R 16 7/8			18 7/8	18 ¼	6/8
18 7/8	R 18 7/8			18 5/8	19 3/8	½
19 3/8	R 18 5/8			18	17 ½	1
t L 17 1/2	R 18			8	9	
L 9	R 8					
esent						2/8
present				7	7 2/8	3/8
ace nts L 7 3/8	R 7			6 5/8	7	1/8
lace ints L 7	R 6 5/8			7 3/8	7 ½	1 1/8
lace ints L 7 1/2	R 7 3/8			6	7 1/8	
Place points L 7 1/8	R 6					6 7/8
			44 3/8	161 3/8	165 1/8	

xact locality where killed Near Golden, British Columbia

ate killed Nov. 1947 By whom killed Lloyd L. Ward, Jr.

resent owner Lloyd L. Ward, Jr.

ddress Box 278, Blytheville, Arkansas

uide's Name and Address Otto Wiedenman

Remarks: (Mention any abnormalities)

2nd Prize - 1947 Comp.

EDITION 17

Boone and Crockett Club
ords of North American Big Game
and
h American Big Game Competition
in care of
can Museum of Natural History
ral Park West at 79th Street
New York 24, N.Y.

Under the Aus
of
The National M
of Heads and H
of the
New York Zoolog
Society

WAPITI

	Right	Left
	55 1/2	55 1/8
& trez B	7	6 7/8
	11	10 7/8
	6	6

N. of Golden, British C
1947
L. Ward Jr
Arkansas
Ward Jr
Arkansas

AWARD WINNER

2ND COMPETITION - 1948

SECOND PRIZE | LLOYD L. WARD, JR.
1948 COMPETITION

Ward submitted his British Columbia elk in the Club's 2nd Competition, where it received a Second Prize in 1948. It was subsequently remeasured under the new system in 1950 and appeared in the 1952, 1958, and 1964 editions of *Records of North American Big Game*, but dropped out of the system when the minimum score for typical American elk was raised to 375 in 1968. At the time, it was the first trophy elk in the program from British Columbia.

~~October 18~~, 1948

Mr. Lloyd L. Ward, Jr.
Red Top Gin Company
Blytheville, Arkansas

Dear Mr. Ward:

Last February you sent us the measurements of your 56-1/4 inch Wapiti taken in British Columbia in 1947. The Committee would like to have this trophy given final consideration by the Board of Judges for the 1948 Big Game Competition.

The Committee wishes to cast no reflections upon the measurements of trophies taken by the owners themselves or any other individuals. However, to make certain the measurements are all taken under standard conditions and are strictly comparable, the Committee has been requiring that the finer trophies be measured at museums or by individuals, known to the Committee and appointed by them to act as official measurers for the Boone and Crockett Club. In making comparisons of trophies which are not present and in relying solely upon the measurement blanks and photographs, the judg need to know that the data is taken under the same formula in every case.

However, in your case, we have no official measurer within a radi of several hundred miles so we are going to ask you to have the measuremen made by some disinterested individual in your community, perhaps a Game ~~Commissioner.~~ Warden The blank should be witnessed and notarized. Complete dire tions for taking the measurements will be found on the back of the sheet. In addition, please have two photographs made of the trophy, one taken fro directly in front and the other from the side. It will be helpful if one photograph shows a yardstick or some other obvious basis for comparis as indicated on the blank.

The deadline date for receipt of this material is December 1st.

We congratulate you upon this trophy and shall appreciate your cooperation in making your entry official.

Very sincerely yours,

Chairman

Enc:1

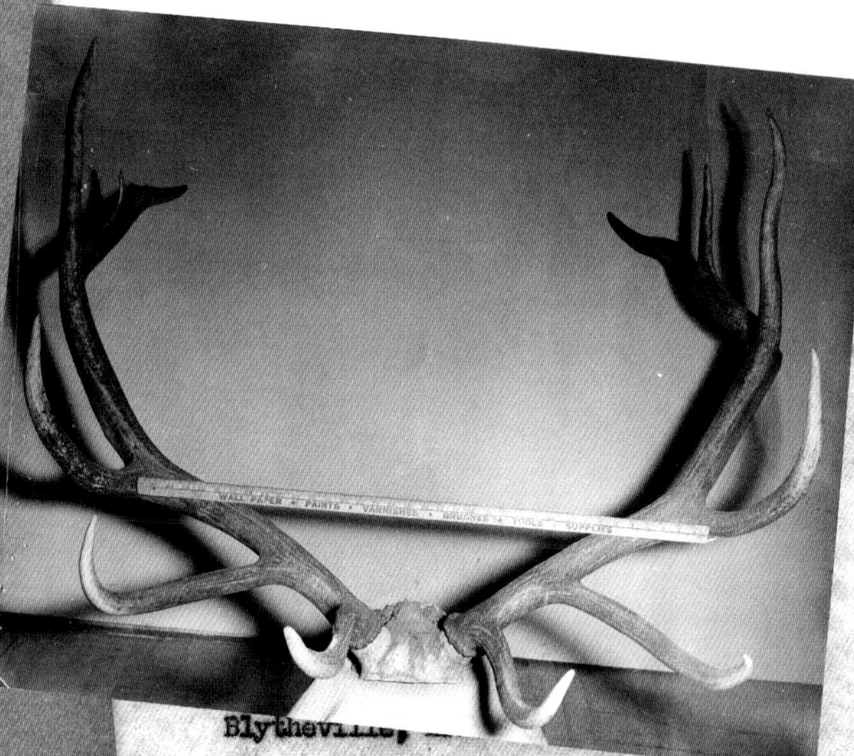

COMPANY

PHONES—

NIGHT—

December 12, 1950

Blytheville,

Dear Mr. Ward:

For some time the Committee on Records of North American Big Game has realized that the system used by the Boone and Crockett Club for measuring trophies and the basis for judging them has left something to be desired.

About a year ago, recognizing the need for a single standard system of accepted authority, an independent committee was appointed for the purpose of developing an Official Scoring System for North American big game trophies. The Committee was made up of Milford Baker, Frederick K. Barbour, Dr. James L. Clark, Grancel Fitz, Samuel B. Webb, as Chairman, and myself.

Before adopting a new system and publishing the final results the measurement charts, as devised by the Scoring Committee were circulated to more than 200 qualified sportsmen, guides, authors, taxidermists, game officials and scientists for constructive criticism and approval. This new scoring system is now the official pattern for the Boone and Crockett Club and it is hoped will come into rather general usage throughout the country.

It is now the desire of the Committee on Records of North American Big Game to have the twenty top trophies in each category listed in our records measured so that we may determine their standing according to this permanent system of measurements.

Your 55-1/2 inch Wapiti which won 2nd Prize in the 1947 Competition is in this group.

Will you therefore record the requested data on the enclosed sheet, have it witnessed, sign the blank and return it to us. Your prompt cooperation will be very much appreciated by the Committee.

FIRST PRIZE | RAY HOLES
1949 COMPETITION

Ray Holes' 7x7 elk received the First Prize at the 1949 Competition held at the American Museum of Natural History in New York. At that time, the Club's big game program was administered under the auspices of the National Museum of Heads and Horns of the New York Zoological Society. The bull was harvested near the Lochsa River, in Idaho's Selway drainage, on October 5, 1945.

AWARD WINNER

3RD COMPETITION - 1949

WAPITI—1st Prize - 1949
Length—(R) 59-1/4 (L) 54-1/4
Spread—46-3/4
Circumference—(R) 8-3/8 (L) 7-15/16
Points—(R) 7 (L) 7
Locality—Idaho Co., Idaho - 1945
Hunter—Ray Holes
Guide—None
Owner—Ray Holes

...Crockett Club
...h American Big Game
...and
...Big Game Competition
...care of
...of Natural History
...West at 79th Street
...ork 24, N.Y.

1st Prize
1949 Comp
Off. meas.
Exhibited

Harold E. Anthony, Chairman
William K. Carpenter
Alfred Ely
Karl T. Frederick
A. C. Gilbert
Catherine Sayers, Secretary

Under the Auspices
of
The National Museum
of Heads and Horns
of the
New York Zoological
Society

WAPITI

Species ....

Measurements

		Right	Left	
Length on outside curve A	59¼	59-1/4	54-1/4	54¼
Circumference between bez & trez B		8-3/8 8⅜	7-15/16	7 15/16 half way
Circumference of burr C	14⅛	14-1/8	14	14 8 near 2 prong
Number of points on antler	7	7	7	7

Greatest spread D ... 46-3/4 46¾

Exact locality where killed ... Lochsa, Selway drainage, Idaho Co., Id.

Date killed ... Oct. 5, 1945

By whom killed ... Ray Holes

Address ... Grangeville, Idaho

Owner ... Ray Holes

Address ... Same

Remarks ....

....

...L

UNDER TH...

THE NATIO...
OF HEADS...
OF...
NEW YORK...
SOC...

...RY

THE BOONE...
CL...

LEFT

54½" ...

8⅛

14"

7

...½"

...vay drainage
...unty, Idaho

...ho

...newhat webbed

...k very massi...

...tographs furnished.)

...bove described trophy
...se measurements are
...f.

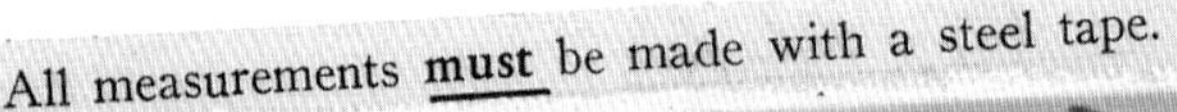

All measurements **must** be made with a steel tape.

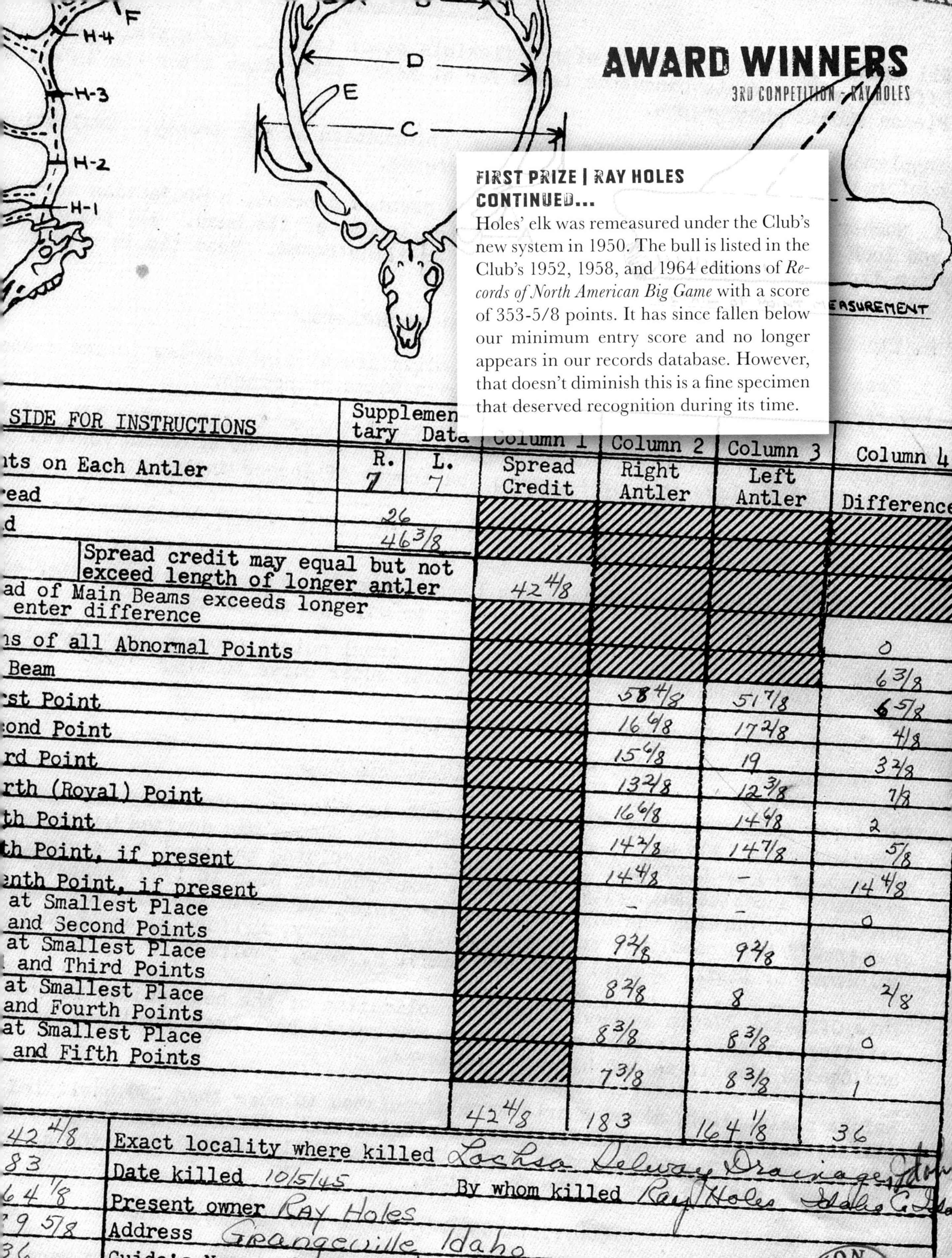

AWARD WINNERS

3RD COMPETITION - RAY HOLES

FIRST PRIZE | RAY HOLES CONTINUED...

Holes' elk was remeasured under the Club's new system in 1950. The bull is listed in the Club's 1952, 1958, and 1964 editions of *Records of North American Big Game* with a score of 353-5/8 points. It has since fallen below our minimum entry score and no longer appears in our records database. However, that doesn't diminish this is a fine specimen that deserved recognition during its time.

SIDE FOR INSTRUCTIONS	Supplementary Data R.	Supplementary Data L.	Column 1 Spread Credit	Column 2 Right Antler	Column 3 Left Antler	Column 4 Difference
nts on Each Antler	7	7				
read	26					
d	46 3/8					
Spread credit may equal but not exceed length of longer antler			42 4/8			
ad of Main Beams exceeds longer enter difference						
ns of all Abnormal Points						0
Beam						6 3/8
st Point				58 4/8	51 7/8	6 5/8
ond Point				16 6/8	17 2/8	4/8
rd Point				15 6/8	19	3 2/8
rth (Royal) Point				13 2/8	12 3/8	7/8
th Point				16 6/8	14 4/8	2
th Point, if present				14 2/8	14 7/8	5/8
enth Point, if present				14 4/8	–	14 4/8
at Smallest Place and Second Points				–	–	0
at Smallest Place and Third Points				9 2/8	9 2/8	0
at Smallest Place and Fourth Points				8 2/8	8	2/8
at Smallest Place and Fifth Points				8 3/8	8 3/8	0
				7 3/8	8 3/8	1
			42 4/8	183	164 1/8	36

42 4/8 Exact locality where killed Lochsa Selway Drainage Idaho

83 Date killed 10/5/45 By whom killed Ray Holes Idaho Co. Ida

64 1/8 Present owner RAY Holes

9 5/8 Address Grangeville Idaho

36 Guide's Na

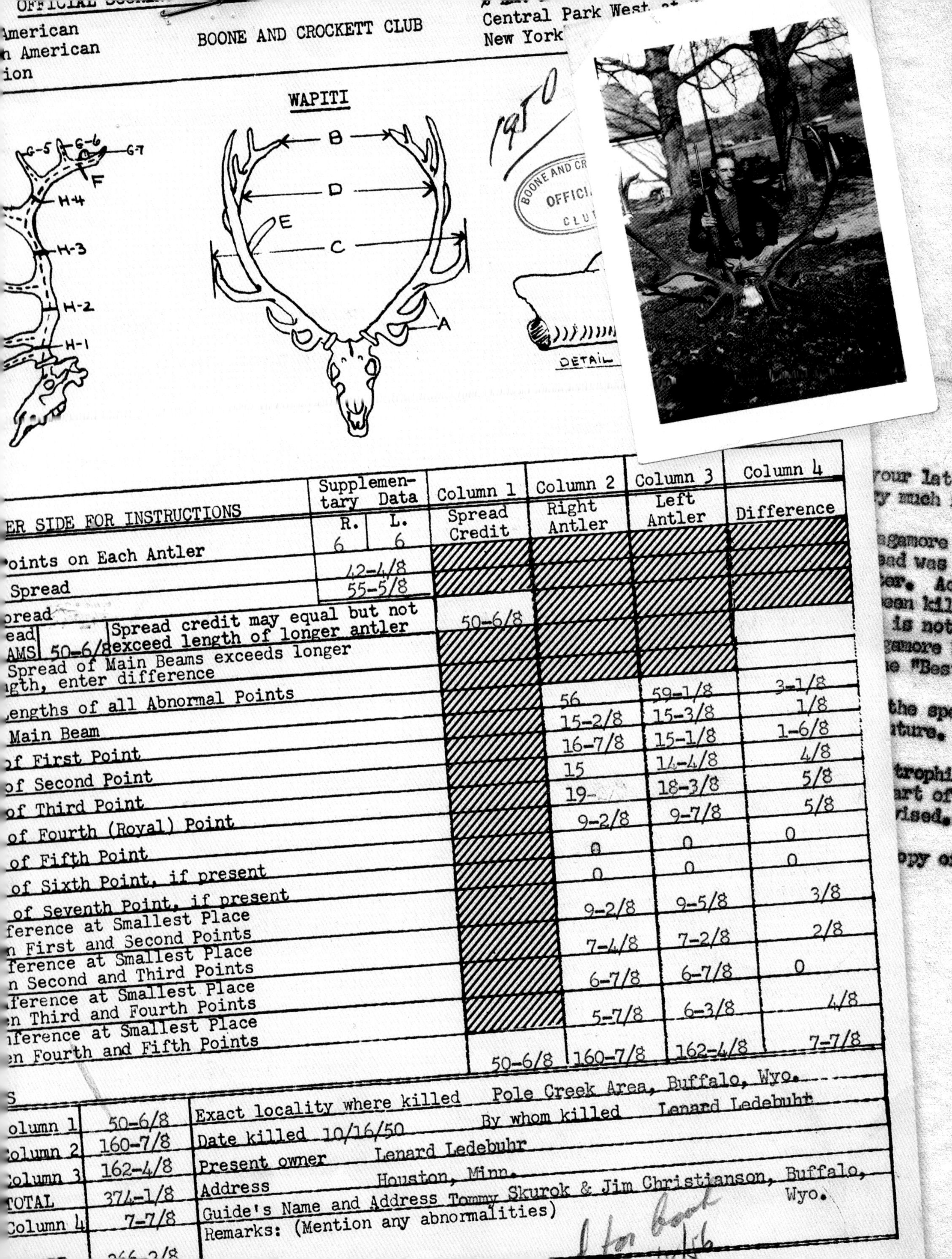

OFFICIAL SCO[...]

American
n American
ion

BOONE AND CROCKETT CLUB

Central Park West at [...]
New York

1950

WAPITI

ER SIDE FOR INSTRUCTIONS

	Supplementary Data R.	Supplementary Data L.	Column 1 Spread Credit	Column 2 Right Antler	Column 3 Left Antler	Column 4 Difference
oints on Each Antler	6	6				
Spread	42-4/8					
Spread	55-5/8					
pread / ead / AMS 50-6/8 — Spread credit may equal but not exceed length of longer antler			50-6/8			
Spread of Main Beams exceeds longer ngth, enter difference						
engths of all Abnormal Points				56	59-1/8	3-1/8
Main Beam				15-2/8	15-3/8	1/8
of First Point				16-7/8	15-1/8	1-6/8
of Second Point				15	14-4/8	4/8
of Third Point				19	18-3/8	5/8
of Fourth (Royal) Point				9-2/8	9-7/8	5/8
of Fifth Point				0	0	0
of Sixth Point, if present				0	0	0
of Seventh Point, if present				0	0	
ference at Smallest Place n First and Second Points				9-2/8	9-5/8	3/8
ference at Smallest Place n Second and Third Points				7-4/8	7-2/8	2/8
ference at Smallest Place n Third and Fourth Points				6-7/8	6-7/8	0
ference at Smallest Place n Fourth and Fifth Points				5-7/8	6-3/8	4/8
			50-6/8	160-7/8	162-4/8	7-7/8

S	
Column 1 50-6/8	Exact locality where killed Pole Creek Area, Buffalo, Wyo.
Column 2 160-7/8	Date killed 10/16/50 By whom killed Lenard Ledebuhr
Column 3 162-4/8	Present owner Lenard Ledebuhr
TOTAL 374-1/8	Address Houston, Minn.
Column 4 7-7/8	Guide's Name and Address Tommy Skurok & Jim Christianson, Buffalo, Wyo.
366-2/8	Remarks: (Mention any abnormalities)

O for book
[...]16

April 16, 1951

' April 8th and the enclosed
is contribution.

Award did not win a prize was
m - in other words, the date
ng to the rules of the compe-
a fair chase during the open
ble for a medal but this
ward which is a medal given
hy of the Show."

of the guides names. This

asured under the new system
year. When this is ready

official measurements of your

Very sincerely yours,

Secretary

AWARD WINNER

4TH COMPETITION - 1950

FIRST PRIZE | LENARD LEDEBUHR
1950 COMPETITION

The 1950 Competition was the first program after the implementation of the Club's current scoring system. Lenard Ledebuhr's elk was awarded First Prize with a score of 366-2/8 points. He had harvested the bull while on a guided hunt near Buffalo, Wyoming, in 1950. Dr. R.C. Bentzen's elk was also part of the 1950 Competition, where it was given the Sagamore Hill Award by the Roosevelt family for the "Best Trophy of the Show." You'll find more information about the Bentzen bull in the Special Trophies chapter.

accordan

Witness:

All meas
Official
Please s

Suppleme
conforma

To simpl

A. Numbe
one inch
from tip
but not

B. Tip t

C. Great
the skul

D. Insid
at wides
column i

E. Total
those no

F. Length
most dist

G-1-2-3-4
measured

H-1-2-3-4

The first
copyright
and publi
system of
committee
members o
Dr. James

This Offi
existing
and neede

Before pu
guides, a
and appro
this grou

2

FIRST PRIZE | BERT ELLIS GEORGE 1951 COMPETITION

Bert Ellis George was hunting with guide Sterling Johnson in Wyoming's Big Horn Mountains when he harvested this bull. It was sent in to the 1951 Competition where it was awarded a First Prize.

...s of North American
Big Game Committee

... NORTH AMERICAN BIG GAME TROPHIES

Address corresp...
Mrs. Grancel Fitz, ...
5 Tudor City ...
New York 17, ...

BOONE AND CROCKETT CLUB

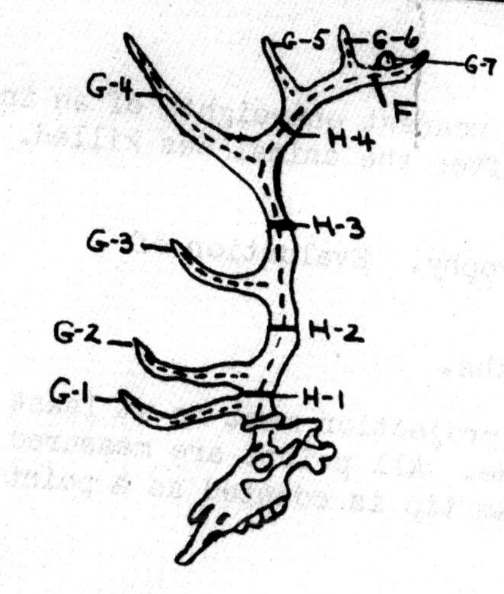

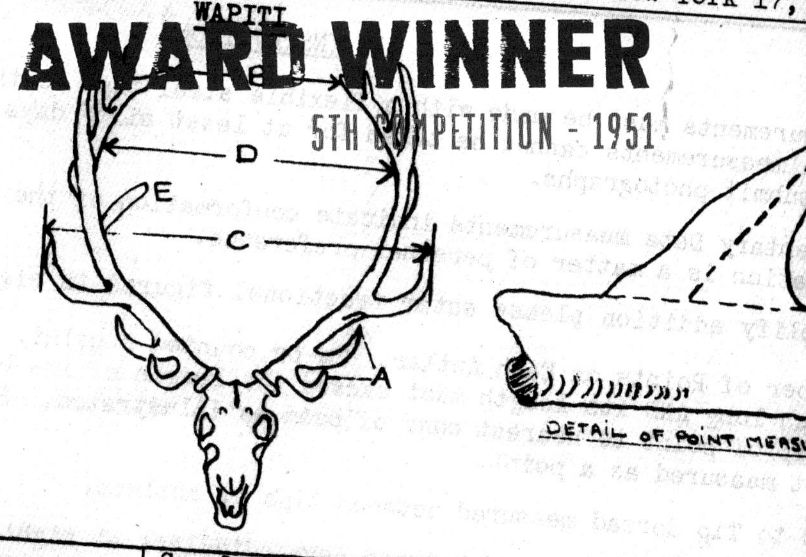

SEE OTHER SIDE FOR INSTRUCTIONS	Supplementary Data R.	Supplementary Data L.	Column 1 Spread Credit	Column 2 Right Antler	Column 3 Left Antler	C... Di...
A. Number of Points on Each Antler	6	6				
B. Tip to Tip Spread	38 2/8					
C. Greatest Spread	46 7/8					
D. Inside Spread of MAIN BEAMS: 43 2/8. Spread credit may equal but not exceed length of longer antler			43 2/8			
IF Inside Spread of Main Beams exceeds longer antler length, enter difference						
E. Total of Lengths of all Abnormal Points						
F. Length of Main Beam				56	57 5/8	1
G-1. Length of First Point				18 1/8	18 1/8	
G-2. Length of Second Point				14 7/8	16 6/8	1
G-3. Length of Third Point				15 4/8	15 4/8	
G-4. Length of Fourth (Royal) Point				20 4/8	18 4/8	2
G-5. Length of Fifth Point				15 2/8	13 [illegible]	2
G-6. Length of Sixth Point, if present						
G-7. Length of Seventh Point, if present						
H-1. Circumference at Smallest Place Between First and Second Points				8 6/8	8 6/8	
H-2. Circumference at Smallest Place Between Second and Third Points				7 3/8	7 3/8	
H-3. Circumference at Smallest Place Between Third and Fourth Points				7	7	
H-4. Circumference at Smallest Place Between Fourth and Fifth Points				6	5 6/8	
TOTALS			43 2/8	169 3/8	168 3/8	8

ADD	Column 1	43 2/8
	Column 2	169 3/8
	Column 3	168 3/8
	TOTAL	381
SUBTRACT	Column 4	8
	FINAL SCORE	373

Exact locality where killed Big Horn Mts., Wyoming

Date killed 10-15-51 By whom killed Bert Ellis George

Present owner *Bert Ellis George*

Address 1823 University Avenue, Berkeley, Calif.

Guide's Name and Address Sterling Johnson, Lovell, Wyoming

Remarks: (Mention any abnormalities)

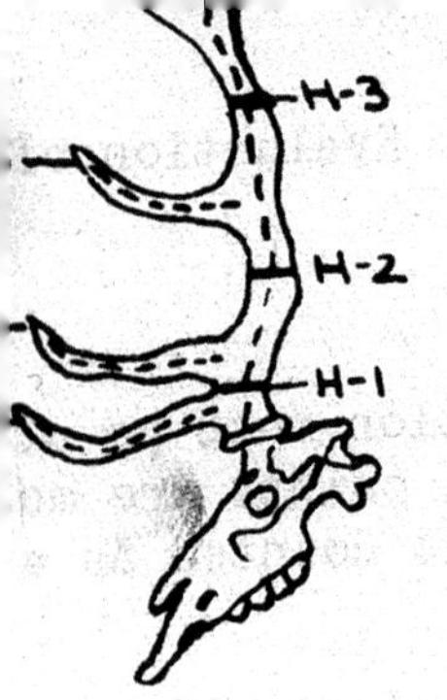

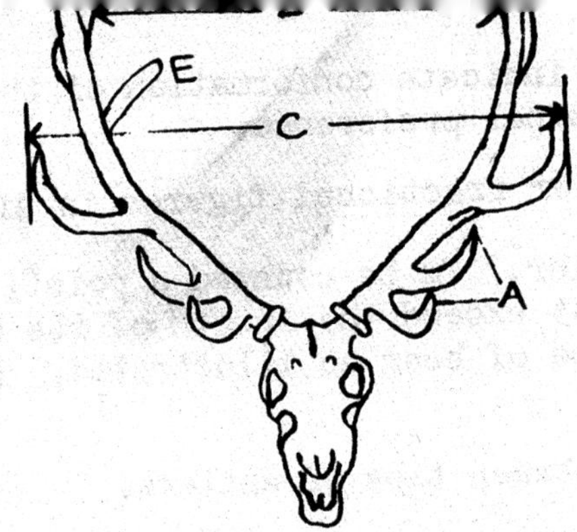

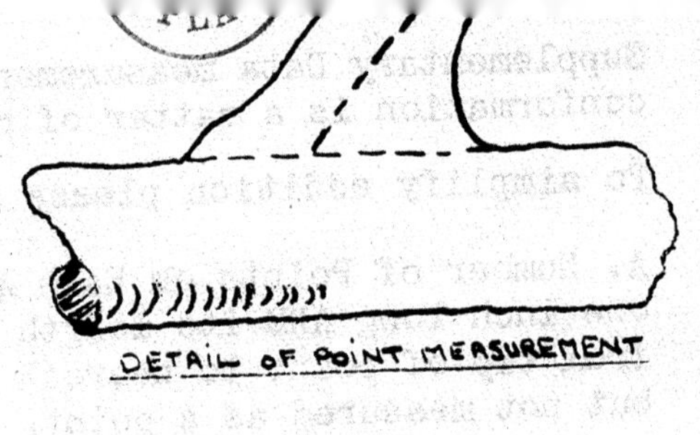

OTHER SIDE FOR INSTRUCTIONS	Supplementary Data R.	Supplementary Data L.	Column 1 Spread Credit	Column 2 Right Antler	Column 3 Left Antler	Column 4 Difference
of Points on Each Antler	8	7				
Tip Spread	48.0					
t Spread	53 2/8					
Spread BEAMS 47 3/8 Spread credit may equal but not exceed length of longer antler			47 3/8			
de Spread of Main Beams exceeds longer length, enter difference						
f Lengths of all Abnormal Points						3 7/8
of Main Beam				59 5/8	57 4/8	2 1/8
h of First Point				17 2/8	16 7/8	3/8
h of Second Point				18 5/8	19 4/8	7/8
h of Third Point				17 2/8	16 4/8	6/8
th of Fourth (Royal) Point				21 4/8	20 5/8	7/8
th of Fifth Point				16 3/8	17 5/8	1 2/8
th of Sixth Point, if present				11 2/8	9	7
th of Seventh Point, if present				—	—	—
umference at Smallest Place een First and Second Points				7 7/8	7 5/8	2/8
umference at Smallest Place een Second and Third Points				6 6/8	6 6/8	—
umference at Smallest Place een Third and Fourth Points				8 2/8	8 6/8	4/8
umference at Smallest Place een Fourth and Fifth Points				7 4/8	7 4/8	
			417 7/8			

ALS

Column 1	47 3/8	Exact locality w
Column 2	182 2/8	Date killed 9/2
Column 3	188 2/8	Present owner Ra
TOTAL	417 7/8	Address Mont
Column 4	18 5/8	Guide's Name and
L SCORE	399 2/8	Remarks: (Mention

AWARD WINNER

6TH COMPETITION - 1953

FIRST PRIZE | RALPH FRY
1953 COMPETITION

Ralph Fry's Alberta bull received the First Prize at the Club's 1953 Competition. His elk still ranks high in the records book and is the fourth-largest American elk ever entered from Alberta with a final score of 399-2/8 points.

Outdoor Life *First Choice of Discriminating Sportsmen*

353 FOURTH AVENUE · NEW YORK 10, N.Y.

Dec. 25, 1954

SHOOTING DEPARTMENT
JACK O'CONNOR, EDITOR

Dear Betty:

I am enclosing some measurements. Herb Klein has the damndest collection of American sheep heads in the world, I thin,--all 4 kinds of sheep with heads over 40. I am enclosing the dope on a good Stone he shot and of an old Wyoming bighorn he killed 20 years ago without a guide and on his first sheep hunt. I think he told me it was the first ram he saw!

The elk head is a hell of a head, as you can see.

My best,

Jack

Box
Lewi
Ida

FIRST PRIZE | ELMER BACUS
1957 COMPETITION

Jack O'Connor took special interest in Elmer Bacus' elk, which he harvested in Adams County, Idaho, in 1954. O'Connor and friend George Pfeffer were responsible for getting the trophy to New York for judging during the 7th Competition, where it was awarded First Prize.

JAN 7 1955

Outdoor Life *First Choice of Discriminating Sportsmen*

353 FOURTH AVENUE · NEW YORK 10, N.Y.

AWARD WINNER

7TH COMPETITION - 1955

January 18, 1955

Mrs. Betty Fitz
c/o"Records of North American
Big Game"
5 Tudor City Place
New York 17, N.Y.

Dear Betty:

That terrific elk head shot by Bacus is at a store called "The Western Outfitters" at Grangeville, Idaho. It's in the custody of George Pfeffer. I am quite sure that you could get the head. Bacus is not interested in it. He is a meat hunter, not a head hunter; but George and I will send it in if you want it. By that time it probably will have shrunk a bit and it can be measured in New York.

I certainly hope Grancel gets his jaguar. I have never shot one of the darned things. How was the Texas deer hunt?

That elk head is the most impressive thing that I have ever seen in the way of an elk head.

Regards to Grancel,

My best wishes,

Jack

Jack O'Connor
Box 382
Lewiston, Idaho

JO'C:DC

Hav

I've had a letter from Bacus See attached

Note Chart

I sent Jack a card & asked him if he cleared the head. He does not answer my question.

This letter not ack.

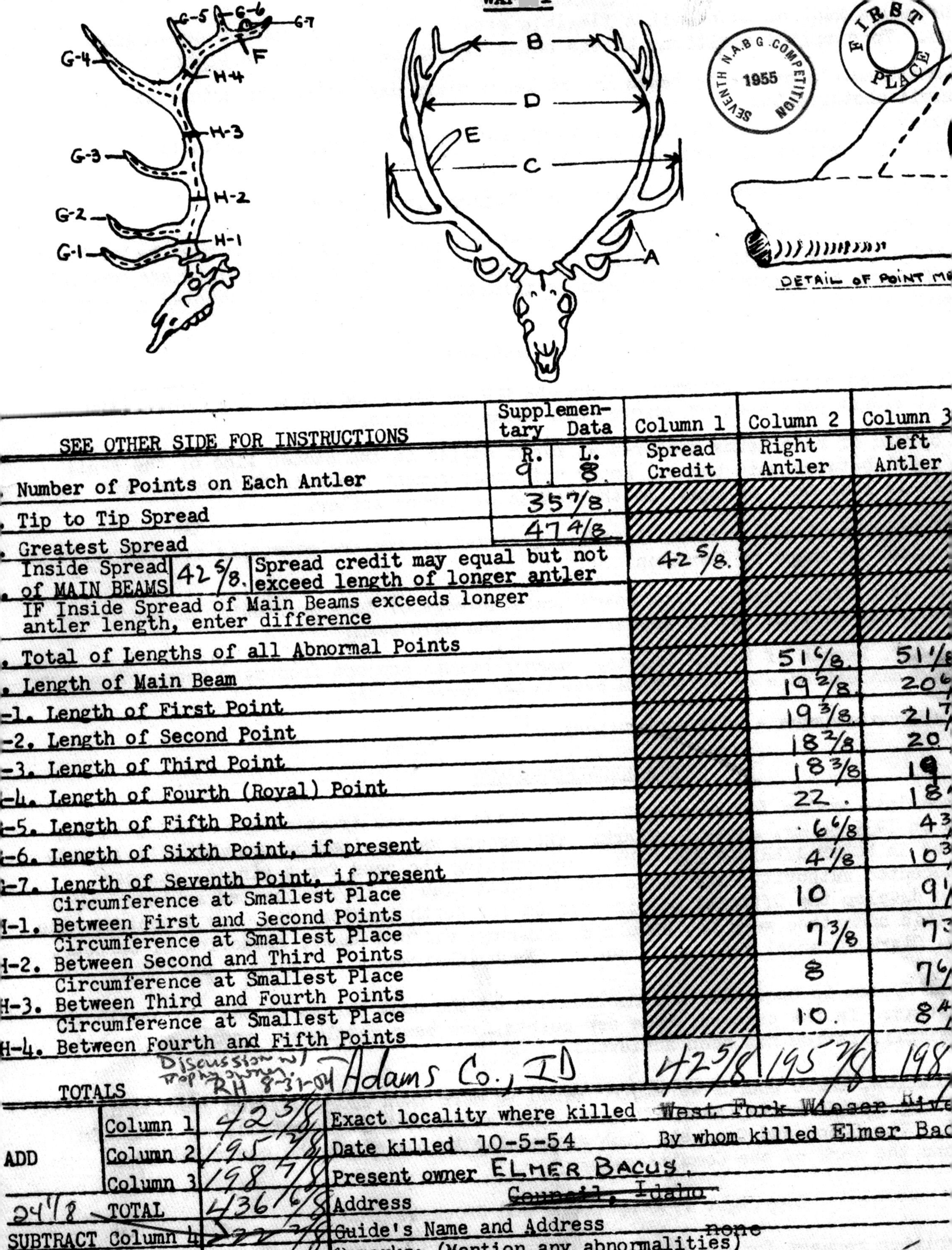

SEE OTHER SIDE FOR INSTRUCTIONS	Supplementary Data R.	Supplementary Data L.	Column 1 Spread Credit	Column 2 Right Antler	Column 3 Left Antler
Number of Points on Each Antler	9	8			
Tip to Tip Spread	35 7/8				
Greatest Spread	47 4/8				
Inside Spread of MAIN BEAMS 42 5/8. Spread credit may equal but not exceed length of longer antler			42 5/8.		
IF Inside Spread of Main Beams exceeds longer antler length, enter difference					
Total of Lengths of all Abnormal Points				51 6/8	51 1/8
Length of Main Beam				19 2/8	20 6
-1. Length of First Point				19 3/8	21 7
-2. Length of Second Point				18 2/8	20
-3. Length of Third Point				18 3/8	19
-4. Length of Fourth (Royal) Point				22.	18
-5. Length of Fifth Point				6 6/8	4 3
-6. Length of Sixth Point, if present				4 1/8	10 3
-7. Length of Seventh Point, if present				10	9
H-1. Circumference at Smallest Place Between First and Second Points				7 3/8	7 3
H-2. Circumference at Smallest Place Between Second and Third Points				8	7 6
H-3. Circumference at Smallest Place Between Third and Fourth Points				10.	8 4
H-4. Circumference at Smallest Place Between Fourth and Fifth Points					
TOTALS — Discussion w/ trophy owner RH 8-31-04 — Adams Co., ID			42 5/8	195 7/8	198

ADD		
	Column 1	42 5/8
	Column 2	195 7/8
	Column 3	198 7/8
24 1/8	TOTAL	436 6/8
SUBTRACT	Column 4	2?? ?/8

Exact locality where killed ~~West Fork Weiser Rive~~

By whom killed Elmer Bac

Date killed 10-5-54

Present owner ELMER BACUS.

Address ~~Council, Idaho~~

Guide's Name and Address none

Remarks: (Mention any abnormalities)

North American Big Game Competition sponsored by THE BOONE AND CROCKETT CLUB

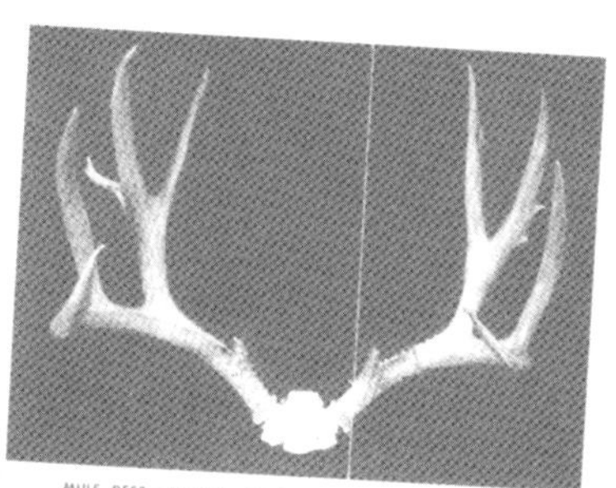

MULE DEER — (typical) — 1st Prize — NEW WORLD'S RECORD

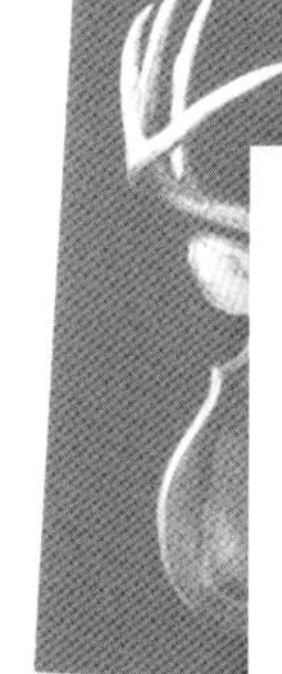

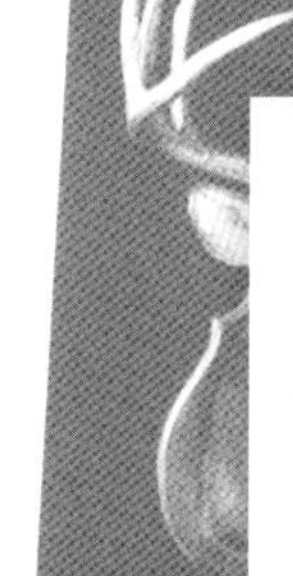

WHITETAIL

FIRST PRIZE | ELMER BACUS CONTINUED...

Bacus' bull has a final score of 412-5/8 points, ranks 15th overall today, and is still the largest elk ever entered from the state of Idaho. If it weren't for O'Connor and Pfeffer, the trophy may have never made it to B&C. O'Connor notes in his letter dated January 18, 1955, to Betty Fitz:

"...Bacus is not interested in it. He is a meat hunter, not a head hunter; but George and I will send it in if you want it. By that time it probably will have shrunk a bit and it can be measured in New York."

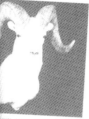

WHITE SHEEP — 1st Prize

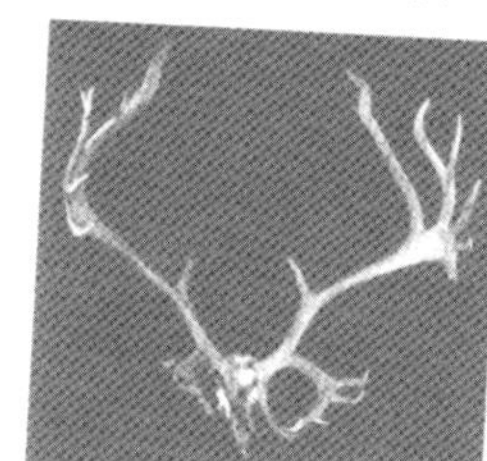

MOUNTAIN CARIBOU — 1st Prize

ROCKY MOUNTAIN GOAT — 1st Prize

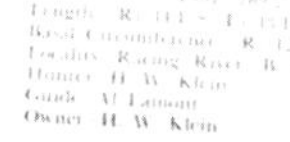

STONE SHEEP — 1st Prize

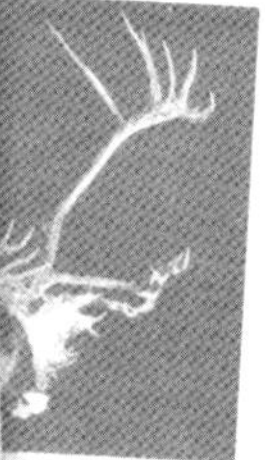

CARIBOU — 1st Prize

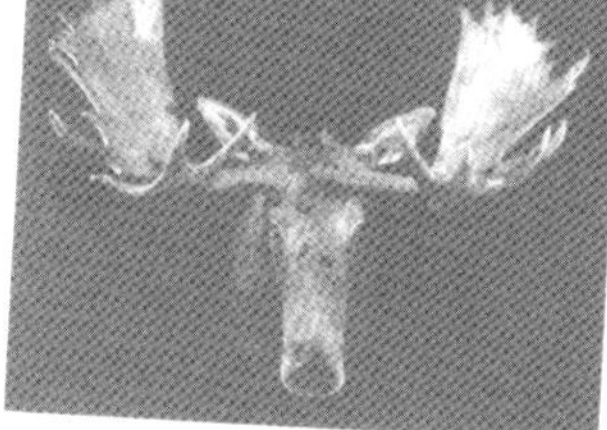

CANADA MOOSE — 1st Prize

ALASKA-YUKON MOOSE — 1st Prize

WAPITI — 1st Prize
Length—(R) 51-6/8 (L) 51-4/8
Inside Spread 42-5/8
Circumference—(R) 10 (L) 9-1/8
Points—(R) 9 (L) 8
Locality—Wieser River, Idaho—1954
Hunter—Elmer Bacus
Owner—Elmer Bacus

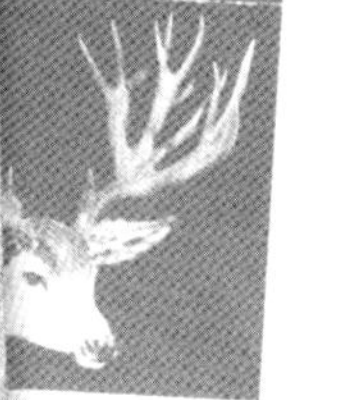

(typical) — 1st Prize

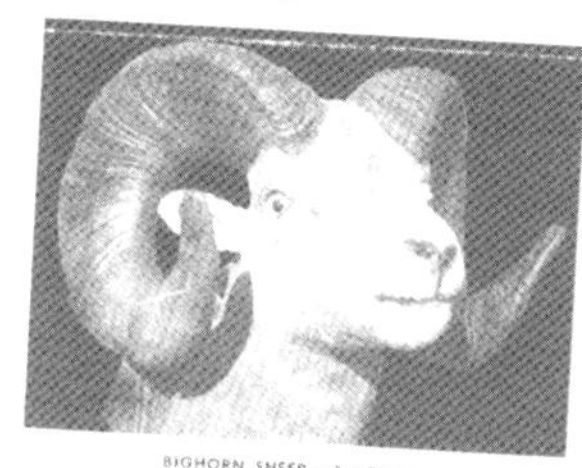

BIGHORN SHEEP — 1st Prize

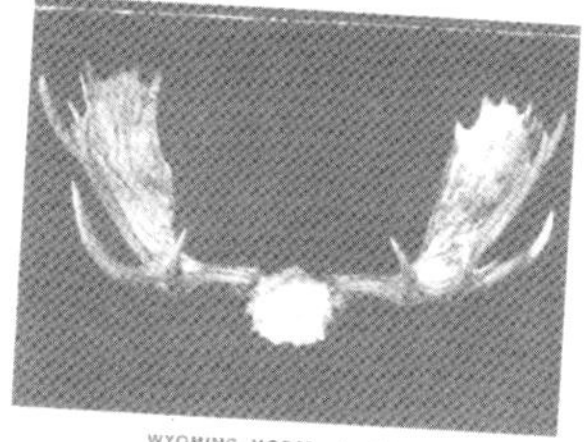

WYOMING MOOSE — 1st Prize

BISON — 1st Prize

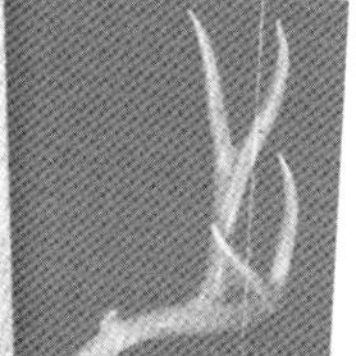

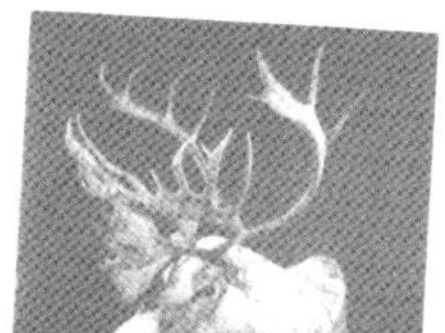

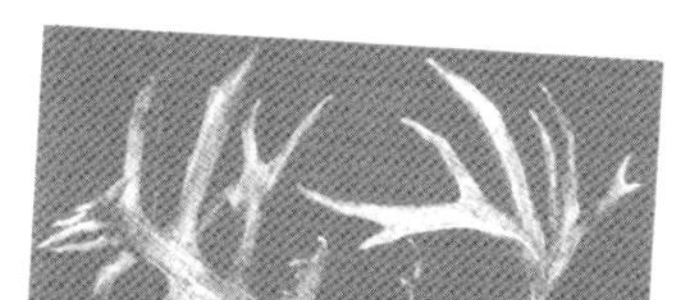

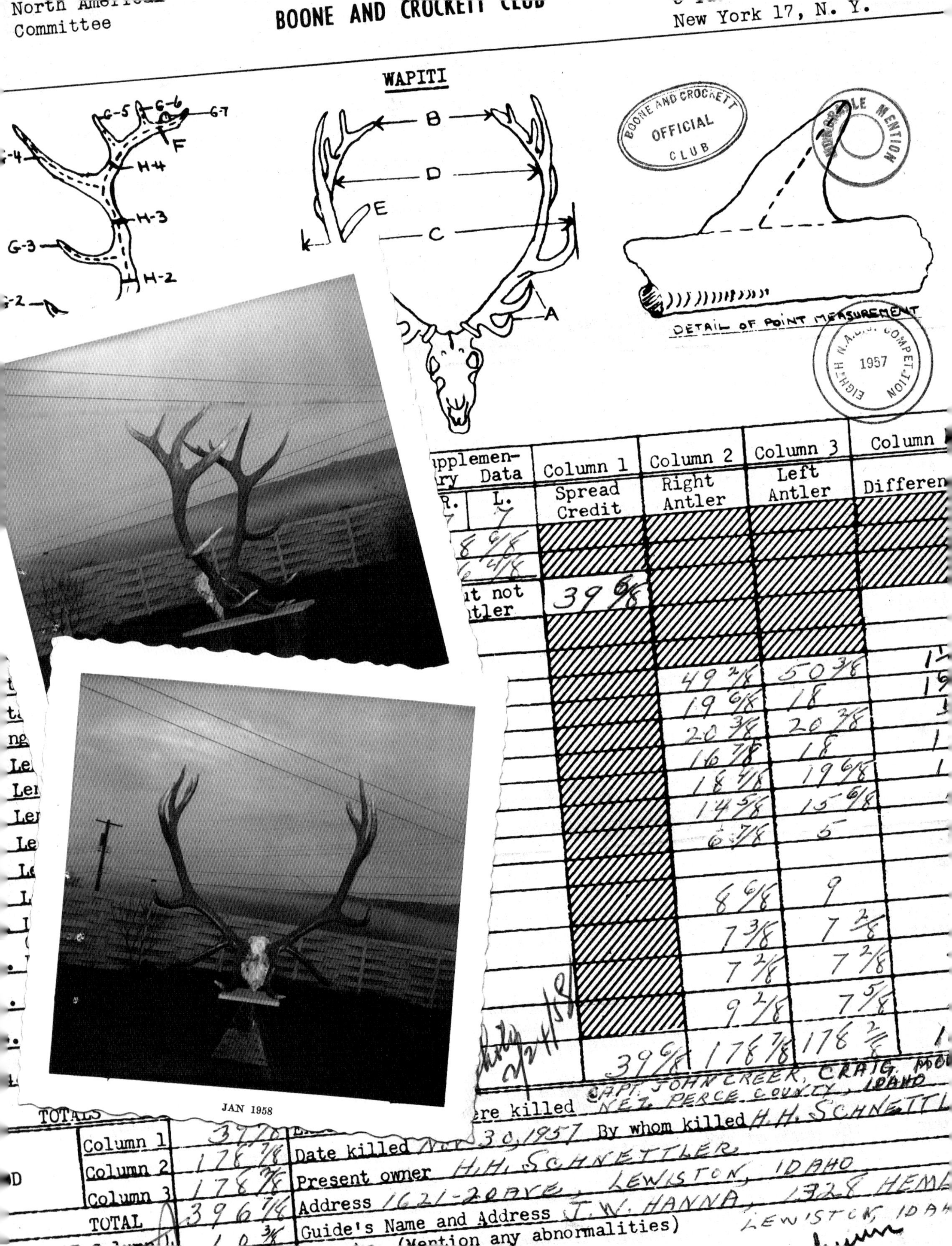

North American
Committee

BOONE AND CROCKETT CLUB

New York 17, N. Y.

WAPITI

Supplementary Data		Column 1	Column 2	Column 3	Column 4
R.	L.	Spread Credit	Right Antler	Left Antler	Difference
7	7				
	8 6/8				
	6 4/8				
...t not ...tler		39 6/8			
			49 2/8	50 3/8	1
			19 6/8	18	1
			20 3/8	20 3/8	
			16 7/8	18	1
			18 4/8	19 6/8	1
			14 5/8	15 6/8	
			6 7/8	5	
			8 6/8	9	
			7 3/8	7 2/8	
			7 2/8	7 2/8	
			9 2/8	7 5/8	
			178 7/8	178 2/8	
		39 6/8	178 7/8	178 2/8	

TOTALS

Column 1	39 6/8
Column 2	178 7/8
Column 3	178 2/8
TOTAL	396 7/8

...ere killed CAPT. JOHN CREEK, CRAIG MOU... NEZ PERCE COUNTY, IDAHO

Date killed NOV 30, 1957 By whom killed H. H. SCHNETTL...

Present owner H. H. SCHNETTLER

Address 1621-20 AVE., LEWISTON, IDAHO

Guide's Name and Address J. W. HANNA, 1328 HEM... LEWISTON, IDAHO

(Mention any abnormalities)

Points—(R) 4 (L) 4
Locality—Canelo Hill, Ariz.—1955
Hunter—Carlos Achoa

COUES DEER — Certificate of Merit

Score—114-6/8

Length—(R) 19-5/8 (L) 19-3/8
Inside Spread—14-5/8
Circumference—(R) 4-4/8 (L) 4-5/8
Points—(R) 6 (L) 8
Locality—Chirichuas Mts., Ariz.—1949
Hunter—John Miller

WAPITI — 1st Prize

Score—392

Length—(R) 58-7/8 (L) 58-4/8
Inside Spread—48-5/8
Circumference—(R) 8-7/8 (L) 9
Points—(R) 7 (L) 7
Locality—Panther River, Alta.—1955
Hunter—Bill Brooks

WAPITI — 2d Prize

Score—390-6/8

Length—(R) 53-5/8 (L) 54-3/8
Inside Spread—49-6/8
Circumference—(R) 9-3/8 (L) 9-5/8
Points—(R) 7 (L) 6
Locality—Clearwater, Alta.—1955
Hunter—Bob Dial

WAPITI — Hon. Men.

Score—389-5/8

Length—(R) 56-5/8 (L) 52-5/8
Inside Spread—52-5/8
Circumference—(R) 9-2/8 (L) 9-2/8
Points—(R) 7 (L) 7
Locality—Fort-A-La-Corn, Sask.—1955
Hunter—Jim Crozier

WAPITI — Hon. Men.

Score—387-6/8

Length—(R) 57-6/8 (L) 56-4/8
Inside Spread—51
Circumference—(R) 8 (L) 7-7/8
Points—(R) 7 (L) 6
Locality—Bighorn Mts., Wyo.—1954
Hunter—Elgin T. Gates

WAPITI — Hon. Men.

Score—386-4/8

Length—(R) 49-2/8 (L) 50-3/8
Inside Spread—39-6/8
Circumference—(R) 8-6/8 (L) 9
Points—(R) 7 (L) 7
Locality—Craig Mt., Idaho—1957
Hunter—H. H. Schnettler
Guide—J. W. Hanna

WAPITI — Certificate of Merit

Score—402-5/8

Length—(R) 59-1/8 (L) 59-6/8
Inside Spread—[illegible]-1/8
Circumference—(R) 9-1/8 (L) 8-5/8
Points—(R) 7 (L) 7
Locality—Red River, Alta.—1946
Hunter—Henry Folkman

Greatest Spread—65-1/8
Length of Palm—(R) 43-3/8 (L) 45-4/8
Width of Palm—(R) 18-1/8 (L) 18-6/8
Normal Points—(R) 15 (L) 14
Locality—Swede Lake, Alaska—1956
Hunter—Paul Bierdeman

AWARD WINNER

8TH COMPETITION 1957

[illegible] — Hon. Men.

Score—22[illegible]

Greatest Spread—69-4/8
Length of Palm—(R) [illegible]-2/8 (L) 44-2/8
Width of Palm—(R) 14-6/8 (L) 15-2/8
Normal Points—(R) 16 (L) 14
Locality—Talkeetna Mts., Alaska—1957
Hunter—Wayne C. Eubank

ALASKA-YUKON MOOSE — Hon. Men.

Score—227-6/8

Greatest Spread—62-2/8
Length of Palm—(R) 44-2/8 (L) 44-3/8
Width of Palm—(R) 14 (L) 13-4/8
[illegible]—1957

HONORABLE MENTION | H.H. SCHNETTLER 1957 COMPETITION

Betty Fitz made reference in a letter to a trophy owner that the 8th Competition had one of the finest groups of wapiti ever assembled. Unfortunately, we were not able to locate several of the photographs from this era in our archives. The elk represented in the score chart at left received an honorable mention at the competition. The bull was harvested by a local Idaho hunter, H.H. Schnettler, in Nez Perce County, Idaho, during the 1957 season.

[illegible]-5/8
[illegible] 11-4/8
[illegible]956

Length of Palm—[illegible]) 29-3/8
Width of Palm—(R) 10-6/8 (L) 11
Normal Points—(R) 11 (L) 11
Locality—Wilson, Wyo.—1955
Hunters—Avon VanNoy and Victor Tullis
Owner—Victor Tullis
Guide—Avon VanNoy

BIGHORN SHEEP — 2d Prize

Score—189-7/8

Length—(R) 40-5/8 (L) 41-4/8
Basal Circumference—(R) 15-4/8 (L) 15-6/[illegible]
Locality—Ribbon Lake, Alta.—1957
Hunter—Ovar Uggen

BIGHORN SHEEP — Hon. Men.

Score—188-5/8

Length—(R) 38-7/8 (L) 39-4/8
Basal Circumference—(R) 15-6/8 (L) 15-6/[illegible]
Locality—Sun River, Mont.—1955
Hunter—Bruce McCracken

BIGHORN SHEEP — Hon. Men.

Score—186-3/8

Length—(R) 38-1/8 (L) 36
Basal Circumference—(R) 16 (L) 16-1/8
Locality—Castleriver, Alta.—1954

Records of North American Big Game Committee

...SCORING SYSTEM FOR NORTH AMERICAN BIG GAME TROPHIES

BOONE AND CROCKETT CLUB

Address correspond... Mrs. Grancel Fitz, 5 Tudor City Pl... New York 17, N. ...

AWARD WINNER

10TH COMPETITION - 1961

FIRST PRIZE | CARL B. SNYDER
1961 COMPETITION

Carl B. Snyder's prize-winning elk was harvested in Mineral County, Montana, during the 1959 season. With a score of 404-6/8 points, this bull remains the third-largest elk entered from Montana and the 27th overall throughout North America.

SEE OTHER SIDE FOR INSTRUCTIONS

	Supplementary Data R.	L.	Column 1 Spread Credit	Column 2 Right Antler	Column 3 Left Antler	Column 4 Difference
A. Number of Points on Each Antler	8	7				
B. Tip to Tip Spread	34 3/8					
C. Greatest Spread	54 -					
D. Inside Spread of MAIN BEAMS 47 2/8 — Spread credit may equal but not exceed length of longer antler			47 2/8			
IF Inside Spread of Main Beams exceeds longer antler length, enter difference						
E. Total of Lengths of all Abnormal Points						
F. Length of Main Beam				58 6/8	57 -	1 6/8
G-1. Length of First Point				16 4/8	17 -	4/8
G-2. Length of Second Point				17 4/8	16 5/8	7/8
G-3. Length of Third Point				18 7/8	21 1/8	2 2/8
G-4. Length of Fourth (Royal) Point				21 4/8	22 2/8	6/8
G-5. Length of Fifth Point				15 1/8	15 -	1/8
G-6. Length of Sixth Point, if present				3 5/8	5 3/8	1 6/8
G-7. Length of Seventh Point, if present				1 2/8	—	1 2/8
H-1. Circumference at Smallest Place Between First and Second Points				9 5/8	9 1/8	4/8
H-2. Circumference at Smallest Place Between Second and Third Points				6 6/8	7 —	2/8
H-3. Circumference at Smallest Place Between Third and Fourth Points				6 4/8	6 4/8	—
H-4. Circumference at Smallest Place Between Fourth and Fifth Points				6 7/8	6 5/8	2/8
TOTALS			47.2	183.4	183.5	9 6/8

ADD	
Column 1	47.2
Column 2	183.4
Column 3	183.5
TOTAL	414.3
SUBTRACT Column 4	9.3
FINAL SCORE	404 6/8

Exact locality where killed Mineral Co. Mont. W. OF ST. REGIS - MINERAL CO. MONT.

Date killed 1959 By whom killed CARL B. SNYDER

Present owner ~~Carl B. SNYDER~~ Warren G. Stone

Address ~~726 WOODFORD St. Missoula, Montana~~

Guide's Name and Address

Remarks: (Mention any abnormalities)

FIRST PLACE

OFFICIAL MEASUREMENT BOONE AND CROCKETT

10th N.A.B.G. COMPETITION 1961 BOONE & CROCKETT

CLEARWATER RESORT

CLEARWATER JUNCTION -:- HIGHWAYS 200-~~209~~ 83

In the Heart of the Beautiful

BLACKFOOT VALLEY

GREENOUGH 59836 -:- PHONE 406 - 244-~~5555~~ 5598

RECEIVED

OCT 20 1983

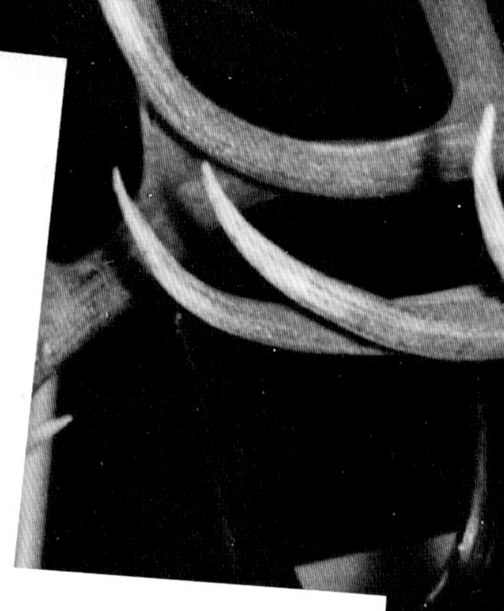

WM. H. NESBITT
ADMINISTRATIVE DIRECTOR.
BOONE & CROCKETT CLUB
205 SOUTH PATRICK STREET
ALEXANDRIA, VIRGINIA 223
703/548/7727

TO WHOM IT MAY CONCERN.

THIS WILL CERTIFY THAT TH
1981 EDITION OF THE BOONE
A SCORE OF 404 6/8, WAS F
MONTANA ON JULY 30, 1971.
TROPHY ELK AND HAS BEEN S

RL B. SNYDER

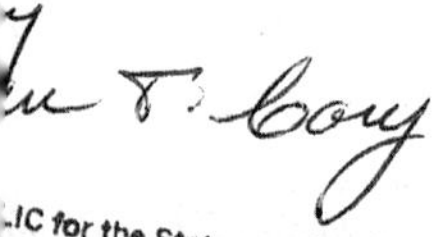

LIC for the State of Montana
t Great Falls, Montana
n Expires 3/8/85

: • STORE AND GIFT SHOP •

1961 North American Big Game Exhibition

sponsored by BOONE AND CROCKETT CLUB

MULE DEER (Non-Typical)—Certificate of Merit
NEW WORLD'S RECORD
Score—207-3/8 + 147-7/8—355-2/8
Length—(R) 26-2/8 (L) 26-1/8
Circumference—(R) 5 (L) 4-7/8
Points—(R) 22 (L) 21
Inside Spread—22-1/8
Locality—Chip Lake, Alta.—1926
Hunter—Ed Broder

SAGAMORE HILL AWARD
WHITE SHEEP—1st Award
NEW WORLD'S RECORD
Score—189-6/8
Length—(R) 48-5/8 (L) 47-7/8
Basal Circumference—(R) 14-5/8 14-6/8
Locality—Wrangell Mts, Alaska—1961
Hunter—Harry L. Swank, Jr.

ALASKA-YUKON MOOSE 1st Award
NEW WORLD'S RECORD
Score—251
Greatest Spread—(R) 77-4/8
Length of Palm (R) 46-3/8 (L) 51
Width of Palm—(R) 17 (L) 20-6/8
Normal Points—(R) 18 (L) 17
Locality—Mt. Susitna, Alaska 1961
Hunter—Bert Klineburger
Guide—Eldon Brandt

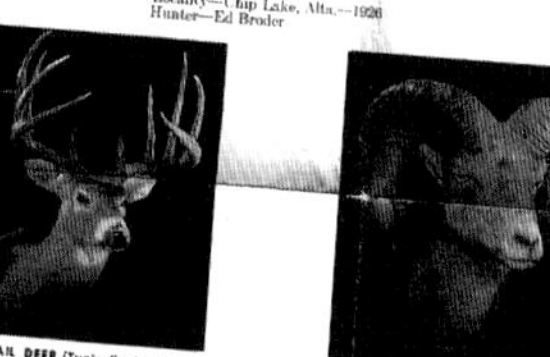

WHITETAIL DEER (Typical)—1st Award
Score—186-1/8
Length—(R) 25-1/8 (L) 26-2/8
Circumference—(R) 4-6/8 (L) 4-7/8
Points—(R) 6 (L) 5
Inside Spread—20-1/8
Locality—Roane Co., Tenn.—1959
Hunter—W. A. Foster

BADLANDS BIGHORN—Certificate of Merit
The finest surviving specimen of an extinct race.
Score—196-6/8
Length—(R) 41-2/8 (L) 40-4/8
Basal Circumference—(R) 16-4/8 (L) 16-4/8
Locality—Badlands, N. Dak.—1880
Hunter—Howard Eaton
Owner—Richard K. Mellon

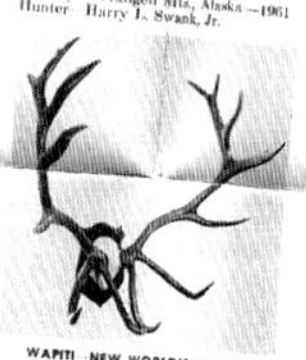

WAPITI—NEW WORLD'S RECORD
Certificate of Merit
Score—442-1/8
Length—(R) 55-5/8 (L) 59-5/8
Circumference—(R) 12-1/8 (L) 11-2/8
Points—(R) 8 (L) 7
Inside Spread—45-4/8
Locality—Dark Canyon, Colo.—1915
Hunter—John Plute
Owner—Tony Rozman

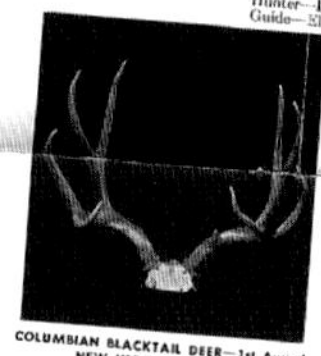

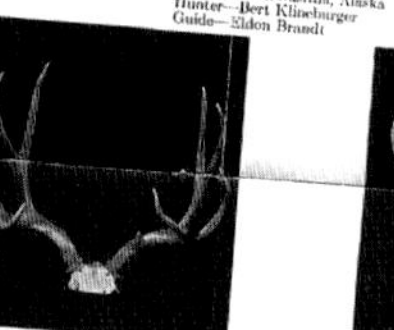

COLUMBIAN BLACKTAIL DEER—1st Award
NEW WORLD'S RECORD
Score—160-5/8
Length—(R) 20-5/8 (L) 21-4/8
Circumference—(R) 4-5/8 (L) 4-5/8
Points—(R) 4 (L) 4
Inside Spread—16-5/8
Locality—Camas Valley, Ore.—1958
Hunter—Bernard L. Den

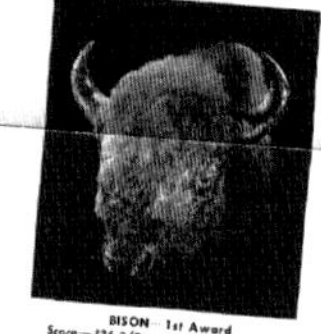

BISON—1st Award
Score—136-2/8
Length—(R) 19 (L) 18-6/8
Basal Circumference—(R) 18-4/8 (L) 18-4/8
Locality—N. W. T., Can.—1961
Hunter—Samuel Israel
Guide—Northern Safari

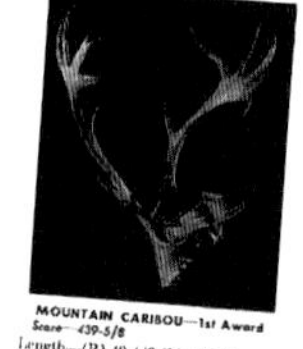

MOUNTAIN CARIBOU—1st Award
Score—439-5/8
Length—(R) 49-4/8 (L) 46-2/8
Width of Brow Palms—(R) 15-3/8 (L) 4-7/8
Points—(R) 24 (L) 19
Inside Spread—33-1/8
Locality—Cold Fish Lake, B.C.—1961
Hunter—Drew W. Getgen
Guide—Rusty Russell

BARREN GROUND CARBIOU—1st Award
Score—450
Length—(R) 47-7/8 (L) 48-5/8
Width of Brow Palms—(R) 13-5/8 (L) 4-3/8
Points—(R) 20 (L) 24
Inside Spread—36-6/8
Locality—Talkeetna Mts, Alaska—1960
Hunter—George L. Clark
Guide—Frenchy Lamoureux

WAPITI—1st Award
Score—404-6/8
Length—(R) 58-6/8 (L) 57
Circumference—(R) 9-5/8 (L) 9-1/8
Points—(R) 8 (L) 7
Inside Spread—47-2/8
Locality—Mineral Co., Mont.—1959
Hunter—Carl B. Snyder

WOODLAND CARIBOU—1st Award
Score—334
Length—(R) 34-4/8 (L) 37-5/8
Width of Brow Palms—(R) 10-6/8 (L) 12-4/8
Points—(R) 25 (L) 16
Inside Spread—29-4/8
Locality—Red Indian Lake, Newfoundland—1960
Hunter—Grancel Fitz
Guide—Gene Manion

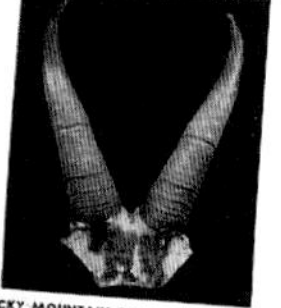

ROCKY MOUNTAIN GOAT—1st Award (Tie)
Score—52
Length—(R) 10-1/8 (L) 10-2/8
Basal Circumference—(R) 5-7/8 (L) 5-7/8
Locality—Kootenay, B.C.—1961
Hunter—Howard Paish

DESERT SHEEP 1st Award
Score—186-2/8
Length—(R) 40-5/8 (L) 38-3/8
Basal Circumference—(R) 16 (L) 16
Locality—Maricopa Co., Ariz.—1961
Hunter—Lt. Ralph Grossman

STONE SHEEP—1st Award
Score—183-3/8
Length—(R) 44-6/8 (L) 441/8
Basal Circumference—(R) 15 (L) 15
Locality—Ketchika Range B.C.—1961
Hunter—John Caputo, Jr.
Guide—Skook Davidson

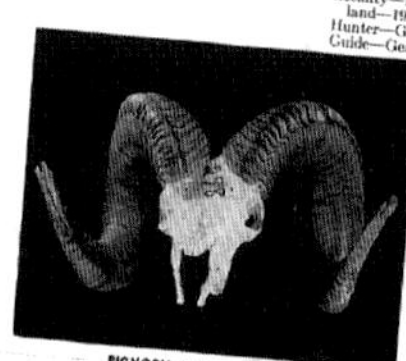

BIGHORN SHEEP—1st Award
Score—196-6/8
Length—(R) 45-2/8 (L) 44-2/8
Basal Circumference—(R) 16-1/8 (L) 15-7/8
Locality—Wardner, B.C.—1961
Hunter—Jim Buss
Guide—Harry Riddell

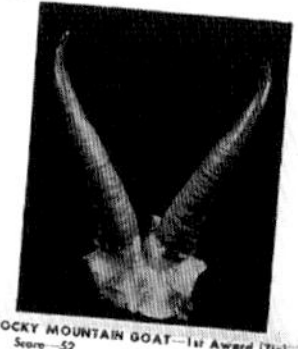

ROCKY MOUNTAIN GOAT—1st Award (Tie)
Score—52
Length—(R) 10-4/8 (L) 11
Basal Circumference—(R) 5-7/8 (L) 6
Locality—Bulkley Range, B.C.—1960
Hunter—Ingvar Wickstrom
Guide—Lefty Gardiner

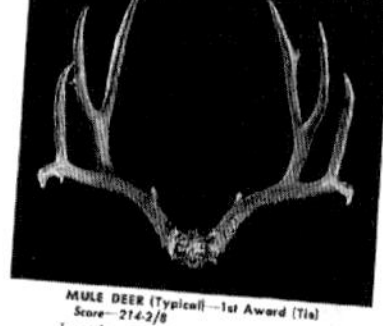

MULE DEER (Typical)—1st Award (Tie)
Score—214-2/8
Length—(R) 27-3/8 (L) 27-1/8
Circumference—(R) 5-4/8 (L) 5-4/8
Points—(R) 5 (L) 6
Inside Spread—28-6/8
Locality—Franklin Co., Idaho—1961
Hunter—Ray Talbot

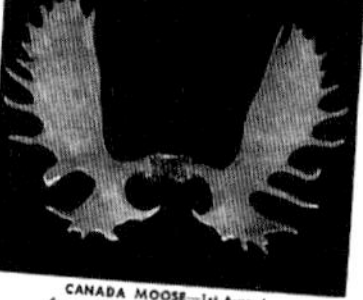

CANADA MOOSE—1st Award
Score—225
Greatest Spread—60
Length of Palm—(R) 45-7/8 (L) 46-1/8
Width of Palm—(R) 14-6/8 (L) 14-3/8
Normal Points—(R) 17 (L) 15

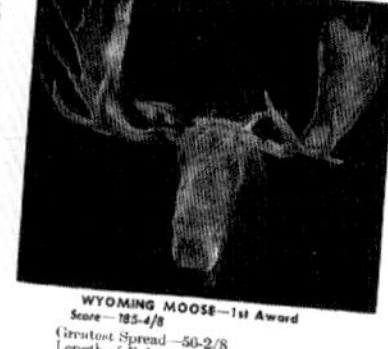

WYOMING MOOSE—1st Award
Score—185-4/8
Greatest Spread—50-2/8
Length of Palm—(R) 41-4/8 (L) 40

MULE DEER (Typical)—1st Award (Tie)
Score—214-2/8

FIRST PRIZE | 1961 COMPETITION CONTINUED...

The quality of wapiti at the 1961 Competition was impressive. Along with Snyder's bull (shown at left), the new World's Record elk taken by John Plute in 1915 was also on display. Snyder sold his award-winning elk to Warren G. Stone, who owned the Clearwater Resort in the heart of Montana's Blackfoot Valley. The bull remained on display in Stone's store for decades.

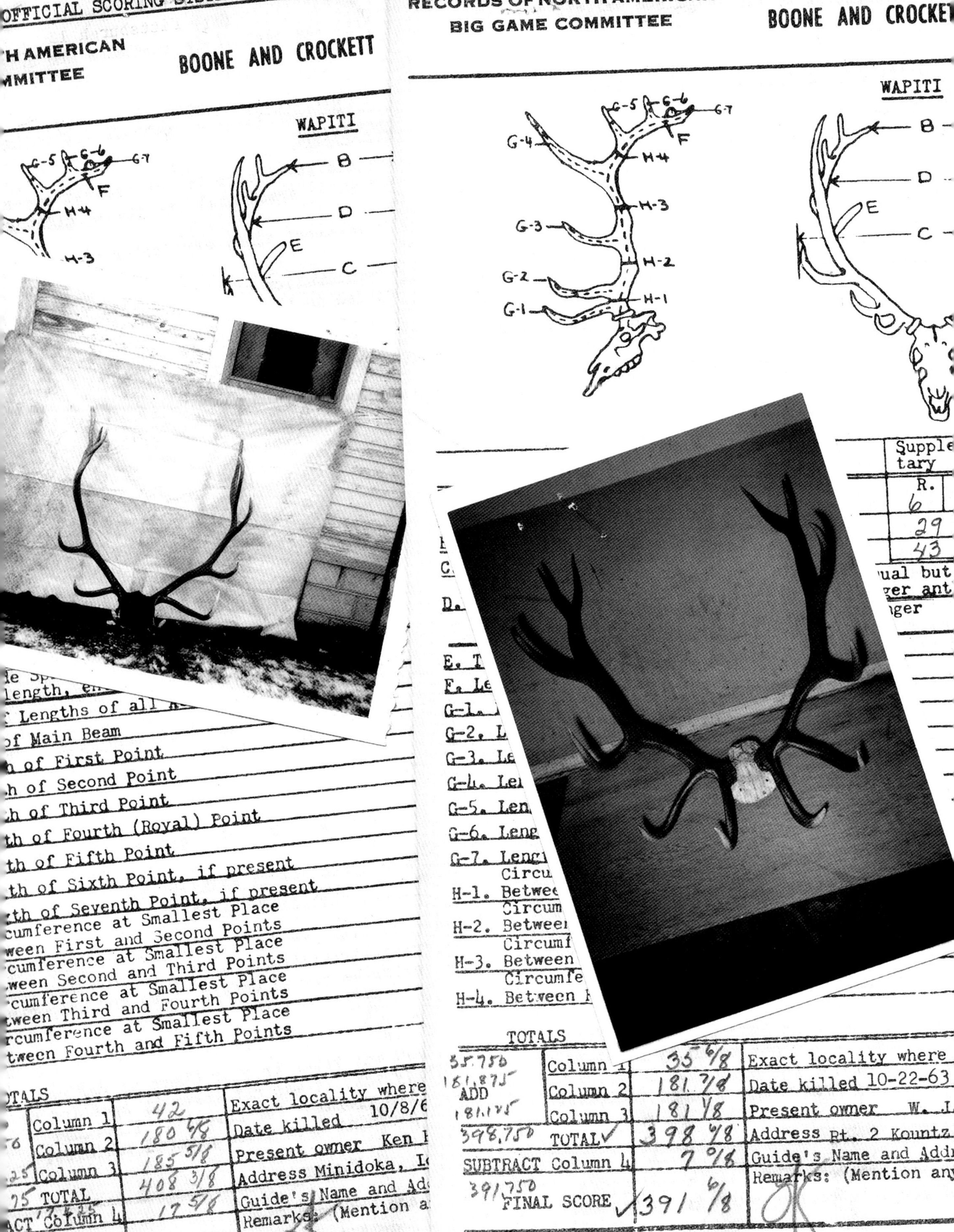
OFFICIAL SCORING SYSTEM FOR
H AMERICAN
MMITTEE
BOONE AND CROCKETT
WAPITI
G-5
G-6
G-7
F
H-4
H-3
B
D
E
C
Lengths of all
of Main Beam
h of First Point
h of Second Point
h of Third Point
th of Fourth (Royal) Point
th of Fifth Point
th of Sixth Point, if present
th of Seventh Point, if present
cumference at Smallest Place
ween First and Second Points
cumference at Smallest Place
ween Second and Third Points
cumference at Smallest Place
tween Third and Fourth Points
rcumference at Smallest Place
tween Fourth and Fifth Points
TALS
Column 1 42
Column 2 180 6/8
Column 3 185 5/8
TOTAL 408 3/8
ACT Column 4 17 5/8
Exact locality where
Date killed 10/8/6
Present owner Ken
Address Minidoka, I
Guide's Name and Add
Remarks: (Mention a
RECORDS OF NORTH AMERICAN
BIG GAME COMMITTEE
BOONE AND CROCKET
WAPITI
G-4
G-3
G-2
G-1
H-1
H-2
Supple
tary
R.
6
29
43
ual but
ger ant
nger
E. T
F. Le
G-1.
G-2. L
G-3. Le
G-4. Le
G-5. Len
G-6. Leng
G-7. Leng
Circu
H-1. Betwee
Circum
H-2. Between
Circumf
H-3. Between
Circumfe
H-4. Between
TOTALS
Column 1 35 6/8
Column 2 181 7/8
Column 3 181 1/8
TOTAL 398 6/8
SUBTRACT Column 4 7 0/8
FINAL SCORE 391 6/8
Exact locality where
Date killed 10-22-63
Present owner W. I
Address Rt. 2 Kountz
Guide's Name and Addr
Remarks: (Mention any

B Mrs. Grancel Fitz, Secretary
5 Tudor City Place, NYC 17, NY.

#26

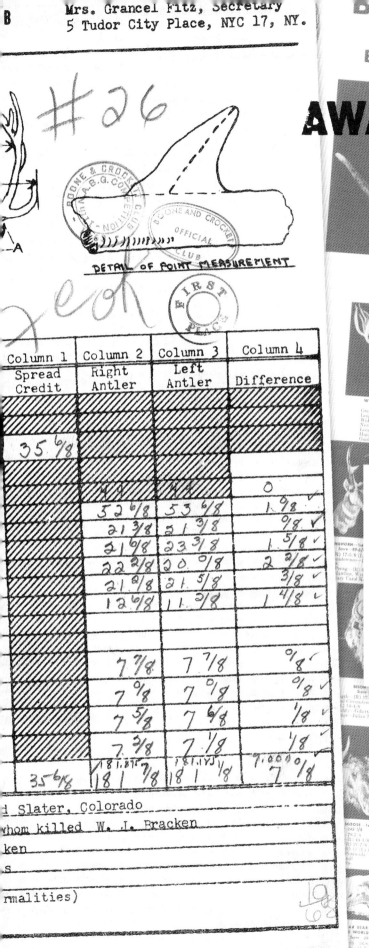

DETAIL OF POINT MEASUREMENT

A

Column 1 Spread Credit	Column 2 Right Antler	Column 3 Left Antler	Column 4 Difference
35 6/8			
	NA	NA	0
	52 6/8	53 6/8	1 0/8
	21 3/8	21 3/8	0/8
	21 6/8	23 3/8	1 5/8
	22 2/8	20 0/8	2 2/8
	21 2/8	21 5/8	3/8
	12 6/8	11 2/8	1 4/8
	7 7/8	7 7/8	0/8
	7 0/8	7 0/8	0/8
	7 5/8	7 6/8	1/8
	7 3/8	7 1/8	1/8
35 6/8	181.875 181 7/8	181.125 181 1/8	7.000 7 0/8

d Slater, Colorado
whom killed W. J. Bracken
ken
s
rmalities)

Big Game Competition

sponsored by
BOONE AND CROCKETT CLUB

AWARD WINNERS

11TH COMPETITION - 1963

SAGAMORE HILL AWARD
STONE SHEEP—1st Award
Score—190
Length—(R) 46-6/8 (L) 46-6/8
Basal Circumference—(R) 15-2/8 (L) 15-1/8
Locality—Sikanni River, B. C.—1962
Hunter—Norman Blank
Guide—R. Lynn Ross

WAPITI—1st Award
Score—391-6/8
Length—(R) 52-6/8 (L) 53-6/8
Circumference—(R) 7-7/8 (L) 7-7/8
Points—(R) 6 (L) 6
Inside Spread—35-6/8
Locality—Slater, Colo.—1963
Hunter—W. J. Bracken

FIRST PRIZE | W.J. BRACKEN
SECOND PRIZE | KEN HOMER
1963 COMPETITION

Two wapiti were awarded prizes at the 11th Competition, which was the last to be held at the American Museum of Natural History in New York City. First Prize went to a bull harvested by W. J. Bracken in Colorado. The Second Prize wapiti was an Idaho bull taken by a local hunter. Both elk were harvested in October 1963.

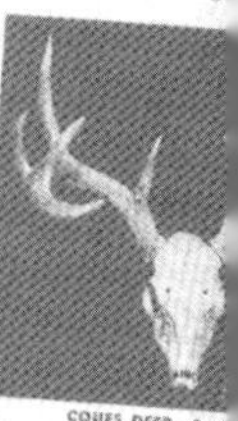

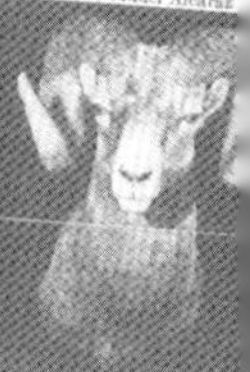

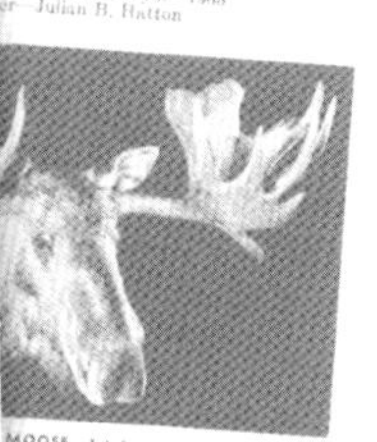

CANADA MOOSE—1st Award

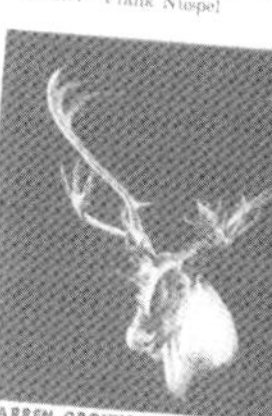

BARREN GROUND CARIBOU—1st Award

ALASKA BROWN BEAR—1st Award

JAGUAR—1st Award

BLACK BEAR—1st Award

OFFICIAL SCORING SYSTEM FOR NORTH AMERICAN BIG GAME TROPHIES

S OF NORTH AMERICAN GAME COMMITTEE

BOONE AND CROCKETT CLUB

Boone and Crockett Club
Records of North American Big Game Committ
c/o Carnegie Museum
4400 Forbes Ave. Pittsburgh, Pa. 15213

WAPITI

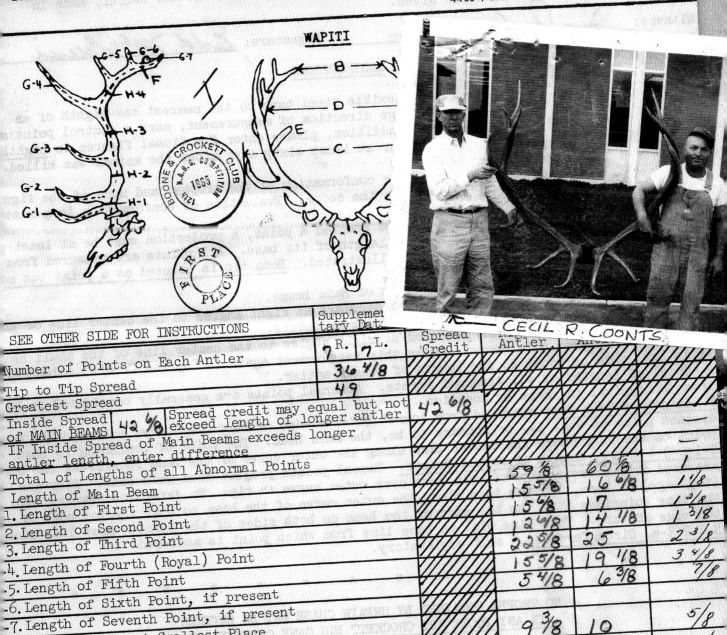

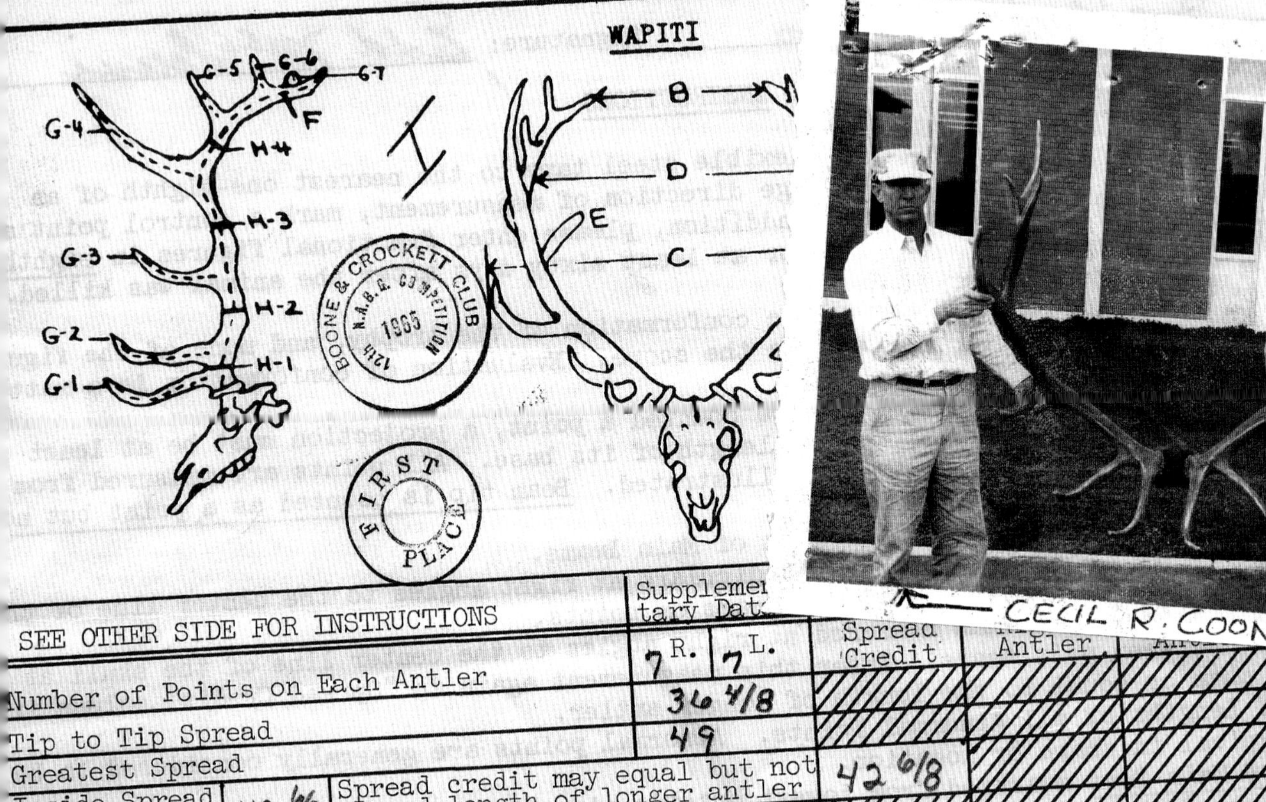

SEE OTHER SIDE FOR INSTRUCTIONS	Supplementary Data R.	L.	Spread Credit	Right Antler	Left Antler	
Number of Points on Each Antler	7	7				
Tip to Tip Spread	36 4/8					
Greatest Spread	49					
Inside Spread of MAIN BEAMS 42 6/8	Spread credit may equal but not exceed length of longer antler		42 6/8			—
IF Inside Spread of Main Beams exceeds longer antler length, enter difference						—
Total of Lengths of all Abnormal Points						
Length of Main Beam				59 1/8	60 1/8	1
1. Length of First Point				15 5/8	16 6/8	1 1/8
2. Length of Second Point				15 6/8	17	1 2/8
3. Length of Third Point				12 4/8	14 1/8	1 3/8
4. Length of Fourth (Royal) Point				22 5/8	25	2 3/8
5. Length of Fifth Point				15 5/8	19 1/8	3 4/8
6. Length of Sixth Point, if present				5 4/8	6 3/8	7/8
7. Length of Seventh Point, if present						
Circumference at Smallest Place 1. Between First and Second Points				9 3/8	10	5/8
Circumference at Smallest Place 2. Between Second and Third Points				7 2/8	7 4/8	2/8
Circumference at Smallest Place 3. Between Third and Fourth Points				8 2/8	8 1/8	1/8
Circumference at Smallest Place 4. Between Fourth and Fifth Points				7 1/8	7 6/8	5/8
TOTALS			42 6/8	179	191 7/8	13 1/8

ADD	Column 1	42 6/8	Exact locality where killed Owyhee Co., Idaho
	Column 2	179	Date killed 10-16-1965 By whom killed Cecil R. Coonts
	Column 3	191 7/8	Present owner Cecil R Coonts
	TOTAL	413 5/8	Address
SUBTRACT Column		13 1/8	Guide's Name and Address
			Remarks: (Mention any abnormalities)

AWARD WINNER

12TH COMPETITION - 1965

FIRST PRIZE | CECIL R. COONTS
1965 COMPETITION

The 12th Competition was the first of four to be held at the Carnegie Museum in Pittsburgh, Pennsylvania. Cecil R. Coonts entered the wapiti he'd taken in 1965 during Idaho's regular hunting season. The bull has a final score of 400-4/8 points and received the First Prize. Coonts' elk is still ranked as the No. 2 elk ever entered from Idaho behind Elmer Bacus' bull taken in 1954.

Record—442-3/8

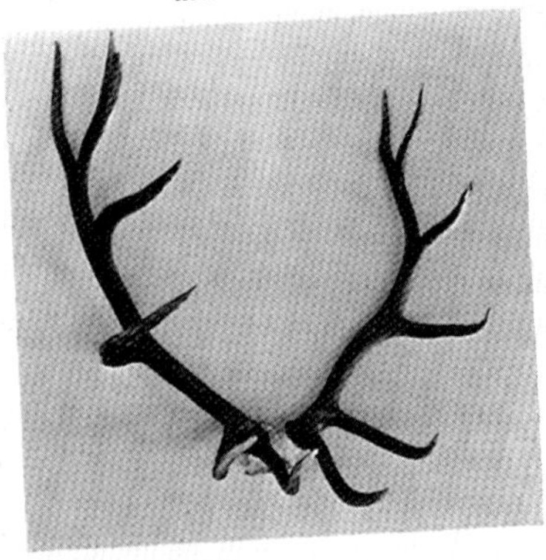

WAPITI—1st Award
Score—395-4/8
Length—(R) 56-2/8 (L) 51-2/8
Inside Spread—43-6/8
Circumference—(R) 10-2/8 (L) 9-5/8
Points—(R) 6 (L) 6
Locality—Silver Bow County, Montana—1966
Wayne Estep

Conservation of our wildlife was not always part of society. Little was done about this until 1887 when Theo Roosevelt organized a group of companions and American men as the Boone and Crockett Club. Since then the Club its members have played a leading role in efforts designe preserve and maintain America's heritage of abundant wil unspoiled scenery and outdoor recreation.

OFFICIAL SCORING SYSTEM FOR NORTH AMERICAN BIG GAME TROPHIES

Called in 1/15/68

$100.00

yes

RECORDS OF NORTH AMERICAN BIG GAME COMMITTEE

BOONE AND CROCKETT CLUB

Boone and Crockett Club
Records of North American Big Game Committee
c/o Carnegie Museum
4400 Forbes Ave. Pittsburgh, Pa. 15213

shipping 2/2/68

ack 2/12/68
Tag # 59

WAPITI

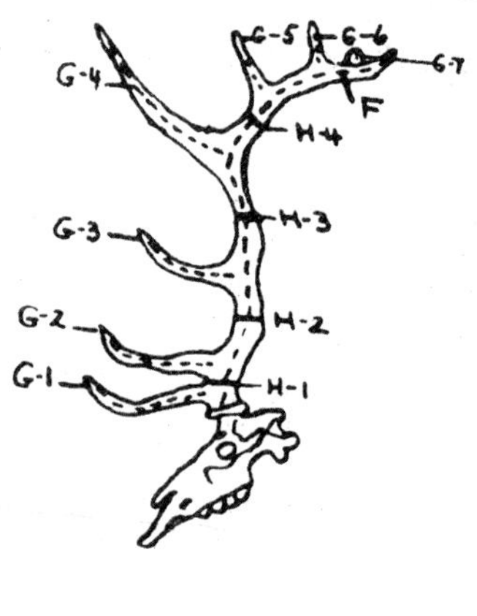

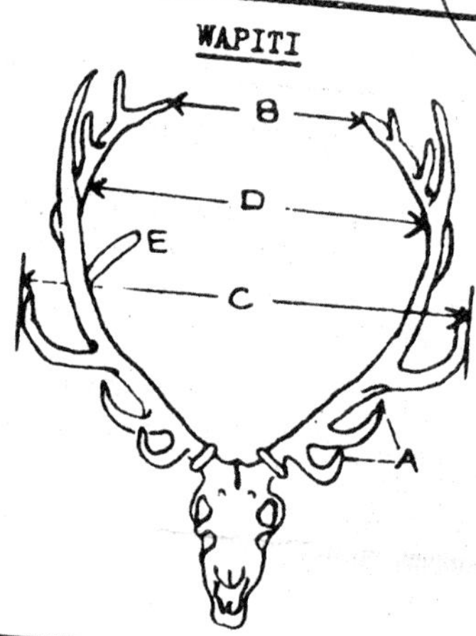

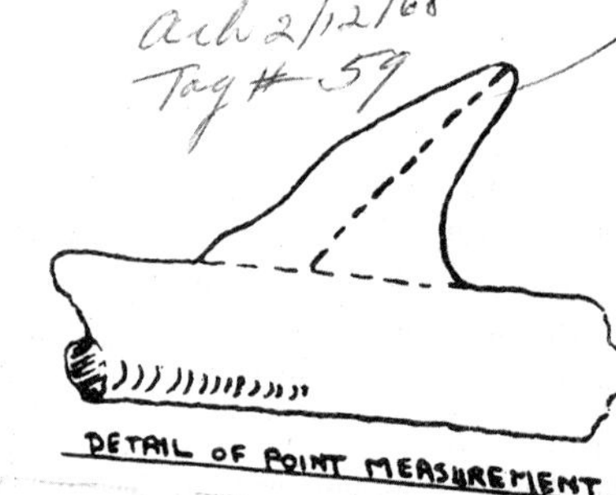

DETAIL OF POINT MEASUREMENT

SEE OTHER SIDE FOR INSTRUCTIONS		Supplementary Data		Column 1	Column 2	Column 3	Column 4
A. Number of Points on Each Antler		6 R.	6 L.	Spread Credit	Right Antler	Left Antler	Difference
B. Tip to Tip Spread		45 7/8					
C. Greatest Spread		46 3/8					
D. Inside Spread of MAIN BEAMS	45	Spread credit may equal but not exceed length of longer antler		45			
IF ... an... Main Beams exceeds longer							
To...							
Le...							
1.							
2.							
3.					55 6/8	51 3/8	4 3/8 ✓
4.					20 2/8	17	3 2/8 ✓
					21 2/8	19 1/8	2 1/8 ✓
					27	22 5/8	4 3/8 ✓
					20 6/8	23	2 2/8 ✓
					17 4/8	13 4/8	4 ✓
					10 2/8	9 5/8	5/8 ✓
					7 5/8	7 3/8	2/8 ✓
					7 6/8	8 2/8	4/8 ✓

AWARD WINNERS

13TH COMPETITION - 1967

FIRST PRIZE | WAYNE ESTEP
1967 COMPETITION

Wayne Estep's wapiti, scoring 395-4/8 points, received the First Prize and still ranks No. 8 in the state of Montana. Estep was hunting Montana's Silver Bow County in 1966 when he harvested the bull. Four other wapitis were on display at the Competition.

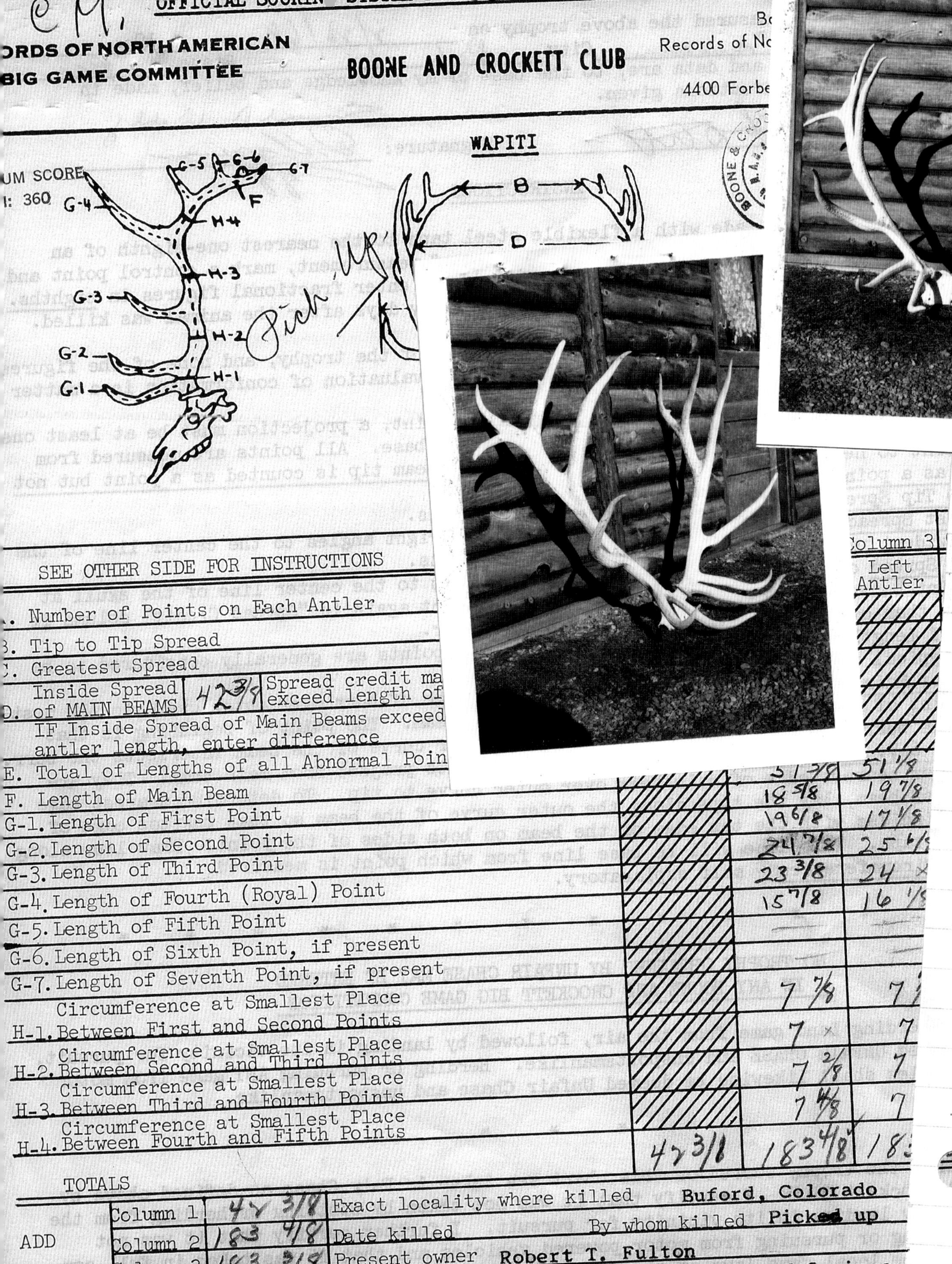

C.M.

OFFICIAL SCORIN...

...ORDS OF NORTH AMERICAN BIG GAME COMMITTEE

BOONE AND CROCKETT CLUB

Bo... Records of No... 4400 Forbe...

WAPITI

...UM SCORE ...: 360

SEE OTHER SIDE FOR INSTRUCTIONS

	Column 1	Column 2	Column 3 Left Antler
A. Number of Points on Each Antler			
B. Tip to Tip Spread			
C. Greatest Spread			
D. Inside Spread of MAIN BEAMS 42 3/8 Spread credit ma... exceed length of...			
IF Inside Spread of Main Beams exceed... antler length, enter difference			
E. Total of Lengths of all Abnormal Poin...			
F. Length of Main Beam		51 3/8	51 1/8
G-1. Length of First Point		18 5/8	19 7/8
G-2. Length of Second Point		19 6/8	17 1/8
G-3. Length of Third Point		24 7/8	25 6/8
G-4. Length of Fourth (Royal) Point		23 3/8	24
G-5. Length of Fifth Point		15 7/8	16 1/8
G-6. Length of Sixth Point, if present		—	
G-7. Length of Seventh Point, if present			
H-1. Circumference at Smallest Place Between First and Second Points		7 7/8	7
H-2. Circumference at Smallest Place Between Second and Third Points		7	7
H-3. Circumference at Smallest Place Between Third and Fourth Points		7 2/8	7
H-4. Circumference at Smallest Place Between Fourth and Fifth Points		7 4/8	7
TOTALS	42 3/8	183 4/8	18...

ADD			
Column 1	42 3/8	Exact locality where killed	Buford, Colorado
Column 2	183 4/8	Date killed	By whom killed Picked up
Column 3	183 3/8	Present owner	Robert T. Fulton

Glenwood Springs, Colorado 81601

Dear Mr. Fulton:

We wish to acknowledge receipt of your letter of December 9, enclosing information regarding your Wapiti measuring 394-7/8.

Your letter crossed ... the Wapiti trophy to P... by our panel of judges for the Thirteenth Competition.

We do hope you will be able to get your trophy from your ... summer camp before February 15th so you could ... This is a fine trophy

AWARD WINNERS

13TH COMPETITION - 1967

CERTIFICATE OF MERIT
ROBERT T. FULTON
1967 COMPETITION

Robert T. Fulton's bull was another entry recognized at the Club's 13th Competition. Fulton, a registered Colorado guide and Chief of Police for Glenwood Springs, found the elk near his summer cabin in Buford County in 1967. The rack was entered as a "picked up" trophy and, with an official score of 392-4/8 points, received a Certificate of Merit. The impressive bull still ranks in Colorado's top ten for trophy elk.

Elmer M. Austen, M.D.
Chairman, Boone & Crockett
C/o Carnegie Museum
4400 Forbes Ave.
Pittsburgh, Pa. 15213

Dear Mr. Austen,
I am enclosing pictures of the
which I have entered in your Co
This is the one that scores 394 7/8
with the form which you previou
I regret that I will be un
this time, to send this head for
measurement, as it is at my
Cabin and it is "snowed in".
probably be late April or t
of May before I can get it
I will ...

BOONE AND CRO
Records of North Am
Commi
c/o Carnegie Museum
4400 Forbes Avenue
Pittsburgh, Pennsylva
BOONE AND CROCKETT CLUB
BIG GAME COMPETITION
Robert G. Young
Wapiti killed 11/4/67 in Summit Co
name appears two ways on the
phy. Please print below exact
name to appear on our record
ert G. Young
E
F.
G-
G-
G-
G-
G-
G-6
G-7
H-1
H-2
H-3.
H-4.
ADD
SUBT
FIN
KODAK SAFETY FILM

c/o Carnegie Museum
4400 Forbes Ave. Pittsburgh, P

WAPITI

FIRST 1970 PLACE

G-1 G-2 G-3 G-4 G-5 G-6 G-7 F H-1 H-2 H-3 H-4 B C E

AWARD WINNERS

14TH COMPETITION - 1970

FIRST PRIZE | ROBERT G. YOUNG
1970 COMPETITION

Boone and Crockett Club member Frank Cook of Anchorage, Alaska, (seated at left reviewing a score chart) was the chairman for the Club's 14th Competition, the last to be held at the Carnegie Museum in Pittsburgh, Pennsylvania. Robert G. Young's wapiti, scoring 407 points, received First Prize. The bull was harvested in Summit County, Colorado, during the 1969 season.

...POINT MEASUREM...

SEE OTHER SIDE FOR INSTRUCTIONS	Sup... tari...	Column 1	Column 2	Column 3 ...eft ...er	Colum... Diff...
...mber of Points on Each Antler	8 R.				
...p to Tip Spread	3...				
...eatest Spread	5...				
...side Spread MAIN BEAMS 43 4/8 — Spread credit may equal but not exceed length of longer antler		43 4/8			
...Inside Spread of Main Beams exceeds longer ...ler length, enter difference					
...al of Lengths of all Abnormal Points					—
...gth of Main Beam			56 ?/8	56 6/8	—
...ngth of First Point			14 4/8	15 4/8	1
...ngth of Second Point			16 5/8	16 3/8	
...ngth of Third Point			24 5/8	21 3/8	3
...gth of Fourth (Royal) Point			24 2/8	23 7/8	
...gth of Fifth Point			15 2/8	14 5/8	5...
...gth of Sixth Point, if present			4	5 3/8	1 3...
...gth of Seventh Point, if present			4 3/8	—	4 3...
...cumference at Smallest Place ...ween First and Second Points			9 4/8	8 4/8	1
...umference at Smallest Place ...een Second and Third Points			7 6/8	7 4/8	...
...umference at Smallest Place ...een Third and Fourth Points			7 1/8	7 1/8	
...umference at Smallest Place ...een Fourth and Fifth Points			7 1/8	7 5/8	4/...
...LS		43 4/8	192	184 5/8	13 1/...

...olumn 1	43 4/8	Exact locality where killed Blue River, Summit Co.,Colo.
...olumn 2	192	Date killed 11-4-67 By whom killed ~~Bob Young~~
...olumn 3	184 5/8	Present owner Robert G. Young
...OTAL	420 1/8	Address Dillon Colorado 80435 BLUE RIVER ROUTE
...olumn 4	13 1/8	Guide's Name and Address none
...ORE	407	Remarks: (Mention any abnormalities)

RDS OF NORTH AMERICAN
G GAME COMMITTEE

BOONE AND CROCKETT CLUB

c/o Carnegie Museum
4400 Forbes Ave. Pittsburgh, Pa.

inimum Score: 375

HONORABLE MENTION 1970

W... ITI

G-5 G-6 G-7
G-4 F
H-4
G-3

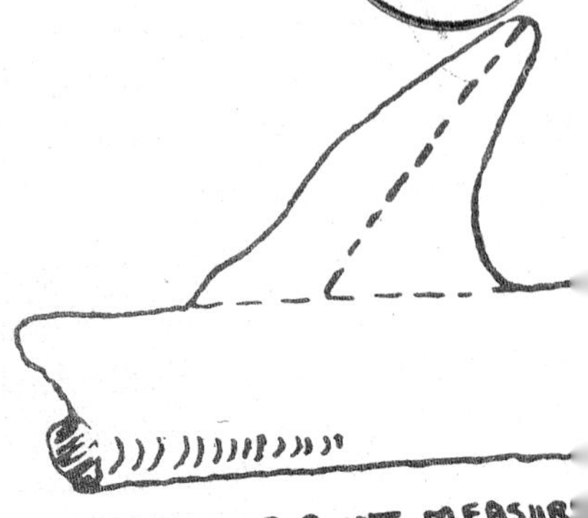

DETAIL OF POINT MEASUR

G-6
second pt
G-5
G-6
G-7

	...1	Column 2	Colu...
SER...	...pread Credit	Right Antler	Le... Ant...
Numbe...			
Tip to...			

G-4 G-5
G-4
G-5 G-6 G-6-7

HONORABLE MENTION
MRS. MILDRED EDER
1970 COMPETITION

Mildred Eder took this fine wapiti down with her .30-30 Model 1894 Winchester shooting a 170-grain bullet. The bull was originally measured by Philip L. Wright, a long-time B&C Club member and future chairman of the Club's Records Program. Wright remarked in his letter dated December 29, 1969, which accompanied the score chart:

"Enclosed are data on a large elk head taken this fall in western Montana. Mrs. Eder, whom I met today, is clearly part Indian, the wife of a rancher. I think it is very appropriate that an Indian woman apparently about 50 years old who has hunted big game for over 35 years should shoot such a fine animal with a .30-30 carbine. I hope she wins first award!"

H-1.
H-2.
H-3.
H-4. Circumference at Smallest Place Between Fourth and Fifth Points

TOTALS

ADD	Column 1	41 6/8	Exact locality ...
	Column 2	186 2/8	Date killed 10-19-69 By whom killed Mrs...
	Column 3	178 2/8	Present owner Mrs. Mildred Eder
	TOTAL	...	Address Helmville, Montana 59843

University of Montana
Missoula, Montana 59801
(406) 243-0211

AWARD WINNERS

14TH COMPETITION - 1970

Mrs. Walter F. Toerge
Secretary, Records Committee
Boone and Crockett Club
Carnegie Museum
4400 Forbes Ave.
Pittsburgh, Pa. 15213

Dear Mrs. Toerge:

Enclosed are data on a large elk head taken this ... whom I met today, is clearly ... I think it very appropriate ... 50 years old who has hunted ... ot such a fine animal with ... rst award!

... G-5 are quite close together ... my mind that all of the long ... el Fitz says in connection ... ng system does not attempt to ... ts."

... rs. Eder to wait until the ... 1971 before having the head ... heir home in Helmville today

...incerely yours,

Philip L. Wright

Philip L. Wright

HUNTER, GUIDE AND HUNT INFORMATION

To be completed by hunter

BOONE AND CROCKETT CLUB

...ecords of North American Big Game Committee

c/o Carnegie Museum
4400 Forbes Avenue
Pittsburgh, Pa. 15213

...unter's name: Mrs. Mildred Eder

Address: Helmville, Montana 59843 (City / State, Province / Zip)

...de's name: None

Address: (City / State, Province / Zip)

...ion of hunt: Powell County, Montana

...of arrival: October 19, 1969 (Month / Day / Year)

...f departure: October 19, 1969 (Month / Day / Year)

...of transportation: On foot (In) ______ (Out)

...otor-powered vehicles used? Yes If so, specify type

...ose: Only to drive to the general area, hunting was done on foot

...ill: October 19, 1969 (Month / Day / Year)

... weapon: .30-30 (Model 94 Winchester)

... bullet: 170 grain

...v if bow and arrow used: --

...te distance from trophy: 80 yards

Mildred Eder

Signature ...

→1
→1A
→2
→2A
→3
062
KODAK SAFETY FILM 5062
KODAK SAFETY

AWARD WINNER

16TH AWARDS - 1977

FIRST AWARD | DOUGLAS SPICER
1977 AWARDS

With no wapiti entries at the 15th Awards Program, Douglas Spicer's Award-winning wapiti was a welcome sight at the 16th Awards Program. His bull from Teton County, Wyoming, is extremely symmetrical with only 3-5/8 inches in deductions and a final score of 401-6/8 points. It is one of seven elk from Wyoming scoring over 400 points.

WAPITI — 1st Award
Score — 401-6/8
Length — (R) 58-3/8 (L) 57-5/8
Circumference — (R) 7-7/8 (L) 8
Points — (R) 6 (L) 6
Inside Spread — 47-2/8
Locality — Targhee National Forest, Teton County, Wyoming — 1972
Hunter — Douglas Spicer

WAPITI — 2nd Award
Score — 386-6/8
Length — (R) 61-6/8 (L) 61-7/8
(R) 8-7/8 (L) 9-1/8

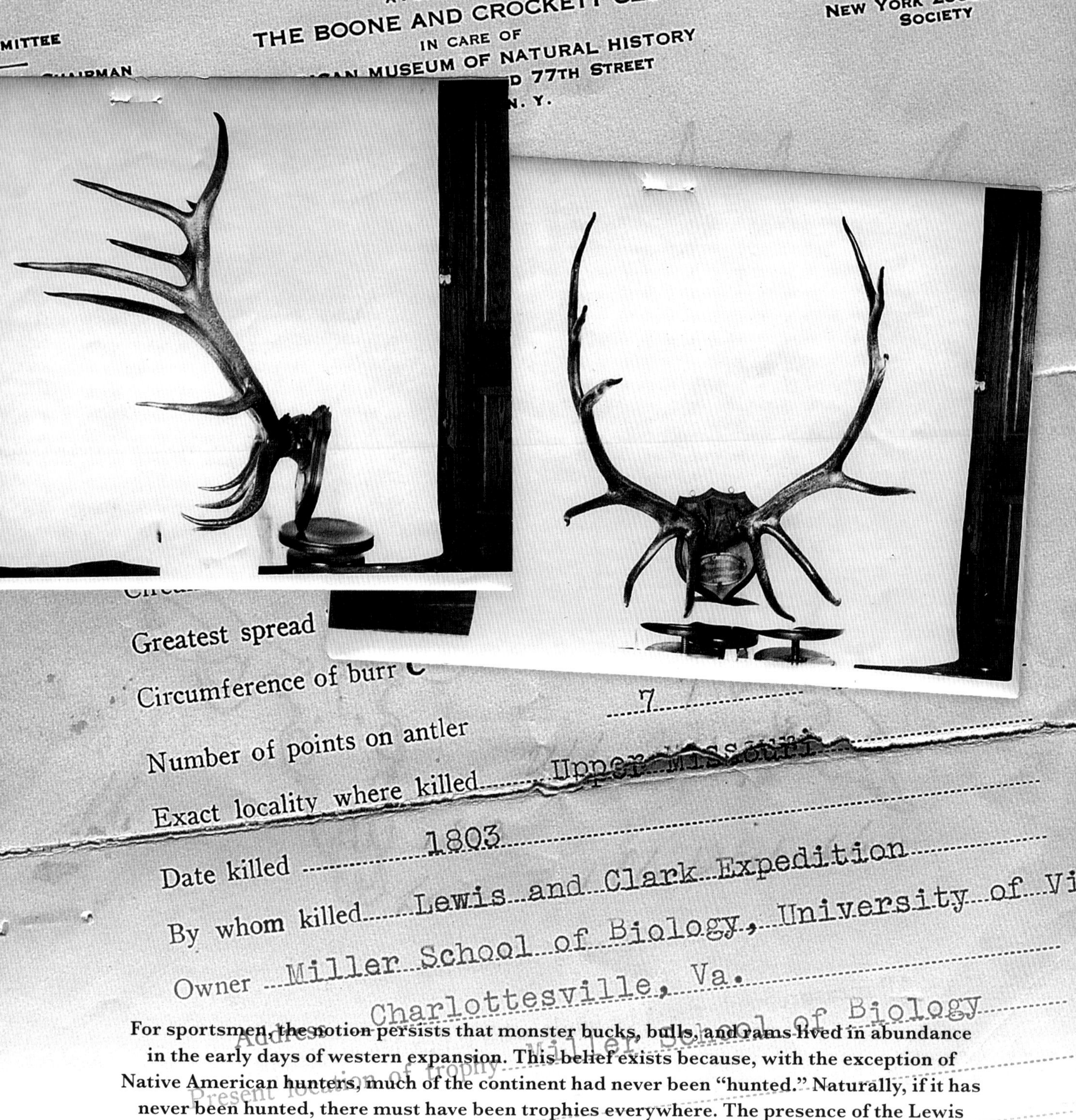

A PUBLICATION OF
THE BOONE AND CROCKETT CLUB
IN CARE OF
...MUSEUM OF NATURAL HISTORY
...D 77TH STREET
...N. Y.

OF THE
NEW YORK ZOOLOGICAL
SOCIETY

...MITTEE
CHAIRMAN

Greatest spread

Circumference of burr

Number of points on antler 7

Exact locality where killed Upper Missouri

Date killed 1803

By whom killed Lewis and Clark Expedition

Owner Miller School of Biology, University of Vi...
Charlottesville, Va.

Address Charlottesville

Present location of trophy Miller School of Biology

Remarks

For sportsmen, the notion persists that monster bucks, bulls, and rams lived in abundance in the early days of western expansion. This belief exists because, with the exception of Native American hunters, much of the continent had never been "hunted." Naturally, if it has never been hunted, there must have been trophies everywhere. The presence of the Lewis and Clark bull, reportedly taken in 1803 from the Upper Missouri River by the Lewis and Clark expedition, is proof only that such trophies did exist, not that they were in every draw. The chart for this bull was submitted in 1938, but was deemed to small to be included in the records book. The paperwork lists the Lewis and Clark expedition, but there is no other evidence to verify this claim. The bull was dropped from B&C records, not because of this fact, but because it was never re-scored after the current scoring system was initiated in 1950.

5: SPECIAL TROPHIES

BY KEITH BALFOURD

A trophy is in the eye of the beholder. It's a true-enough statement that has carried on in our hunting culture for decades. And while it's also true that big game and extreme examples of nature do not exist to be judged, our society is and has been achievement-driven. Definitions, classifications and re-classifications have to be made to satisfy the curious, to settle the debate, to categorize and place things in order.

Boone and Crockett records were never intended for such, but the pure nature of records-keeping breeds setting apart the best of the best. Therefore, within B&C data, segmenting can and does occur, but this is not a bad thing. On the contrary, pulling from the files and singling out trophies deemed "special" is yet another useful benefit of the historical record of big game hunting in North America.

Trophies with a high score and corresponding high ranking will clearly stand out when the numbers are stacked end to end. Some of these trophies carry the "special" label because they sat at the top of all trophies for a species or category known to Boone and Crockett and, therefore, the rest of the sporting community. Separate still are those trophies that were recognized by the records-keepers with the highest honor given: the Roosevelt family's Sagamore Hill Award. Even rarer still are those total oddities of nature that fascinate with signature headgear similar to the human fingerprint: No two are the same, or even close. And while being outsized in antler can make the book, among these there are tales of the hunt that, in and of themselves, make certain trophies fascinating to learn about and special among the rest.

Some special trophies get names. These come not from B&C, but from fans. They are used as identifiers in conversation and reflect respect for the animal, the hunter, and sometimes for the region. The Dark Canyon Bull, the Elk Rapids Bull, the Mercer Bull all have their places in history.

Truly special trophies are not in the eye of the beholder: They are special to everyone. Across a body of work listing American and Roosevelt's elk, there exist such trophies that stop those leafing through cabinets full of files. All in this chapter have been celebrated as an initial entry. Some have been singled out at the time they were listed as special and given extra attention; some you may be learning about for the first time.

Regardless of individual opinions about whether "special" should be more special, there is no denying the significance of starting the campfire discussion with, "Have you seen the ____________ Bull?
(insert name)

GAME AND FISH
COMMISSION

CLARENCE W. BAKER
PRESIDENT
LAKEWOOD DIST. 1

HENRY BLEDSOE
VICE PRES.
YUMA, DIST. 3

PAT GRIFFIN
SECRETARY
FT. COLLINS, DIST. 2

Mrs. Gr
Boone
5 Tudo
New Yo

Dear M

conse
new r
I bel
antle
a cho

JEW:
Encl

SPECIAL TROPHY

THE DARK CANYON BULL

We know John Plute's former World's Record typical American elk has for years been labeled as the Dark Canyon Bull. What we do not know is: Why not the Plute Bull? Maybe Dark Canyon was more ominous and befitting of a trophy that stood unchallenged for 36 years. The bull was taken from Dark Canyon, Colorado, in 1899 and was finally entered and declared a new World's Record at the Club's 10th Competition in 1962. The bull scores 442-3/8. This elk was bumped to No. 2 in 1998 by the surfacing of the Alonzo Winters' Bull taken in 1968. Only 2/8 inches separates these two monarchs.

Somerset, Colo.
April 16, 1964

Dear Sir:

It is almost impossible to get any authentic information or to check out the stories that are told about John Plute's hunt on this short of attime. Although for a later date I will be glad to check out and interview all persons that may know anything concerning this hunt to obtain as accurate a report as possible. If you would care to have this information latter please let me know.

As I have wrote you in the past all of your first information concerning this huge trophy was sent by our State Game and Fish Dept. officer and I do not know if it is correct as they did not interview any reliable source. To the best of our knowledge this trophy was taken prior to 1916 in the Dark Canyon of the Anthracite River drainage in Gunnison county. Killed with a 30-40 Krag rifle, magnificiant animal in size it was packed out by horses. Antlers being of this size required one pack horse ust for them. They are now on exihibit at the Hotchkiss Elks odge 1807, with all proceeds of pictures and postcards of them ing sent to Laradon Hall of Denver, Home of Retarded children.

Another error as first reported, present owner is not ny Rozman", myself, Albert Rozman, but the Rozman Brothers.

I have a picture of 4 hunters in a group and John Plutte ne of the hunters, would this be of any value to you?

Albert A. Rozman "Tony"

STEVE MCNICHOLS, GOVERNOR

TATE OF COLORADO

DEPARTMENT OF GAME AND FISH

HARRY R. WOODWARD
EXECUTIVE DIRECTOR

GAME AND FISH COMMISSION
C. DEWEY BROWN, CORTEZ, DIST. 6
DR. T. O. PLUMMER, MONTROSE, DIST. 7
RALPH L. WHITE, CRAIG, DIST. 8
PARKER SOOTER, ALAMOSA, DIST. 5
ROY ECKLES, LAMAR, DIST. 4

209 N. Townsend Ave.
Montrose, Colorado

December 15, 1961

tz, Secretary
kett Club
ace
ew York

:

ike this is a new world's record. I was rather in my measurements; however, in that this is a ssibly you might want to check my measurements. t the Elks Lodge in Hotchkiss would send the u if you request it. However, it would be quite rt them up in that they are so large.

Very truly yours,

Jesse E. Williams
by JB

Jesse E. Williams,
Regional Information Officer

Rozman displayed the trophy at B.P.O.E. Elk's Lodge 1807 in Hotchkiss, Colorado. In 1962, it was crated and sent to New York City for the Club's 10th Competition held at the American Museum of Natural History. The measurements were verified by a panel of judges, who determined its final score at 442-3/8 points and declared it the official new World's Record wapiti.

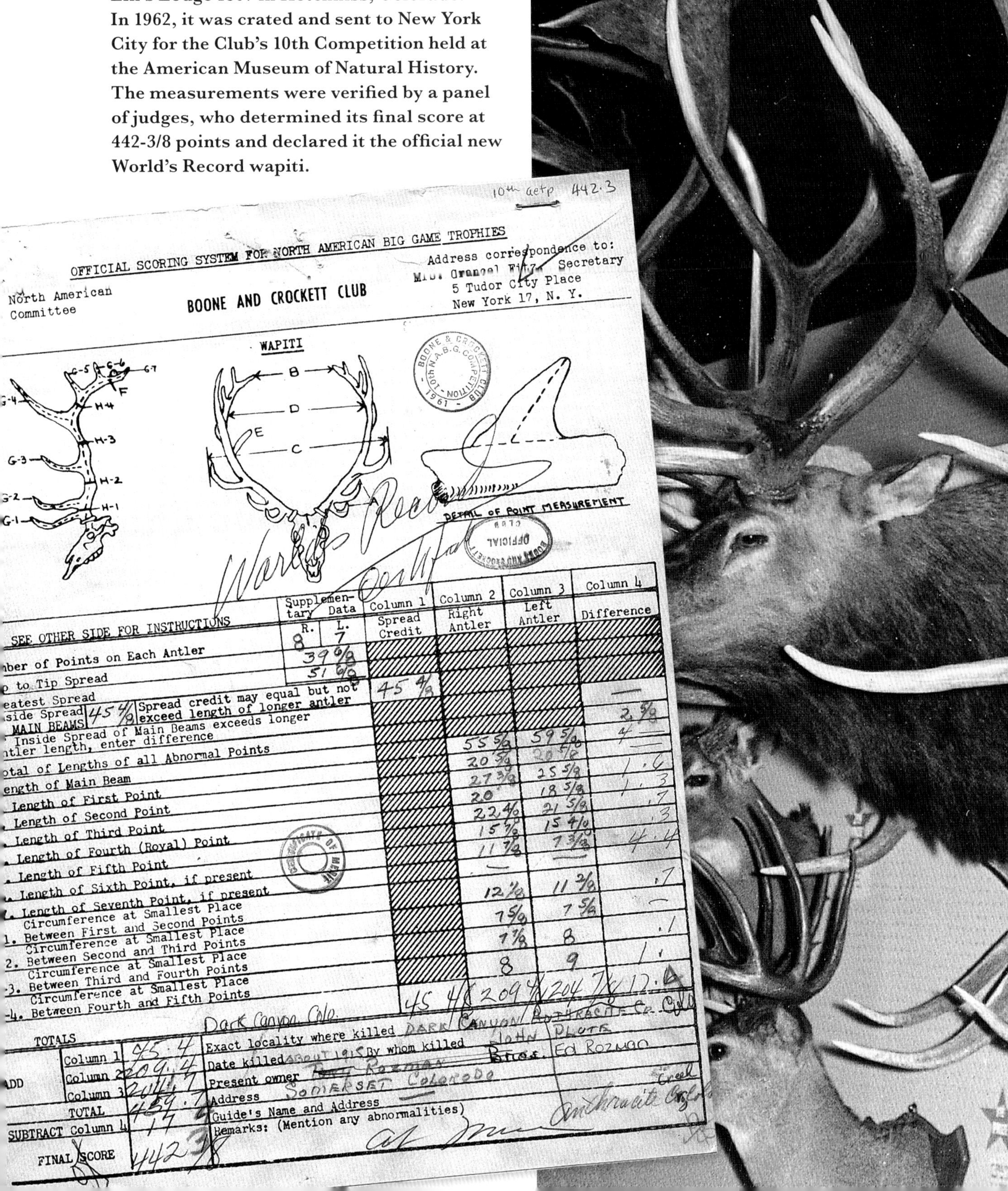

10th actp 442.3

OFFICIAL SCORING SYSTEM FOR NORTH AMERICAN BIG GAME TROPHIES

North American Committee

BOONE AND CROCKETT CLUB

Address correspondence to:
Mis. Grancel Fitz, Secretary
5 Tudor City Place
New York 17, N. Y.

WAPITI

SEE OTHER SIDE FOR INSTRUCTIONS	Supplementary Data R.	Supplementary Data L.	Column 1 Spread Credit	Column 2 Right Antler	Column 3 Left Antler	Column 4 Difference
…ber of Points on Each Antler	8	7				
…p to Tip Spread	39 6/8					
…eatest Spread	51 6/8					
…side Spread of MAIN BEAMS 45 4/8 — Spread credit may equal but not exceed length of longer antler			45 4/8			
… Inside Spread of Main Beams exceeds longer …ntler length, enter difference						—
…otal of Lengths of all Abnormal Points						2 5/8
…ength of Main Beam				55 5/8	59 5/8	4
… Length of First Point				20 5/8	20 5/8	—
… Length of Second Point				27 3/8	25 5/8	1.6
… Length of Third Point				20	18 5/8	1.3
… Length of Fourth (Royal) Point				22 4/8	21 5/8	.7
… Length of Fifth Point				15 7/8	15 4/8	.3
… Length of Sixth Point, if present				11 7/8	7 3/8	4.4
… Length of Seventh Point, if present				—	—	
…1. Circumference at Smallest Place Between First and Second Points				12 1/8	11 3/8	.7
…2. Circumference at Smallest Place Between Second and Third Points				7 5/8	7 5/8	—
…3. Circumference at Smallest Place Between Third and Fourth Points				7 7/8	8	.1
…4. Circumference at Smallest Place Between Fourth and Fifth Points				8	9	1.
TOTALS			45 4/8	209 4/8	204 7/8	12.4

ADD	Column 1	45.4
	Column 2	209.4
	Column 3	204.7
	TOTAL	459.7
SUBTRACT	Column 4	17
FINAL SCORE		442 3/8

Exact locality where killed Dark Canyon Colo. DARK CANYON ANTHRACITE Cr. Colo

Date killed ABOUT 1915 By whom killed JOHN PLOTE Bros. Ed Rozman

Present owner ~~Tony~~ ROZMAN

Address SOMERSET COLORADO

Guide's Name and Address Anthracite Creek Colo

Remarks: (Mention any abnormalities)

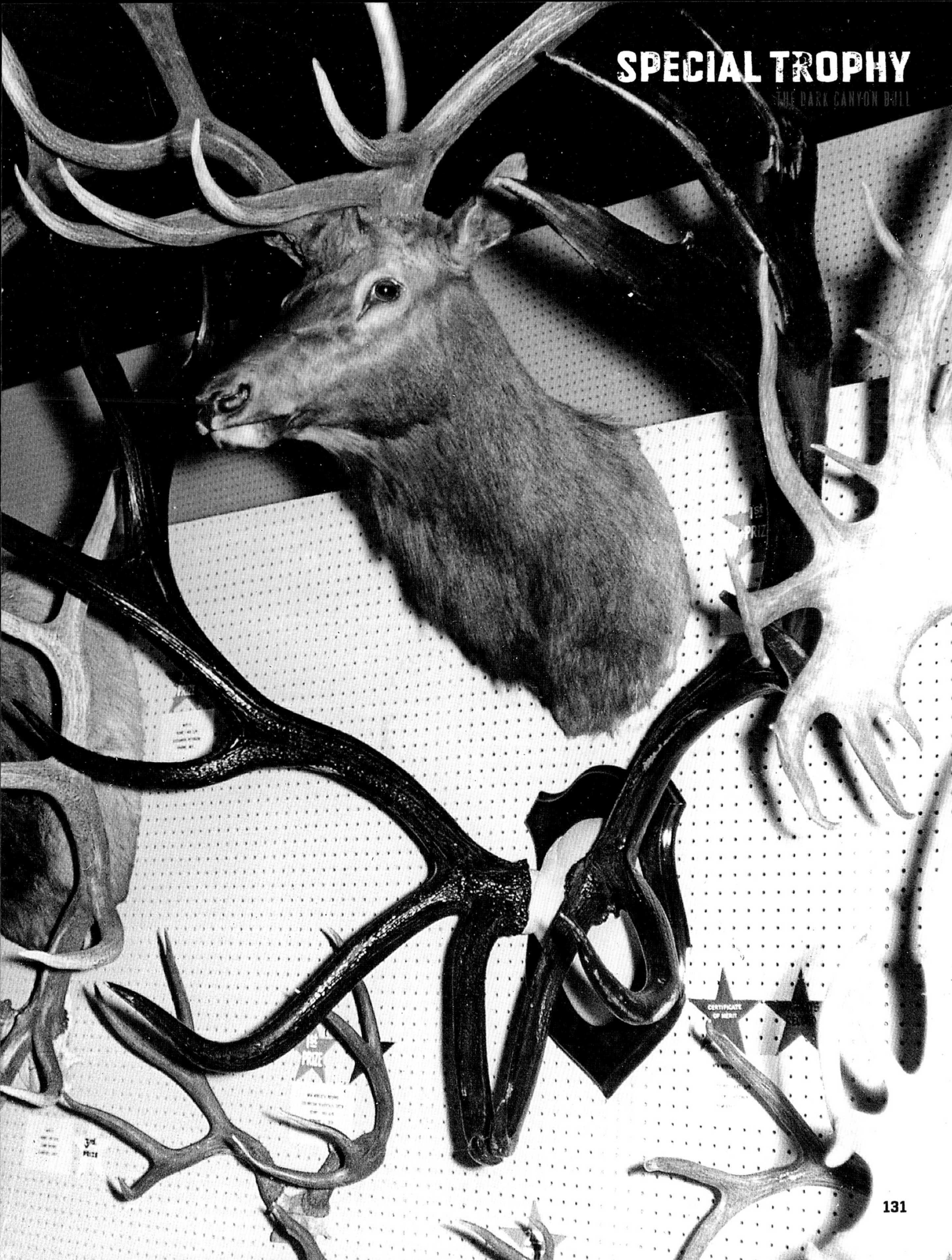
1st PRIZE
CERTIFICATE OF MERIT
3rd PRIZE

SUCCESSFUL HUNTERS!
Among The Elk, Bear
And Deer.
Boy's Successful Hunt
Game in The Rockies.
Colo., Sept. 1888.
Clark Bros., Williamson,
Huber :—
Your letters were
and he came nearer and nearer
was within 200 yards of the camp.
he bugled and repeated, striking
note in the staff in a loud, clear,
whistling tone that echoed from
woodland. It was indeed a grand
nade, but we were
his elkship that we did not
clusion. Hastily
ets we hurriedly dressed and
a march on him. There
was quite dark,

SPECIAL TROPHY
THE DEWEESE BULL

The year was 1888. The conservancy that Theodore Roosevelt founded was in its first year of trying to place conservation in the minds of the people. A Colorado man, having just returned from a subalpine elk-hunting adventure in Colorado, wrote his Nimrod friends who could not make the trip. There is nothing that can be told about this bull, nor the hunt, that isn't better said by the hunter himself, other than to say that the existence of such a story may as well be more of a treasure than this great bull of record. It is worth pointing out that even in a lawless time of abundance, true sportsmen did have an appreciation for all things wild and did follow a personal code of restraint.

SUCCESSFUL HUNTERS!

TEN DAYS AMONG THE ELK, BEAR, AND DEER.

A Former Tipp Boy's Successful Hunt After Big Game in The Rockies.
Camp Big Horns, Colo., Sept. 1888.
Messrs. Bowman, Clark Bros., Williamson, Hawver, and Huber: --

My Dear Nimrods – Your letters were received in due time stating that it was impossible for you to join me this fall in an elk hunt in the Rocky Mountains. I regretted much to receive this word and think you "tender-feet" will regret sending it after reading of our grand time.

Mr. J. E. Brown, Mr. L. E. Franck (county treasurer), both "old-timers" here, and myself took train September 3d, crossed the Rockies to the mouth of Eagle River where I had saddle horses and pack animals (jacks) awaiting us. There are no toll pikes in this country but simply a jack trail leading here and there up into the cedars and pinons, then up to the quakenasps, thence higher to the spruce-covered mountain tops and timber line peaks, and into the very heart of the Rocky Mountains. We soon packed our bedding and supplies on our jacks and took the trail leading up Sweetwater (Turret Creek.) We reached Sweetwater Lake the same evening and camped for the night. The lake is one mile long and half a mile wide, located in a canon between two great mountains; its waters are full of the beautiful speckled trout and our jointed rods, lines, leaders and flies were quickly adjusted and seventeen of the speckled beauties were landed and prepared for supper.

The next morning the bright face of Old Sol found us in the saddle and two miles up the steep ascending trail. What fresh invigorating atmosphere and how grand the scenery of this forenoon ride! We climbed higher through groves of quakenasp and the grassy mountainsides until noon when we reached the "flat tops," or summit of the range. I wish I could picture this landscape for you so you could imagine the grand surroundings of our camp, but I can only say that these flat tops are timbered with dense groves of the stately spruce and are broken here and there with open parks which are covered with a luxuriant growth of the tall gramma grass. Notwithstanding the altitude is 10,000 feet, fine springs, small streams and lakes are everywhere. Turret Peak and Shingle Peak tower up to 12,000 feet – 1000 feet above timber line – and on their North sides lays perpetual snow. From these peaks you can see *forever!* You can see

UCCESSFUL HUNTERS!

n Days Among The Elk, Bear And Deer.

Former Tipp Boy's Successful Hunt After Big Game in The Rockies.

CAMP BIG HORNS, Colo., Sept. 1888.

ssrs. Bowman, Clark Bros., Williamson, Fawver and Huber:—

Y DEAR NIMRODS—Your letters were eived in due time stating that it was im- sible for you to join me this fall in an hunt in the Rocky Mountains. I re- tted much to receive this word and k you "tender-feet" will regret sending fter reading of our grand time.

r. J. E. Brown, Mr. L. E. Franck, unty treasurer,) both "old-timers" here, myself took train September 3d, cross- he Rockies to the mouth of Eagle er where I had saddle horses and pack nals (jacks) awaiting us. There are no pikes in this country but simply a jack leading here and there up into the ars and pinons, then up to the quaken- s, thence higher to the spruce covered untain tops and timber line peaks, and the very heart of the Rocky Moun- s. We soon packed our bedding and plies on our jacks and took the trail ing up Sweetwater (Turret Creek.) We ched Sweetwater Lake the same even- and camped for the night. The Lake ne mile long and half a mile wide, lo- d in a canon between two great moun- s; its waters are full of the beautiful ckled trout and our jointed rods, lines, lers and flies were quickly adjusted and enteen of the speckled beauties were led and prepared for supper.

he next morning the bright face of Old found us in the saddle and two miles the steep ascending trail. What fresh igorating atmosphere and how grand scenery of this forenoon ride! We nbed higher and higher through groves quakenasp and the grassy mountain es until noon when we reached the "flat s," or summit of the range. I wish I ld picture this landscape for you so could imagine the grand surroundings our camp, but I can only say that these tops are timbered with dense groves of stately spruce and are broken here and re with open parks which are covered h a luxuriant growth of the tall gram- grass. Notwithstanding the altitude is 000 feet fine springs, small streams and es are everywhere. Turret Peak and ngle Peak tower up to 12,000 feet— 00 feet above timber line—and on their rth sides lays perpetual snow. From se peaks you can see *forever!* You can into the Egeria Park, the head waters

"bugle"—probably a half mile and he came nearer and neare was within 200 yards of the ca he bugled and repeated, striki note in the staff in a loud, cle whistling tone that echoed fro woodland. It was indeed a nade, but we were so eager for his elkship that we did not aw clusion. Hastily kicking aside ets we hurriedly dressed and tri a march on him. There being was quite dark, and we stole edge of the spruce near the ope he was crossing. We could hea ing and down we crouched nea of willows. All was still as de rustle of the tall grass at his f casionally a musical bugle, but ing at right angles from us a within 80 yards—close enough t breathe. But alas! we could out the outline of his "darned ol and he gained the shelter of and bugled again. I tried to but my "bugle" was evidently ure, or else he heard one fro congenial mate, for he bugle "good-bye" or "some other e grew fainter and fainter, and with cold we crept back to be an emphatic good-night to bull

In the morning we were o all keeping together we follow high ridge near the lakes. Fr seen on all favorable groun a sharp lookout. Presently th of water near at hand attracte tion and looking down we band of elk in a little lake ju grove of spruce. The wind w us, and silently we stole aroun posite edge of the timber. He sight met our eyes—a band of all cows and calves except on bull. Some were in the wa others in an open park. The 300 yards and it was impossib shot at the bull to kill. Ho chanced it, and, taking care no cows and calves, we singled h fired together. Off they went under cover of the spruce, and ed, finding blood on the trail lowing the trail half a mile we it was a flesh wound and return —thinking we might have don feeling like shooting some e deer we saw while coming bac

Next morning before sun u off in different directions. At t of the year the elk are beginnin together, the velvet has just shed antlers of the bulls, and the bar quently be seen off of spruce t feet from the ground where they

into Egeria Park, the head waters of the Grand, Piney, Eagle, Roaring Fork, Muddy and Bear Rivers, and at their base heads the great White River. This was the Ute Indians' paradise for summer and fall hunting, and here is the home of the elk, mountain sheep, silver tip grizzly and cinnamon bear, and the gamey black tail [mule] deer. Three o'clock p.m. found our jacks and horses unpacked and picketed out in the rich grass, dinner over, tents up, hunting equipments in place, and then we started out after fresh meat for supper, although we had a goodly supper of bacon.

Sundown found us all back in camp with three deer packed in and hung on the spruce [in] back of the tent. I killed a big buck that weighed 200 pounds, fat an inch thick over the rump, horns in the velvet which makes for a fine trophy.

Having all the camp meat necessary the next day was spent in looking for elk sign through the spruce forests on the North and shady sides of the breaks on the flat tops. Our notes compared favorably on our return at night, and after camp-fire stories we retired fully convinced that we were in the land of the "wapiti," and believing that our desire to kill a bull elk would soon be gratified.

The next day we discovered quite a chain of small lakes about six miles Northward, with no end to elk and bear sign in their vicinity. We saw dozens of fine fat deer at close range but killed none as we were not out to see how much game we could slaughter and let lay in the mountains – as is too often done. We returned to camp early that day, boned our meat, salted it down in the hides under the spruce trees where the sun never shines and covered it up with boughs. Then we folded our bedding, packed some supplies on our jacks, saddled our horses and made a branch camp at one of the newly discovered lakes by 8 o'clock the same evening.

After we had retired we heard a bull elk "bugle" – probably a half mile distant – and he came nearer and nearer until he was within 200 yards of the camp. Here he bugled and repeated, striking every note in the staff in a loud, clear, shrill, whistling tone that echoed from park to woodland. It was indeed a grand serenade, but we were so eager for a crack at his elkship that we did not await its conclusion. Hastily kicking aside the blankets we hurriedly dressed and tried to steal a march on him. There being no moon it was quite dark, and we stole along the edge of the spruce near the open park that he was crossing. We could hear him coming and down we crouched near a clump of willows. All was still as death save the rustle of the tall grass at his feet and occasionally a musical bugle, but he was going at right angles from us and passed within 80 yards – close enough to hear him breathe. But alas! We could not make out the outline of his "darned old carcass," and he gained the shelter of the spruce and bugled again. I tired to answer him but my "bugle" was evidently a sad failure, or else he heard one from a more congenial mate, for he bugled us a loud "good-bye" or "some other evening" that grew fainter and fainter, and shivering with cold we crept back to bed muttering an emphatic good-night to bull elks.

In the morning we were out early and all keeping together we followed along a high ridge near the lakes. Fresh sign was seen on all favorable ground and we kept a sharp lookout. Presently the splashing of water near at hand attracted our attention and looking down we discovered a band of elk in a little lake just beyond a grove of spruce. The wind was against us, and silently we stole around to the opposite edge of the timber. Here a grand sight met our eyes – a band of forty elk, all cows and calves except on fair sized bull. Some were in the water and others were in an open park. The distance was 300 yards and it was impossible to get a shot at the bull to kill. However we chanced it, and, taking care not to hit the cows and calves, we singled him out and fired together. Off they went like a flash under cover of the spruce, and we followed, finding blood on the trail. After following the trail half a mile we concluded it was a flesh wound and returned to camp – thinking we might have done better and feeling like shooting eight or ten deer we saw while coming back.

Next morning before sun up we were off in different directions. At this season of the year the elk are beginning to band together, the velvet has just shed from the antlers of the bulls, and the bark can frequently be seen off of spruce trees eight feet from the ground where they have been rubbing their antlers. I made a long trip and struck the fresh trail of a band of elk, mostly bulls as the tracks were large. I followed the trail a mile or more somewhat toward camp and saw they were headed for a large body of spruce timber. As it was about noon and being close to camp I concluded to go in, get something to eat and then ride my horse over to the location of the elk and take my evening hunt, for one hour at sun down is worth the balance of the day in elk hunting. On reaching camp I was joined by Mr. Brown who asked if I had moved the jacks from where he had picketed them out in the morning. I had not and went to the park where they should have been. Gone? Yes, gone! Our Rocky Mountain Mocking Birds had "broke" camp and struck out for home, their pace doubtless accelerated by the scent of a gray silver tip. Mr. Franck and myself, after lunch, saddled our horses and rode over in the direction I had tracked the elk. After going a mile we rode out of the spruce on a point to look over the country. The sun was half an hour high and the shadows of the spruce groves were stretching out over the parks – and this is *the* hour for the elk to come from the forests and feed in the parks. Sitting quietly in the saddle, our gaze roving over the beautiful landscape, we sighted a band of elk a mile away just emerging from the spruce. We counted eleven; all were large, one in particular, and we remarked that there was an "Old Towser." He stopped and looked square at us – then moved on. Now was our opportunity. Slipping away from our saddles and leaving the horses for a "blind," we started on a run through the spruce groves, open parks, up, then down the ravines, across another park and finally reached the last spruce grove that separated us from the game. Stealing quietly through this we reached the edge that fringed the park. Peeping out I saw a great bull elk lying down in the tall grass 140 yards away and looking right at us. I saw he was a monster, and we gave him a double shot. Over he went – then he was up and off into the spruce like a flash! The others fled to the top of the hill and were gone in a second. We followed their trail in a forest of spruce twenty miles wide, found no blood, and the sun went down. We stared blankly into each others faces and wondered if it was possible to miss such a monster. Finally we decided to return to camp and pick up the trail early the next morning. We kicked ourselves back to camp and declared that if we had really missed that elephant we would fold our blankets, go to Canon City and never say elk again.

The next morning we were up with the stars and rode over to where we had left the trail. Staking our horses we were soon tracking the "Monarch of the Glen." Although the dense spruce forest was tracked by elk, we could easily follow the right one as it was almost an inch deeper and much larger than the other tracks. After tracking 200 yards we saw that one of us had our brand on him for occasionally we found a drop of blood. He kept in the heaviest timber, and I knew that was a good sign for the Indians say, "Heap hurt when go through heap brush!" We tracked him a mile into the heart of the forest to where the ground and logs were covered with a rich, green, velvet-like moss, and where the sun never penetrates. Here we "jumped" him and away he went; we fired five shots after him, and then I ran to the left about forty yards and gained a higher spot of ground from where I got a broadside shot, the ball breaking his left shoulder and down he went! We rushed up to him; he still struggled, shook those massive antlers and eyed us with vengeance. A merciful shot through the heart ended his career. We then gazed in astonishment at his gigantic size. He measured 15 feet and 4 inches from the point of horn to the hind hoof, and girted 9 feet. His antlers are the largest I ever saw; the beams are six feet long and are five feet between the points, having nine perfect points on one beam and eight on the other – hence the name of our camp, "Big Horns." Old hunters came to see him and they say he is the biggest elk ever killed in this country. He dressed over 700 lbs. of meat. We

Detail of Point Measurement

				SUBTOTALS			7 7/8
				E. TOTAL		7 7/8	
SEE OTHER SIDE FOR INSTRUCTIONS				COLUMN 1	COLUMN 2	COLUMN 3	COLUMN 4
No. Points on Right Antler	8	No. Points on Left Antler	9	Spread Credit	Right Antler	Left Antler	Difference
Tip to Tip Spread	40 5/8	C. Greatest Spread	56 6/4				
Inside Spread of Main Beams	4[illegible]	SPREAD CREDIT MAY EQUAL BUT NOT EXCEED LONGER MAIN BEAM		49 7/8			
Length of Main Beam					56 0/8	55 7/8	1/8
1. Length of First Point					18 7/8	19 6/8	7/8
2. Length of Second Point					22 0/8	22 5/8	5/8
3. Length of Third Point					12 2/8	12 3/8	1/8
4. Length of Fourth Point					18 7/8	18 6/8	1/8
5. Length of Fifth Point					14 0/8	13 5/8	3/8
6. Length of Sixth Point, If Present					8 3/8	9 7/8	1 4/8
7. Length of Seventh Point, If Present					5 6/8	5 1/8	5/8
1. Circumference at Smallest Place Between First and Second Points					7 7/8	8 2/8	3/8
2. Circumference at Smallest Place Between Second and Third Points					7 2/8	7 2/8	—
3. Circumference at Smallest Place Between Third and Fourth Points					8 1/8	8 2/8	1/8
4. Circumference at Smallest Place Between Fourth and Fifth Points					8 3/8	8 1/8	2/8
			TOTALS	49 7/8	187 4/8	189 7/8	5 1/8
Column 1	49 7/8	Exact Locality Where Killed:					

The Royal Gorge Regional Museum and History Center of Canon City, Colorado, currently owns DeWeese's trophy elk. They entered bull in the Club's 25th Big Game Awards Program in 2003, 115 years after it was harvested. It was recognized with a Certificate of Merit in the non-typical American elk category with a final score of 430-2/8 points.

found that one of us had hit him in the neck the evening before, and on cutting out the bullet, which was imbedded in the neck-bone, it proved to be a Winchester – and my comrade used a Sharps.

After dressing him we returned to camp, taking some of his meat with us for supper, and as we kindled our camp-fire that night we gave three cheers for the Monarch Bull Elk, Harrison and Morton, and the boys of Tippecanoe.

The next day Mr. Brown returned with our "mocking birds" and we packed in our elk and boned the meat. The next morning we started to move camp again; our animals were packed and we were in the saddle at daylight. We struck a trail and had only gone half a mile when I caught a glimpse of three silver tip bears on the opposite side of an open park we were just entering. Hastily notifying Mr. Brown, who was just behind me, we slipped out of our saddles and started for the game. I gained a bunch of willows between the bears and myself, and Mr. B. kept to the right along the trees. I opened fire and down went a bear. I advanced and continued firing to keep him down. Mr. B. got into position and began shooting, while the other two bears slowly retreated up the hill snarling and stopping occasionally to snap viciously at us. I expected them to come at us, for the one I had shot lay kicking on the ground and squalling terribly; and so I filled the magazine of my gun with cartridges as I ran, expecting a dozen more bears to appear at any moment (I am glad they did not for I was out in the open park with no trees handy.) Mr. Franck, who was some 300 yards behind us fixing his saddle when the rumpus started, came riding into the fight on the dead run, and the first shot from his old Sharps rifle hit a bear in the neck and silenced him forever. The other bear carried off our lead and escaped. I tell you there was music in the air for a few minutes, the constant bang! bang! bang! of our rifles, the snapping and squalling of the bears, the bray of our jacks as they rushed terror-stricken from the scene, and our shouts to each other to "stand your ground and give 'em h—l!" made up a scene at once exhilaratingly exciting. But it was over in half the time it takes to write it. We came out without a scratch and got two bears out of the three. Their robes are fine and we will have them made into rugs to keep as mementos of a most thrilling experience.

After a close search for an hour we found our jacks huddled together with a part of their packs off and frightened nearly to death. We were soon on the move again and came down to our first camp, satisfied with our day's sport.

In the early morning we were up early and rode six miles to another locality, and then swung around to a "salt lick" where we had seen a band of mountain sheep several days before. It was sundown when we reached the ridge in front of the "licks," and we dismounted and quietly crept to the top. Three hundred yards distant was a band of eleven elk standing around the lick. It was too dark to see the antlers, but we were satisfied several of the larger ones were bulls, and singling out our targets we fired. At the first round they rushed up the mountain which was very steep. This gave us an advantage, although we were firing a distance of over three hundred yards. We continued firing until each of us succeeded in killing an elk – Mr. Brown bringing down a fine bull. We dressed them and returned to camp, arriving at 11:30, where we prepared a meal from the fat of the land.

In the morning we decided that the swelling was out of our necks, broke camp and started for home. We reached the railroad on the 16th and sent eight pack animals and two packers back to camp to bring out the balance of our game. Reached home on the 17th ready for business and feeling that we have a new lease on life which could not be had only through an elk hunt in the Rocky Mountains.

Dall DeWeese.
Canon City, Colorado.

REPRINTED FROM CANNON CITY CLIPPER, OCTOBER 31, 1888.

ZE WINNING TROPHIES

1950

AMERICAN BIG GAME COMPETITIO

Sponsored by

BOONE AND CROCKETT CLU

WAPITI — Sagamore Hill Award
Score — 441-6/8

Length—(R) 61-6/8 (L) 61-2/8
Greatest Spread—50-2/8
Basal Circumference—(R) 10-2/8 (L) 9-7/8
Points—(R) 8 (L) 7

Locality—Big Horn Mts., Wyo. - 1890
Hunter—Unknown
Guide—Unknown
Owner—Dr. R. C. Bentzen

SPECIAL TROPHY

WYOMING SATE RECORD

Dr. R.C. Bentzen of Wyoming found the set of antlers of an old, neglected bull in a barn near the Big Horn Mountains and brought it to the attention of the Boone and Crockett Club. No other information was ever made available. It was entered and accepted with a score of 441-6/8 at the Club's 4th Competition in 1950 with a harvest date of 1890. It is the first wapiti to win the Boone and Crockett Club's highest honor, the Sagamore Hill Award. Since the 1950 Competition the criteria for the Sagamore Hill Award has changed. This is the only pick-up trophy to have won this award.

BIGHORN SHEEP — 1st Prize
Score — 190-6/8
Length—(R) 42-4/8 (L) 44-4/8
Basal Circumference—(R) 14-7/8 (L) 15
Greatest Spread—23-3/8
Locality—Fernie, B. C. - 1950
Hunter—J. J. Osman
Guide—None
Owner—J. J. Osman

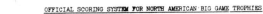

OFFICIAL SCORING SYSTEM FOR NORTH AMERICAN BIG GAME TROPHIES

Records of North American Big Game Committee

BOONE AND CROCKETT CLUB

Address correspondence to:
Mrs. Grancel Fitz, Secretary
5 Tudor City Place
New York 17, N. Y.

WAPITI

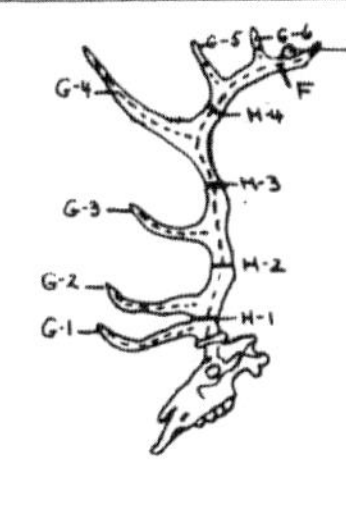

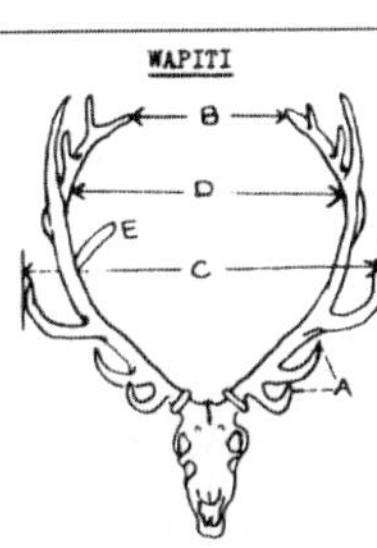

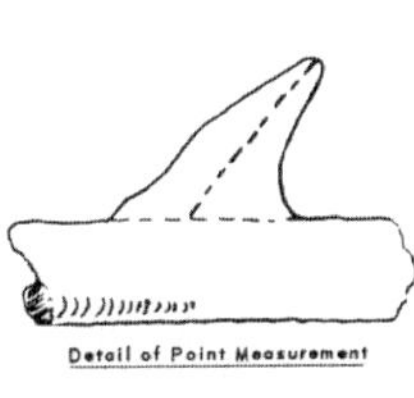

SEE OTHER SIDE FOR INSTRUCTIONS	Supplementary Data R.	Supplementary Data L.	Column 1 Spread Credit	Column 2 Right Antler	Column 3 Left Antler	Column 4 Difference
A. Number of Points on Each Antler	8	7				
B. Tip to Tip Spread	28 2/8					
C. Greatest Spread	50 2/8					
D. Inside Spread of MAIN BEAMS 47 — Spread credit may equal but not exceed length of longer antler			47			
IF Inside Spread of Main Beams exceeds longer antler length, enter difference						
E. Total of Lengths of all Abnormal Points						
F. Length of Main Beam				61 6/8	61 2/8	4/8
G-1. Length of First Point				20 3/8	20	3/8
G-2. Length of Second Point				21 4/8	20 4/8	1
G-3. Length of Third Point				26 6/8	18 2/8	8 4/8
G-4. Length of Fourth (Royal) Point				24 2/8	25	6/8
G-5. Length of Fifth Point				16 1/8	19 6/8	3 5/8
G-6. Length of Sixth Point, if present				5 2/8	5 2/8	---
G-7. Length of Seventh Point, if present				2	---	2
H-1. Circumference at Smallest Place Between First and Second Points				10 2/8	9 7/8	3/8
H-2. Circumference at Smallest Place Between Second and Third Points				7 6/8	7 7/8	1/8
H-3. Circumference at Smallest Place Between Third and Fourth Points				7 2/8	7 5/8	3/8
H-4. Circumference at Smallest Place Between Fourth and Fifth Points				6 7/8	7	1/8
TOTALS			47	210 1/8	202 3/8	17 6/8

ADD	Column 1	47	Exact locality where killed Cookstove Basin, Big Horn Mts., Wyoming
	Column 2	210 1/8	Date killed 1890 By whom killed Unknown
	Column 3	202 3/8	Present owner Dr. R. C. Bentzen
TOTAL		459 4/8	Address 244 N. Main Street, Sheridan, Wyoming
SUBTRACT Column 4		17 6/8	Guide's Name and Address Unknown
FINAL SCORE		441 6/8	Remarks: (Mention any abnormalities)

SECOND AND

PRIZE TROP

AND

hat I have m...
s) A.M.N.H.
ese measurements and data are, to the best
with the instructions given.

Signatu... T. DONALD CARTER

ED McGUIRE

INSTRUCTIONS

...o the nearest one-eighth of an inch.
...lays after the animal was killed.

...urements m... ...he trophy. Evaluation of
measureme...
...ubmit phot...

...entary Data ..., a projection must be at least
...ation is a ... base. All points are measured
... Beam tip is counted as a point

...ber of Point...
...ch long AND...
...ip of point...
...t measured a... ...t angles to the center line of
...ts.

...o to Tip Spre... the center line of the skull
...t again in "Spread Credit"
...eatest Spread... antler.
...skull at wides...

...nside Spread o... ...ts are generally considered to b...
...idest point be...
...mn if it is le... ...f burr over outer curve to the

Total of Length... They a...
...se nontypical i...

Length of Main...
...st distant point...

...-1-2-3-4-5-6-7. L...
...easured from near...

...-1-2-3-4. Circumferences - self e...

The first complete system for sc...
copyrighted in 1935 by Dr. James...
and published in NORTH AMERICAN...
system of accepted authority, t...
committee to develop the Offici...
members of this committee were...
Dr. James L. Clark, Grancel Fi...

This Official System is basic...
existing systems: In the pr...
and needed simplification ha...

Before publication, these c...
guides, authors, taxidermis...
... The Boone a...

Late City Edition 3/15/51

18 L+

BIG GAME CONTEST WON BY 1/4 INCH

Fractional Difference in the Spread of Alaska Moose Antlers Decides Prize

An Alaska moose squeaked by on a margin of a quarter of an inch to win first prize over another in the Third Annual North American Big Game Competition of the Boone and Crockett Club, which last night awarded its coveted medals and citations to hunters from all parts of the country.

As it was explained at the American Museum of Natural History, where the event took place, the difference of a quarter of an inch in the spread of a moose's antlers is much more than meets the eye.

Dr. Harold E. Anthony of the museum, who was the competition's committee chairman and who awarded the prizes in the fitting setting of the Hall of North American Mammels, said that hunters "don't think any more of giving up a fraction of an inch than of giving up their left leg."

Brought down in "fair chase" according to approved standards of sportsmen and conservationists, the moose was the prize of Dan Auld Jr., a young Texas rancher from Kerrville. His wife, who was with him on his trip to New York for his reward, revealed that the hunting expedition occurred on their honeymoon in September, 1949. Mrs. Auld remained in Canada while Mr. Auld went after big game. The spread of Mr. Auld's head was 66¾ inches; of the runner-up's, Arthur C. Popham Jr. of Kansas City, Mo. ...

SOME OF THE AWARD WINNERS AT BIG GAME CO...

THE NEW...

Dr. R. C. Bentzen displays his trophy, a head of a wapiti, which won him the Sagamor... at the American Museum of Natural History.

pronghorn, and Alaska brown bear. The icing on the cake came with the presentation of a special prize for an unrecorded Wapiti, which it was thought likely would set a new world record by the club's new and complicated method of scoring...

would add to the date of scientists and sportsmen, it received the Sagamore Hill Award, given by the Roosevelt family in memory of Theodore Roosevelt, first president of the club. Theodore...

French Free Lauza...

Special to The New Yo...

PARIS, March 1... Lauzanne, pre-war e... Parisian newspape...

SPECIAL TROPHY

WYOMING STATE RECORD - SAGAMORE HILL AWARD WINNER

This award-winning elk was originally owned by Dr. R. C. Bentzen, who was responsible for entering it in the Club's Records Program. The bull was sold to the Jackson Hole Museum in 1959, where it currently resides.

f North Am
he Committe

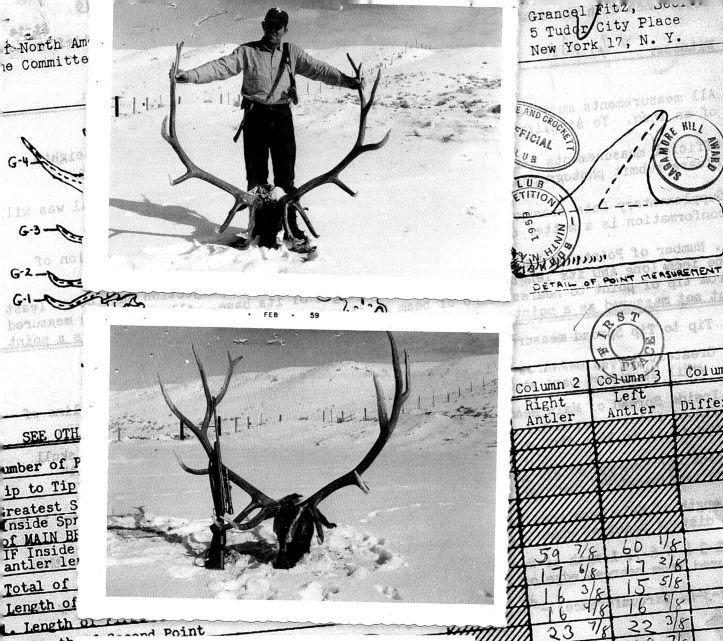

Grancel Fitz, Secre
5 Tudor City Place
New York 17, N. Y.

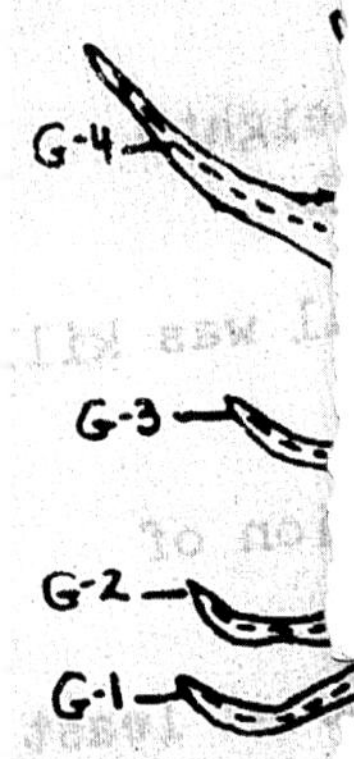

G-4
G-3
G-2
G-1

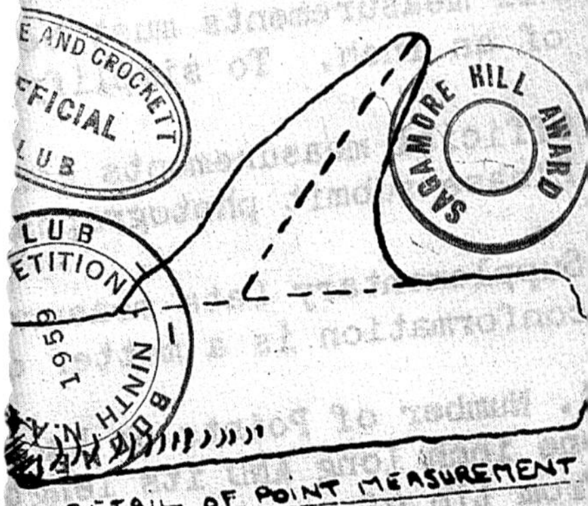

BOONE AND CROCKETT OFFICIAL CLUB

SAGAMORE HILL AWARD

CLUB COMPETITION 1959 NINTH N.A. BIG GAME

DETAIL OF POINT MEASUREMENT

FIRST PLACE

• FEB • 59

SEE OTH

	Column 2 Right Antler	Column 3 Left Antler	Colum Differ
Number of P			
Tip to Tip			
Greatest S			
Inside Spr of MAIN BE			
IF Inside antler le			
Total of			
Length of	59 7/8	60 1/8	
1. Length of	17 6/8	17 2/8	
2. Length of Second Point	16 3/8	15 5/8	
3. Length	16 4/8	16 6/8	
4. Length	23 7/8	22 3/8	
5. Length	18 3/8	19 7/8	
6. Length	4	4 2/8	
7. Length	—		
Circu H-1. Betwe	9 2/8	9 3/8	
Circu H-2. Betwe	7 1/8	7 2/8	
Circu H-3. Betwe	7 1/8	6 7/8	
Circ H-4. Betw	6 1/8	6	
TOTA	186 3/8	185 6/8	

53

Madison County, Mont.
By whom killed Fred C. Mer
~~same~~
ont. 59754 Missou
none

ADD

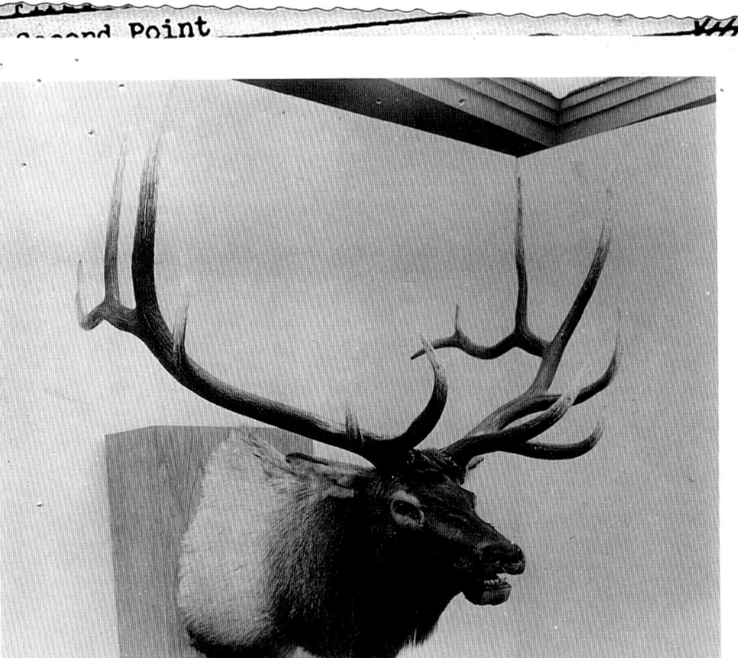

SPECIAL TROPHY

THE MERCER BULL

For the great elk state of Montana, there are only four typical elk on record that score over 400 inches. Fred C. Mercer took the largest, at 416-4/8, in 1958. The third-largest was taken one year later and scores 404-6/8. The Mercer Bull was the second and last American elk to date to receive the Sagamore Hill Award at the 9th Competition in 1959. The inside spread of this bull is an impressive 53-inches. The bull is now owned by the Rocky Mountain Elk Foundation and is in its rightful home in Missoula, Montana.

(Air Mail) March 22, 1960

Mr. Fred C. Mercer
Twin Bridges, Montana

Dear Mr. Mercer:

This will confirm my conversation with you following the Awards Dinner of the Boone and Crockett Club in New York last Tuesday, in which I indicated that if you should decide to make available your magnificent Wapiti trophy to a museum outside the State of Montana, the Carnegie Museum, Pittsburgh, Pennsylvania, would appreciate receiving first refusal.

Rec'd. 3/28/60

In order to bring our clipping file up-to-date, I would greatly appreciate your sending me copies of publicity articles appearing in your local newspapers, as well as those surrounding Twin Bridges.

Again, my warmest congratulations on your splendid trophy and your being awarded the Sagamore Hill Medal.

Cordially yours,

Robert S. Waters, Chairman,
Records of North American Big Game Committee
218 Franklin Street
Johnstown, Pennsylvania

RSW/rds

SPECIAL TROPHY

THE SHARP BULL

Robert Sharp took this Roosevelt's elk bull from Clatsop County, Oregon, in 1949. It was entered in the 19th Awards (1986) and declared the new World's Record at a score of 384-3/8. For a time, there was a fuss over the ownership of this great bull, but credit has always been given to Robert Sharp as the hunter. This bull was the World's Record for only one Awards period, having been surpassed by a bull taken from Vancouver Island, British Columbia, in 1989. It currently ranks 4th.

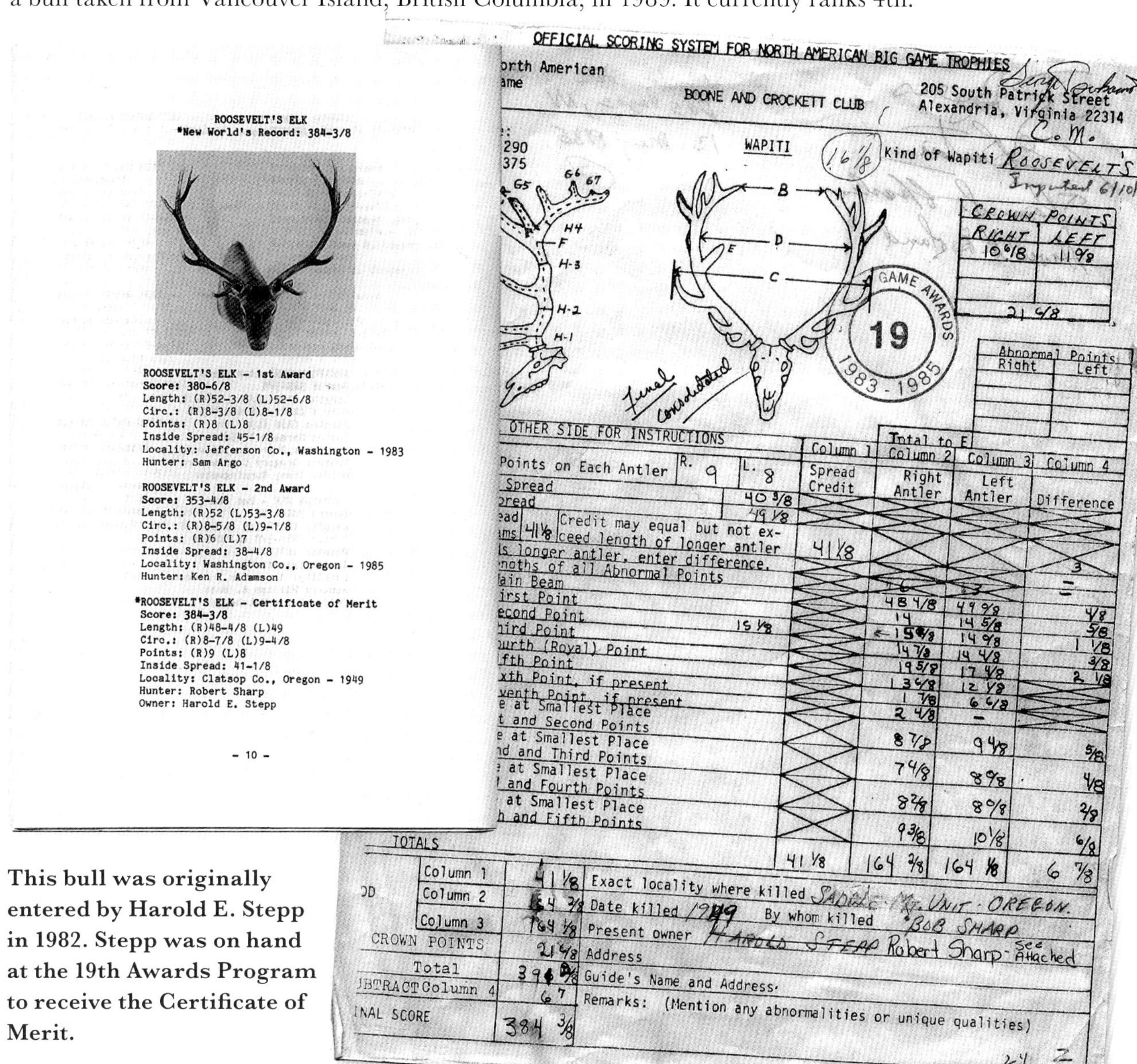

ROOSEVELT'S ELK
*New World's Record: 384-3/8

ROOSEVELT'S ELK - 1st Award
Score: 380-6/8
Length: (R)52-3/8 (L)52-6/8
Circ.: (R)8-3/8 (L)8-1/8
Points: (R)8 (L)8
Inside Spread: 45-1/8
Locality: Jefferson Co., Washington - 1983
Hunter: Sam Argo

ROOSEVELT'S ELK - 2nd Award
Score: 353-4/8
Length: (R)52 (L)53-3/8
Circ.: (R)8-5/8 (L)9-1/8
Points: (R)6 (L)7
Inside Spread: 38-4/8
Locality: Washington Co., Oregon - 1985
Hunter: Ken R. Adamson

*ROOSEVELT'S ELK - Certificate of Merit
Score: 384-3/8
Length: (R)48-4/8 (L)49
Circ.: (R)8-7/8 (L)9-4/8
Points: (R)9 (L)8
Inside Spread: 41-1/8
Locality: Clatsop Co., Oregon - 1949
Hunter: Robert Sharp
Owner: Harold E. Stepp

- 10 -

OFFICIAL SCORING SYSTEM FOR NORTH AMERICAN BIG GAME TROPHIES

orth American
ame

BOONE AND CROCKETT CLUB

205 South Patrick Street
Alexandria, Virginia 22314

290
375

WAPITI

Kind of Wapiti ROOSEVELT'S

CROWN POINTS	
RIGHT	LEFT
10 6/8	11 0/8
21 6/8	

Abnormal Points	
Right	Left

OTHER SIDE FOR INSTRUCTIONS

		Column 1	Column 2	Column 3	Column 4
Points on Each Antler	R. 9 L. 8	Spread Credit	Right Antler	Left Antler	Difference
Spread	40 3/8				
oread	49 1/8				
ead / ams 41 1/8	Credit may equal but not exceed length of longer antler	41 1/8			
ls longer antler, enter difference.					
ngths of all Abnormal Points					3
ain Beam					
irst Point			48 4/8	49 0/8	4/8
econd Point			14	14 5/8	5/8
hird Point	15 1/8		15 1/8	14 0/8	1 1/8
urth (Royal) Point			14 7/8	14 4/8	3/8
fth Point			19 5/8	17 4/8	2 1/8
xth Point, if present			13 4/8	12 1/8	
venth Point, if present			1 7/8	6 6/8	
e at Smallest Place / t and Second Points			2 4/8	–	
e at Smallest Place / nd and Third Points			8 7/8	9 4/8	5/8
at Smallest Place / and Fourth Points			7 4/8	8 0/8	4/8
at Smallest Place / h and Fifth Points			8 2/8	8 0/8	2/8
			9 3/8	10 1/8	6/8
TOTALS		41 1/8	164 2/8	164 1/8	6 7/8

Column 1	41 1/8	Exact locality where killed SADDLE MT. UNIT · OREGON.
Column 2	164 2/8	Date killed 1949 By whom killed BOB SHARP
Column 3	164 1/8	Present owner HAROLD STEPP Robert Sharp · See Attached
CROWN POINTS	21 6/8	Address
Total	391 2/8	Guide's Name and Address·
JBTRACT Column 4	6 7/8	Remarks: (Mention any abnormalities or unique qualities)
INAL SCORE	384 3/8	

This bull was originally entered by Harold E. Stepp in 1982. Stepp was on hand at the 19th Awards Program to receive the Certificate of Merit.

THE HORNS THAT GOT AWAY

It was opening day of Roosevelt Elk season, Oct. 25 th. 1949. I was hunting alone in the southern part of Clatsop County, approximately nine miles south west of Saddle MT. on the Oregon coast.

I had walked in on an old Railroad grade and was walking through a Bracken Fern jungle. Looking across a draw I saw an enormous Bull Elk which was facing away from me. Not wanting to shoot him in the hind quaters I hesitated, then just a short distance from this Bull I saw another large Bull looking toward me. I raised my 30:06 Enfield and shot just past his ear, hitting him in the neck. The Bull was still standing so I placed another in his lower neck and dropped him.

When I reached the Bull I remember how amazed I was at the size of his Antlers. They were so large it prevented me from rolling him on his back to dress out the animal. I had a pack with me which contained some food and a meat cleaver. I used this cleaver to cut off the head to allow me to get the Bull on his back. When I was cutting off the head I accidently missed and hit the base of the right Antler. This knocked a small chunk out of the base and left a meat cleaver mark in the Antler.

. After packing the meat out and getting it all home, the word spread about the large Bull I had killed. Several friends came to see the Antlers and if any of them were alive today they might recognize them.

Then in 1952 or 1953, some fellows in St. Helens asked to borrow the horns. There was a Parade being held and they wanted to put them in it. After the Parade was over I expected the Antlers would be returned. This wasn't to be, and Thirty years would pass before I saw them again.

On Jan. 12 th. 1984 I was reading the local Newspaper. A photo of a set of Elk Antlers appeared and the owner, Harold Stepp, of St. Helens was asking if anyone had any information about them. I couldn't believe it, but I was certain it was my set of Antlers. I called my son and told him to look in the paper also. There was a phone number listed, so I called Mr. Stepp right away.

When I reached Mr. Stepp he asked if there was any way I could be sure these were my antlers. I remembered the cleaver mark in the Antler base and told him to look there. He placed the phone down for a moment and then returned, stating that this set of Antlers had the missing chunk and the mark where I said it should be.

Later on I went and looked at the Antlers and Im positive it's my missing Antlers. These were so big and unusual that it would be difficult not to recognize them even after that many years.

Im not interested in any claim to the Antlers after this long, Im just glad and satisfied to know I located my horns that got away.

Signed: Robert J Sharp

Mr. BoB Sharp

In the late 1980s, the case of ownership for the World's Record bull was settled by Oregon's Columbia County Circuit Court. Hunter Robert Sharp was officially deemed owner of the trophy he'd harvested over forty years earlier..

NOTARY PUBLIC:

Comm. Expires 4-30-88

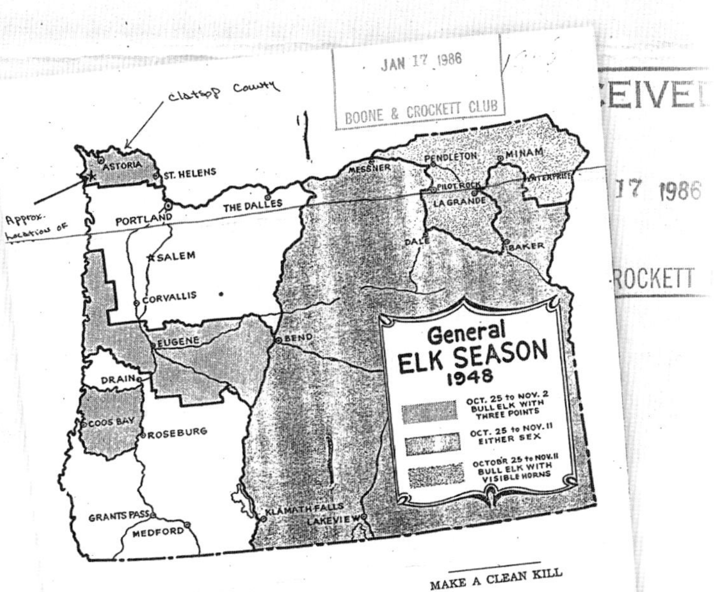

SPECIAL TROPHY

THE MELK BULL

Half moose? Half elk? It has been pieced together without the aid of photographic support that this bull elk was killed in Wyoming, sometime in the late 1800s, possibly by Col. Archibald Rogers. These links were made based on his writing of a great 7x7 bull he had taken, but no one knows for sure if this is the same elk he referenced. We do know that Mrs. Archibald Rogers donated the elk to the Boone and Crockett Club's National Collection of Heads and Horns in 1910 and clearly it is one of the most unusual elk known.

This interesting elk was featured in a special chapter titled "Freak Antlers" from the Club's 1952 records book. In 1996, the Club loaned the trophy to Roger Selner, who had it mounted (above). The elk was part of Selner's World Record Elk tour for several years until it was returned the Club's headquarters.

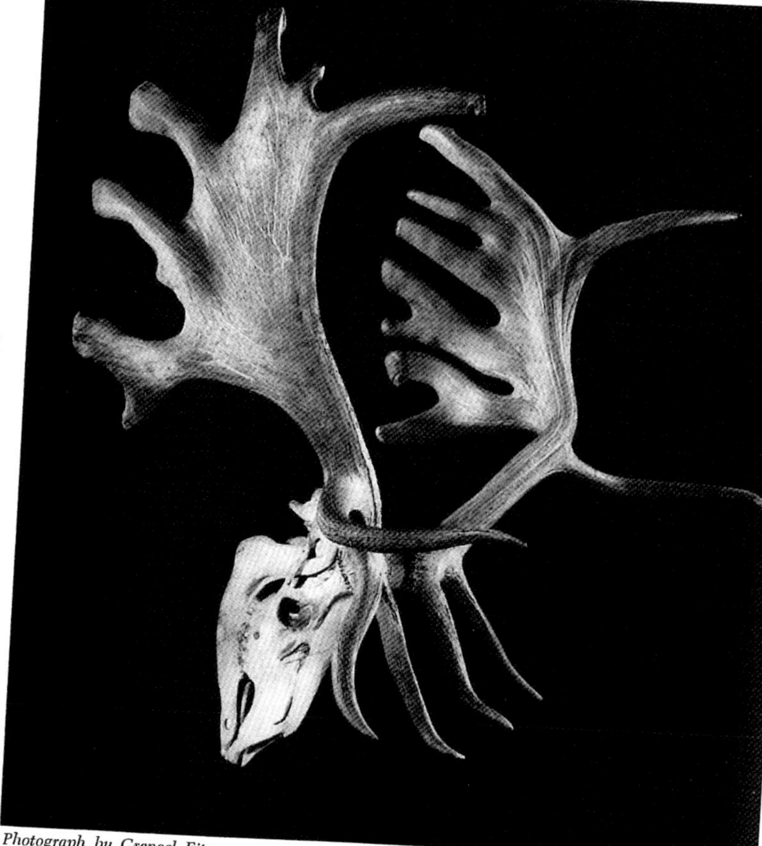

Photograph by Grancel Fitz

In the National Collection

FREAK PALMATED WAPITI ANTLERS

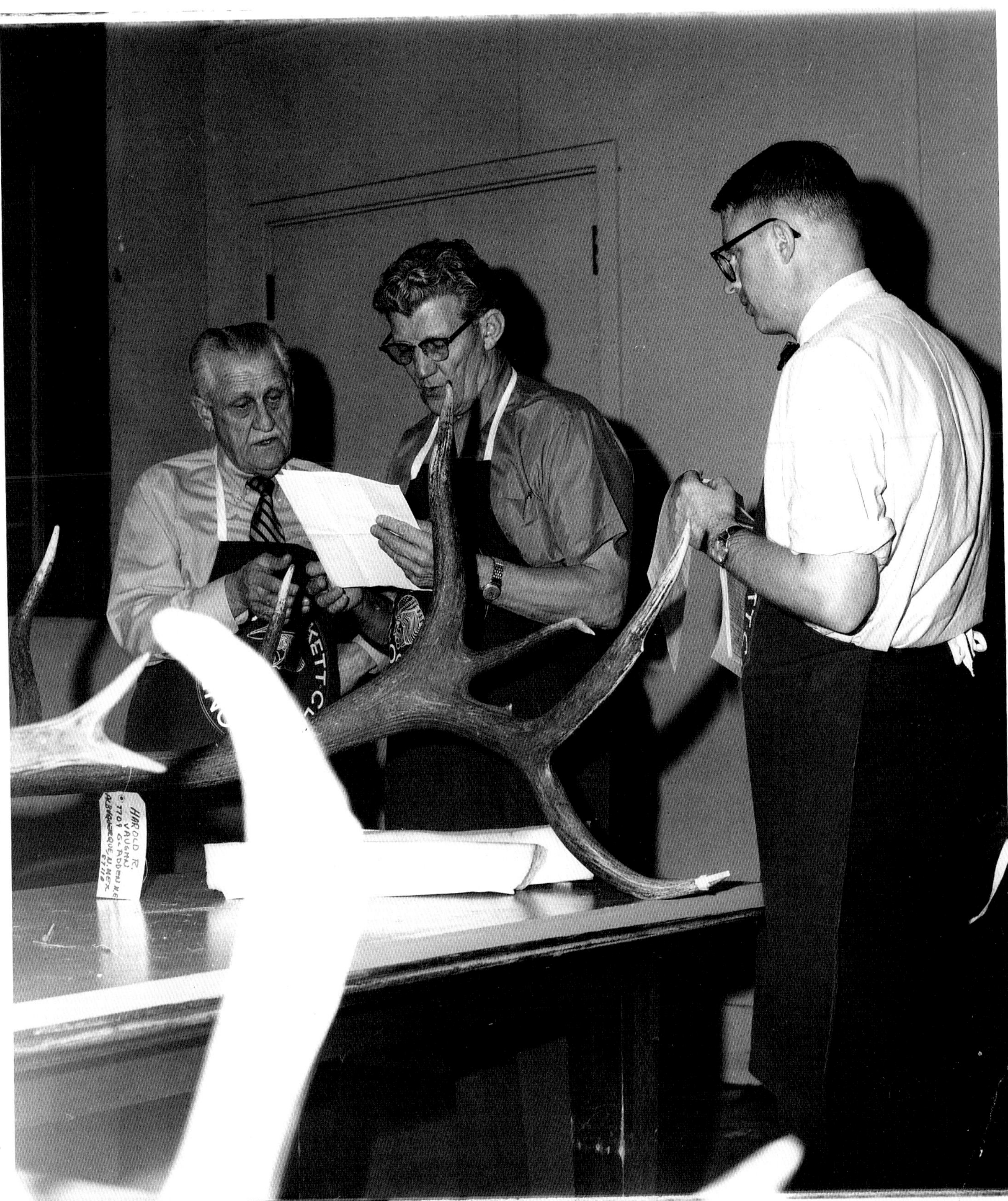
HAROLD R.
VAUGHN

SPECIAL TROPHY

THE HAROLD VAUGHN BULL

Not all entries make it their first time around. In the early days of Boone and Crockett records-keeping, things were a bit fluid. Adjustments had to be made as more data were collected. A bull taken near Rock Lake, Alberta, in 1968 was entered into the 14th Competition as a typical. Unfortunately, after panel scoring, its final score dropped below the entry minimum and it was sent home. At the time of the 14th Competition (1971), B&C did not yet have a category for non-typical American elk. This category was added in 1986. At the urging of Phil Wright, then director of Big Game Records, the Vaughn Bull was re-entered as a non-typical with a score of 401-6/8. The bull currently ranks No. 5 out of a total of six non-typical American elk entries from this province.

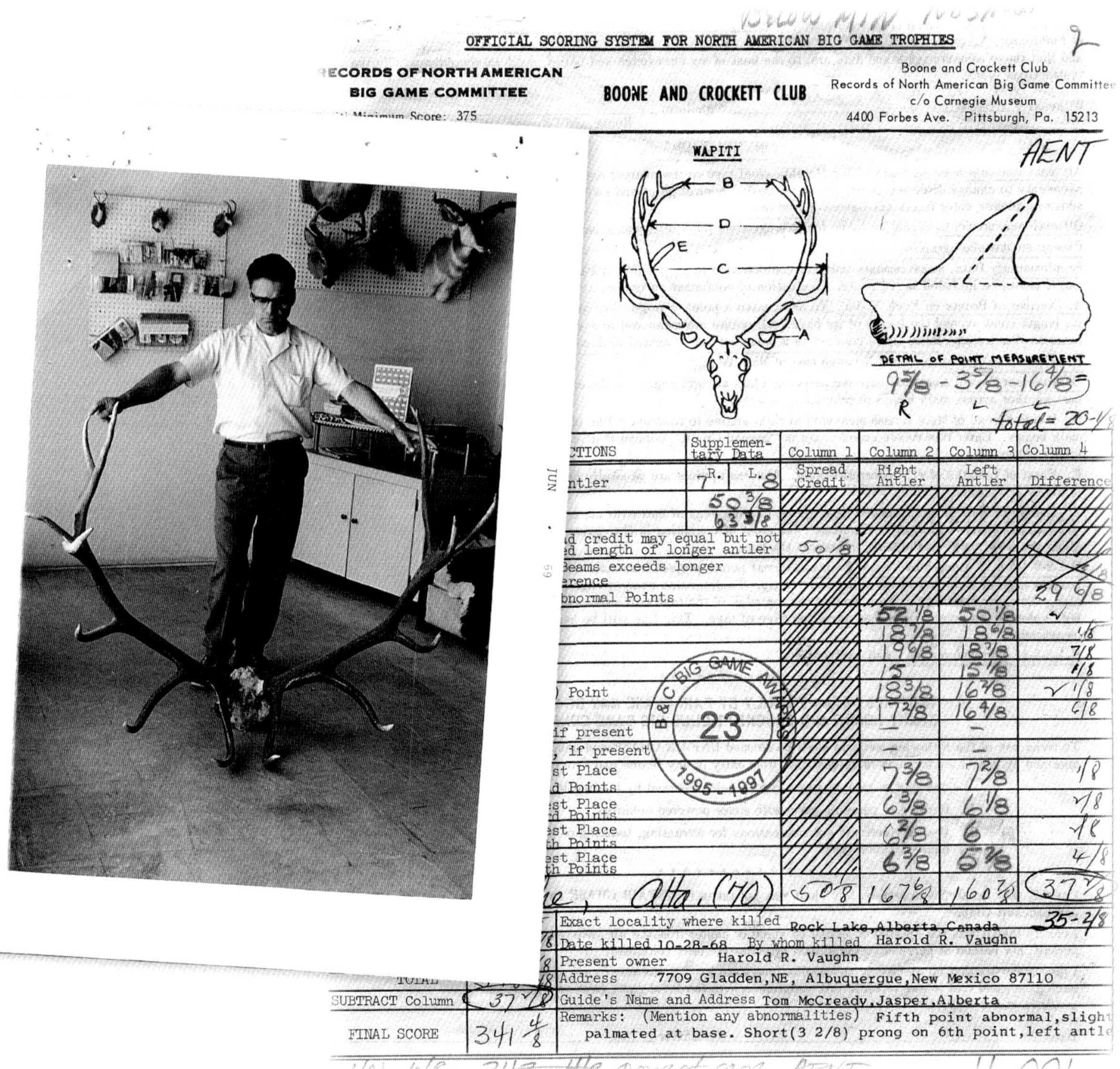

OFFICIAL SCORING SYSTEM FOR NORTH AMERICAN BIG GAME TROPHIES

RECORDS OF NORTH AMERICAN BIG GAME COMMITTEE

BOONE AND CROCKETT CLUB

Boone and Crockett Club
Records of North American Big Game Committee
c/o Carnegie Museum
4400 Forbes Ave. Pittsburgh, Pa. 15213

Minimum Score: 375

WAPITI

DETAIL OF POINT MEASUREMENT

Supplementary Data	Column 1	Column 2	Column 3	Column 4
	Spread Credit	Right Antler	Left Antler	Difference

TOTAL

SUBTRACT Column 37 2/8

FINAL SCORE 341 4/8

Exact locality where killed Rock Lake, Alberta, Canada

Date killed 10-28-68 By whom killed Harold R. Vaughn

Present owner Harold R. Vaughn

Address 7709 Gladden, NE, Albuquerque, New Mexico 87110

Guide's Name and Address Tom McCready, Jasper, Alberta

Remarks: (Mention any abnormalities) Fifth point abnormal, sligh[t] palmated at base. Short(3 2/8) prong on 6th point, left antle[r]

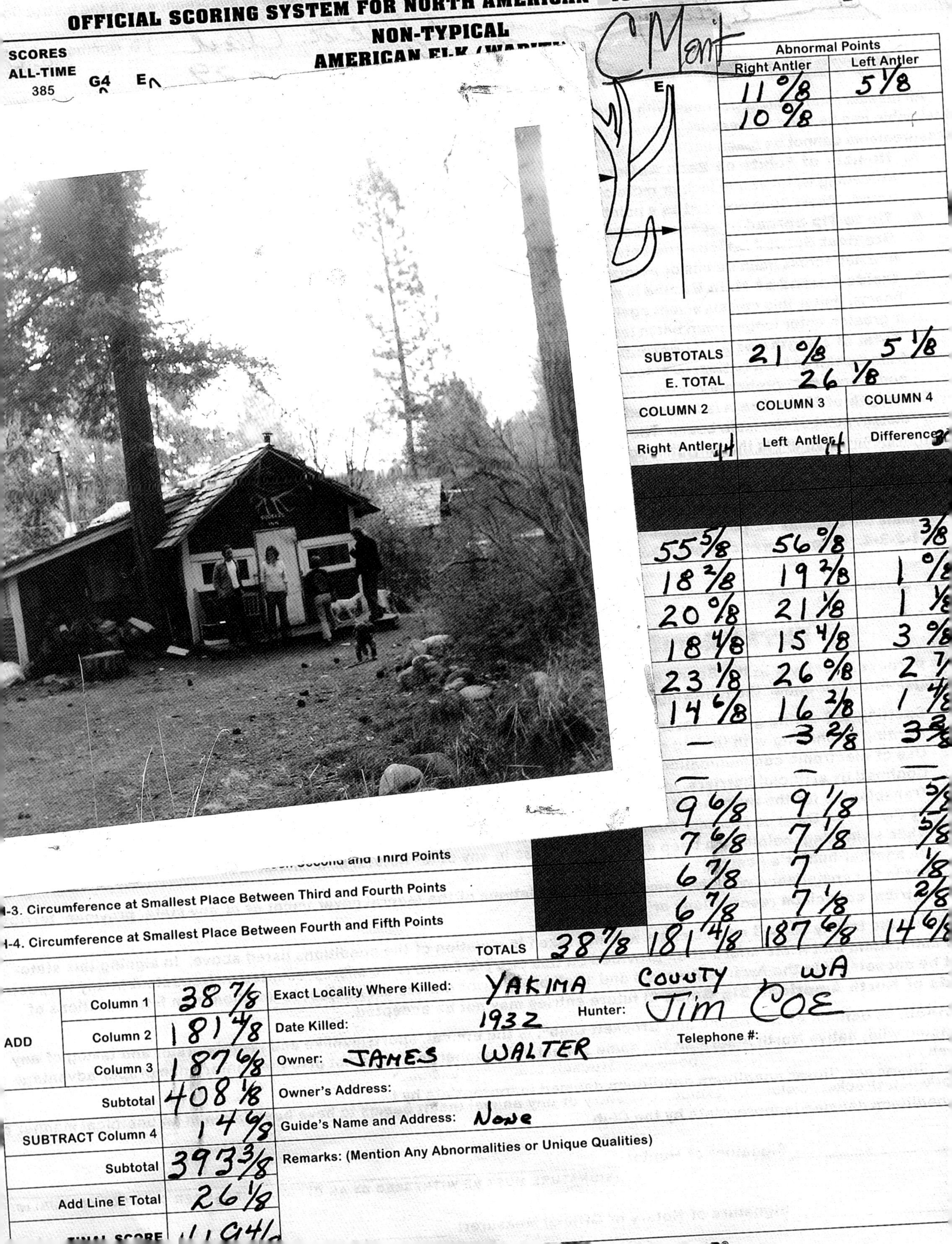

OFFICIAL SCORING SYSTEM FOR NORTH AMERICAN

NON-TYPICAL

AMERICAN ELK (WAPITI)

SCORES
ALL-TIME
385

C Mont

Abnormal Points	
Right Antler	Left Antler
11 0/8	5 1/8
10 0/8	
SUBTOTALS 21 0/8	5 1/8
E. TOTAL 26 1/8	

Column 1	Column 2	Column 3	Column 4
	Right Antler 14	Left Antler 14	Difference
	55 5/8	56 0/8	3/8
	18 2/8	19 2/8	1 0/8
	20 0/8	21 1/8	1 1/8
	18 4/8	15 4/8	3 0/8
	23 1/8	26 0/8	2 7/
	14 6/8	16 2/8	1 4/8
	—	3 2/8	3 2/8
	—	—	—
	9 6/8	9 1/8	5/8
	7 6/8	7 1/8	5/8
...Second and Third Points	6 7/8	7	1/8
H-3. Circumference at Smallest Place Between Third and Fourth Points	6 7/8	7 1/8	2/8
H-4. Circumference at Smallest Place Between Fourth and Fifth Points			
TOTALS 38 7/8	181 4/8	187 6/8	14 6/8

ADD		
	Column 1	38 7/8
	Column 2	181 4/8
	Column 3	187 6/8
	Subtotal	408 1/8
SUBTRACT Column 4		14 6/8
	Subtotal	393 3/8
	Add Line E Total	26 1/8
	FINAL SCORE	[illegible]

Exact Locality Where Killed: YAKIMA COUNTY WA

Date Killed: 1932 Hunter: JIM COE

Telephone #:

Owner: JAMES WALTER

Owner's Address:

Guide's Name and Address: None

Remarks: (Mention Any Abnormalities or Unique Qualities)

SPECIAL TROPHY
THE JAMES COE BULL

At 418-2/8 points B&C, this bull taken in 1932 from Chinook Pass was the Washington State record non-typical American elk for only two years. It would have been the state record for at least 50 years if it had been discovered and entered after the 1950 B&C scoring system. It was entered and accepted in 2000 and currently ranks 3rd for non-typical American elk from the Evergreen State. It is one of only five bulls to score over 400 inches from Washington.

James Walter, Jim Coe's grandson, submitted the following account about his grandfather and his hunt for "Jim" Bull.

James Richard Coe (born February 8, 1890 – died August 12, 1933) hunted in the Cascades for most of his 43 years living in the state of Washington. The particulars of the story surrounding the hunt which brought him and his camp face-to-face with Jim "Bull" were never passed down in the family because of his early death at the age of 43 and a shooting accident in the family that left a 12 year old, close family friend dead.

Jim Coe was a tall man, strongly built, congenial, and friendly, indeed assertive (not a bit passive). He seemed to have a passion for life, the type of restless adventurer that inevitably needed to get out of town (Yakima) because of his scrappy, high-spirited demeanor. His destiny was to be in the mountains of Chinook Pass, hunting on horseback in early mountain mornings 'til dusk then sitting around evening campfires by the Naches River with hunting buddies.

Finally in 1932 a three-acre piece of land on the Naches River opened up for sale. It was part of the Anderson Homestead 35 miles up Chinook Pass from Yakima. It was here Jim Coe and company set up camp on weekends and eventually built his hunting cabin, Squeeze Inn, between two towering Douglas firs. Early one morning on an outing, he came face-to-face with Jim "Bull" and took him down in a clap of thunder that echoed off the surrounding ridges; Gold Creek, Edgar Rock, and others unnamed along the Cascade chain.

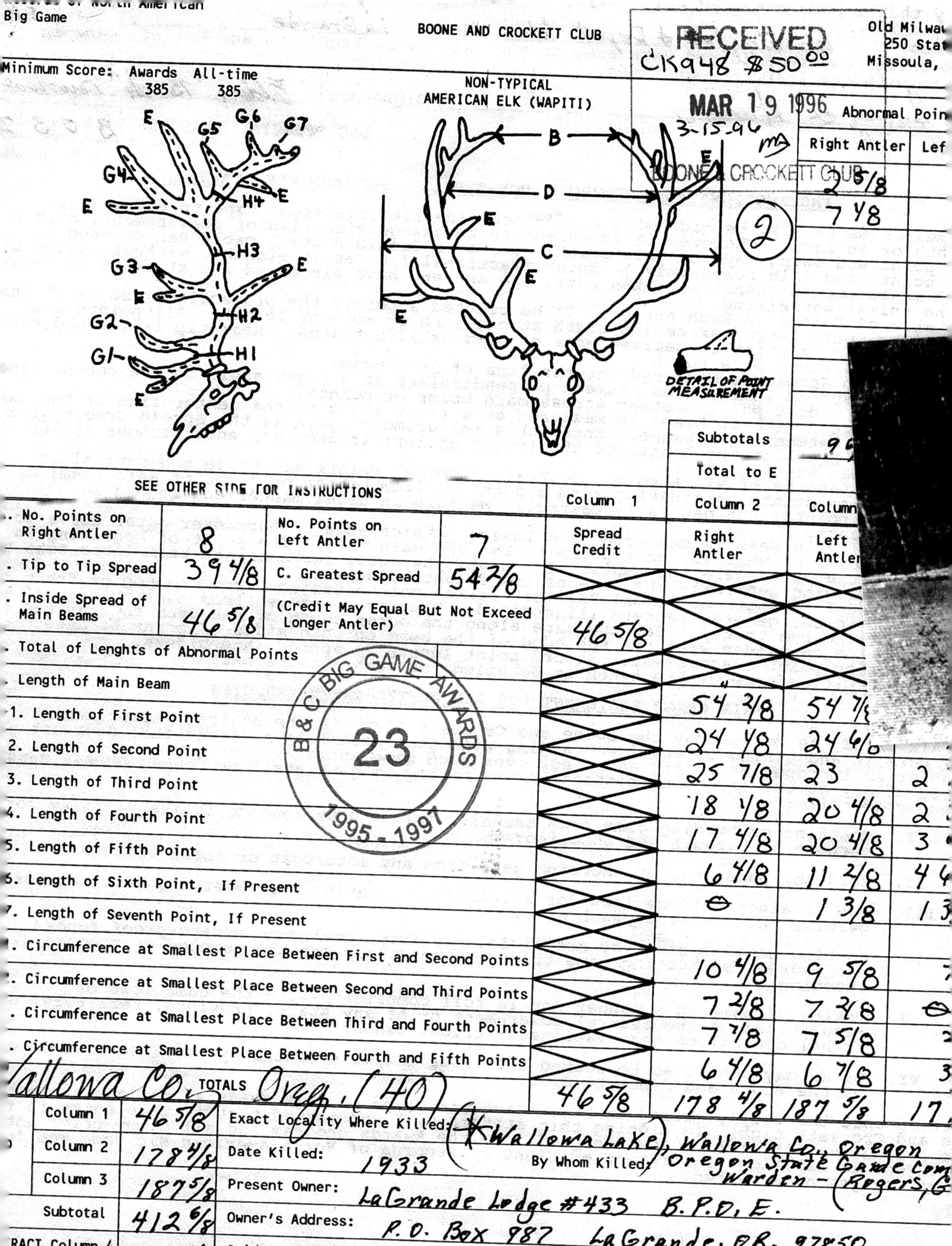

Records of North American Big Game

BOONE AND CROCKETT CLUB

Old Milwau... 250 Stat... Missoula, ...

RECEIVED CK948 $50.00 MAR 19 1996 BOONE & CROCKETT CLUB

3-15-96

Minimum Score: Awards 385 All-time 385

NON-TYPICAL AMERICAN ELK (WAPITI)

(2)

Abnormal Points	
Right Antler	Left Antler
2 5/8	
7 4/8	

		Subtotals	9...
		Total to E	

SEE OTHER SIDE FOR INSTRUCTIONS

				Column 1	Column 2	Column 3	
A. No. Points on Right Antler	8	No. Points on Left Antler	7	Spread Credit	Right Antler	Left Antler	
B. Tip to Tip Spread	39 4/8	C. Greatest Spread	54 2/8				
D. Inside Spread of Main Beams	46 5/8	(Credit May Equal But Not Exceed Longer Antler)		46 5/8			
E. Total of Lenghts of Abnormal Points							
F. Length of Main Beam					54 2/8	54 7/8	
G-1. Length of First Point					24 1/8	24 4/8	
G-2. Length of Second Point					25 7/8	23	2
G-3. Length of Third Point					18 1/8	20 4/8	2
G-4. Length of Fourth Point					17 4/8	20 4/8	3
G-5. Length of Fifth Point					6 4/8	11 2/8	4 4
G-6. Length of Sixth Point, If Present					0	1 3/8	1 3
G-7. Length of Seventh Point, If Present							
H-1. Circumference at Smallest Place Between First and Second Points					10 4/8	9 5/8	
H-2. Circumference at Smallest Place Between Second and Third Points					7 2/8	7 2/8	0
H-3. Circumference at Smallest Place Between Third and Fourth Points					7 7/8	7 5/8	
H-4. Circumference at Smallest Place Between Fourth and Fifth Points					6 4/8	6 7/8	3
TOTALS				46 5/8	178 4/8	187 5/8	17...

Wallowa Co. Oreg. (40)

Column 1	46 5/8
Column 2	178 4/8
Column 3	187 5/8
Subtotal	412 6/8
SUBTRACT Column 4	

Exact Locality Where Killed: (*Wallowa Lake), Wallowa Co. Oregon

Date Killed: 1933 By Whom Killed: Oregon State Game Com... Warden - (Rogers, G...

Present Owner: LaGrande Lodge #433 B.P.O.E.

Owner's Address: P.O. Box 987 LaGrande, OR. 97850

SPECIAL TROPHY

MR. TAFT

The state of Oregon and its elk were not immune from the unregulated over-harvest of the late 1800s. Similar to other places that lost their great elk, Oregon received a transplant of elk from the Jackson Hole, Wyoming, herd that landed by railcar and then by horse-drawn wagon to the upper reaches of Wallowa Lake. The year was 1911. One elk in particular, the ruler of this growing herd, became local legend for his antler size, ornery disposition, and, ultimately, his death. His genes, the mounts of his sheds, and last set of antlers are a living testament to his dominion and the role he played in restoring elk to this region of eastern Oregon.

TAFT'S ILLUSTRIOUS LIFE

As remembered by the Hudson family,

Howard Hudson was a handyman who lived in one of the secluded cabins at the head of Wallowa Lake. He helped build the Wallowa Lake Lodge. Several elk were to be brought in by rail from Jackson, Wyoming. Howard and the other Hired hands set to work at building corrals that would hold the elk (including Taft).

Howard was to be the caretaker of the elk for many years. All the elk were special, but Taft had grown to be a magnificent animal sporting an awe inspiring set of antlers. Howard would record Taft's antler measurements during the winter feeding ritual. These measurements were needed in case Howard happened to find Taft's tremendous shed antlers.

One christmas, Howard's two boys, one six years of age and the other nine years of age received BB guns. Of course, boys being boys, they soon tired of shooting cans and targets, and decided that Taft represented of formidable trophy. The boys thought it was funny, the way Taft reacted as though being stung by a swarm of yellow jackets. As the months passed, Taft wisened up. The boys would stalk Taft, hiding behind trees and shooting when the opportunity arose. Taft would proceed to chase the boys clear back to Howard's cabin. When Howard found out what the mischievous boys were up to, he instantly reprimanded the boys by taking the BB guns away from them.

As the years went by, the elk no longer feared the people at the park. One season, Taft and one of his offspring dueled to the death during the annual rut. Taft won, and the mount of his offspring now hangs in the LaGrande Elk's Lodge Adjacent to Taft's magnificent mount. Another time, Taft mauled an 11 year old boy. Taft had become extremely aggressive, so the game commission was called upon to dispose of Taft. Taft's tremendous antlers were taken to a taxidermist for a full head mount. This mount is displayed in the LaGrande Elk's Lodge.

The Hudson family knows of only two sets of Taft's shed antlers that Howard found and mounted. Howard carefully carved out a special form and plaque to display Taft's shed antlers. One set of Taft's shed antlers remains at the Wallowa Lake Lodge, while the other set has been passed down through the family for the last 66 years. The first set ofTaft's shed antlers were passed on to Howard's son, Edward (the six year old). Edward let Payless Drug in LaGrande, Oregon, display the horns for more than 20 years. Then Edward passed them on to his son, Jerry, where they have been displayed for the last 25 years, along with the origional photographs of Taft in the corrals. There were postcards made of Taft at the lake.

Jerry Hudson 1-19-9

SPECIAL TROPHY

MR. TAFT

A framed account of Taft hangs with the mount at the LaGrande Elks Club.

"TAFT"

This beautiful bull was the leader of a herd of fourteen cow elk, which La Grande BPOE No. 433 was instrumental in bringing from Jackson Hole, Wyoming to Eastern Oregon in 1911. These elk arrived in La Grande in late winter in a railroad stock-car. At Joseph, the elk were transferred into three stock-rack bob-sleds pulled by four-horse teams for the thirty mile trip to Billy Meadows in Wallowa County where the elk were turned loose.

Taft maintained leadership of the herd until 1932 when one of his sons Tarazan, challenged him. The ensuing battle, which occurred at the head of Wallowa Lake was a fight to the death. Tarazan was killed by Taft, who later became so mean and dangerous that he had to be killed a year later.

La Grande Lodge No. 433 is proud of its part in the history of these elk and was fortunate to acquire this beautiful trophy for display in the Lodge room.

Written by J. Dale Standley
Exalted Ruler 1952

1947

COMMITTEE

ALFRED ELY, CHAIRMAN

HAROLD E. ANTHONY

R. R. M. CARPENTER

Records of North American Big Game

OFFICIAL

UNDER THE AUSPICES OF THE NATIONAL MU[SEUM] OF HEADS AND H[ORNS] OF THE NEW YORK ZOOLO[GICAL] SOCIETY & THE BOONE & CRO[CKETT] CLUB

A ... TORY

... LY

MICHIGAN'S INTERMEDIATE CHAIN OF LAKES

The Indians called this land "Ma Shabee" (much water and land of birds). There is no other small chain of lakes to compare with it in the entire world.

Throughout hundreds of years, the great Algonquin tribe, of which the local Chippewas are a part, reserved this region for a "happy hunting ground," a resort where they came to hunt, fish, swim, and make gardens. From 1600 no battles were fought in this territory.

It was the Indians fishing at night with torches that gave Torch Lake its name, "Was-wagonink," Lake of Torches.

By the treaty of 1825, signed by Lewis Cass and Chief Meguzee, (meaning Eagle) this region was ceded to the United States.

In 1846 Abram Wadsworth, the first white settler, came here prospecting. He surveyed and planned the town of Elk Rapids, naming the town, the river and the lake from a pair of elk horns he found at the mouth of the river, one of the largest sets of horns on record. These are to be seen at present at the Elk Rapids library.

Then came the lumber and iron industry. The first pig iron to be shipped from America to England was shipped from Elk Rapids.

Now acres and acres of cherry orchards border these lakes, their blossoms making it a beautiful garden in spring and a rich red harvest in summer.

LEFT

... in. 58 1/2 in.

...d trez B ... 8 " 8 3/8 "

12 5/8 " 12 5/8 "

6 8

66 3/4 "

Unknown

"

"

Albert St. E Lansing, Mac

...arks: Elk Rapids Library

Photographs: Front view.............. Profile..............
(Please place ✓ mark to indicate photographs furnished.)

I We hereby certify that we have measured the above describ...

on... March 20 1948

SPECIAL TROPHY

THE ELK RAPIDS BULL

In the 1800s, if you were the first white settler/prospector to an area, it was customary that you named it or that the town be named after you. Abram Wadsworth settled on the eastern shore of Lake Michigan and promptly named his new home Elk Rapids. Obviously, he thought this name was befitting considering that, early on, he found a huge set of elk antlers at the mouth of a nearby river. The year was 1846. This bull was listed in B&C records before the new scoring system was introduced, but never re-scored. The bull is currently on display at the Elk Rapids Chamber of Commerce.

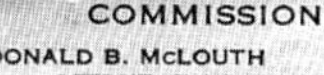

COMMISSION:
DONALD B. McLOUTH, DETROIT, CHAIRMAN
H. J. RICHARDS, CASPIAN
HAROLD TITUS, TRAVERSE CITY
HARRY H. WHITELEY, DOWAGIAC
JOSEPH P. RAHILLY, NEWBERRY
RICHARD H. FLETCHER, JR., BAY CITY
HAROLD W. GLASSEN, LANSING
WAYLAND OSGOOD, SECRETARY

STATE OF MICHIGAN

DEPARTMENT OF CONSERVATION

P. J. HOFFMASTER, DIRECTOR

STAFF:
C. A. PAQUIN, EDUCATION
DURWARD ROBSON, FIELD ADMINISTRATION
F. A. WESTERMAN, FISH AND FISHERIES
MARCUS SCHAAF, FORESTRY
H. D. RUHL, GAME
G. A. WALKER, GENERAL OPERATIONS
G. E. EDDY, GEOLOGICAL SURVEY
F. P. STRUHSAKER, LANDS
ARTHUR C. ELMER, PARKS AND RECREATION
S. G. FONTANNA, DEPUTY DIRECTOR

Bellaire, Michigan
March 20, 1948

American Museum of Natural History
Columbus Avenue and 77th. Street
New York, N.Y.

Gentlemen:

At the request of a group of Village Officials of the Village of Elk Rapids, Michigan I have this date measured a set of Elk antlers which have been in the posession of the village for a number of years and are now on display at the library in that village. I wish to state that I used care in these measurements and followed the instructions contained on the inclosed form.

In case you might be further interested I know of two single Elk antlers that have been found in recent years in waters of this County, which I think establishes the fact that Elk once were native to this part of Michigan.

Yours very truly,

Leslie L. Miles

LM

Leslie L. Miles
Conservation Officer
Antrim County

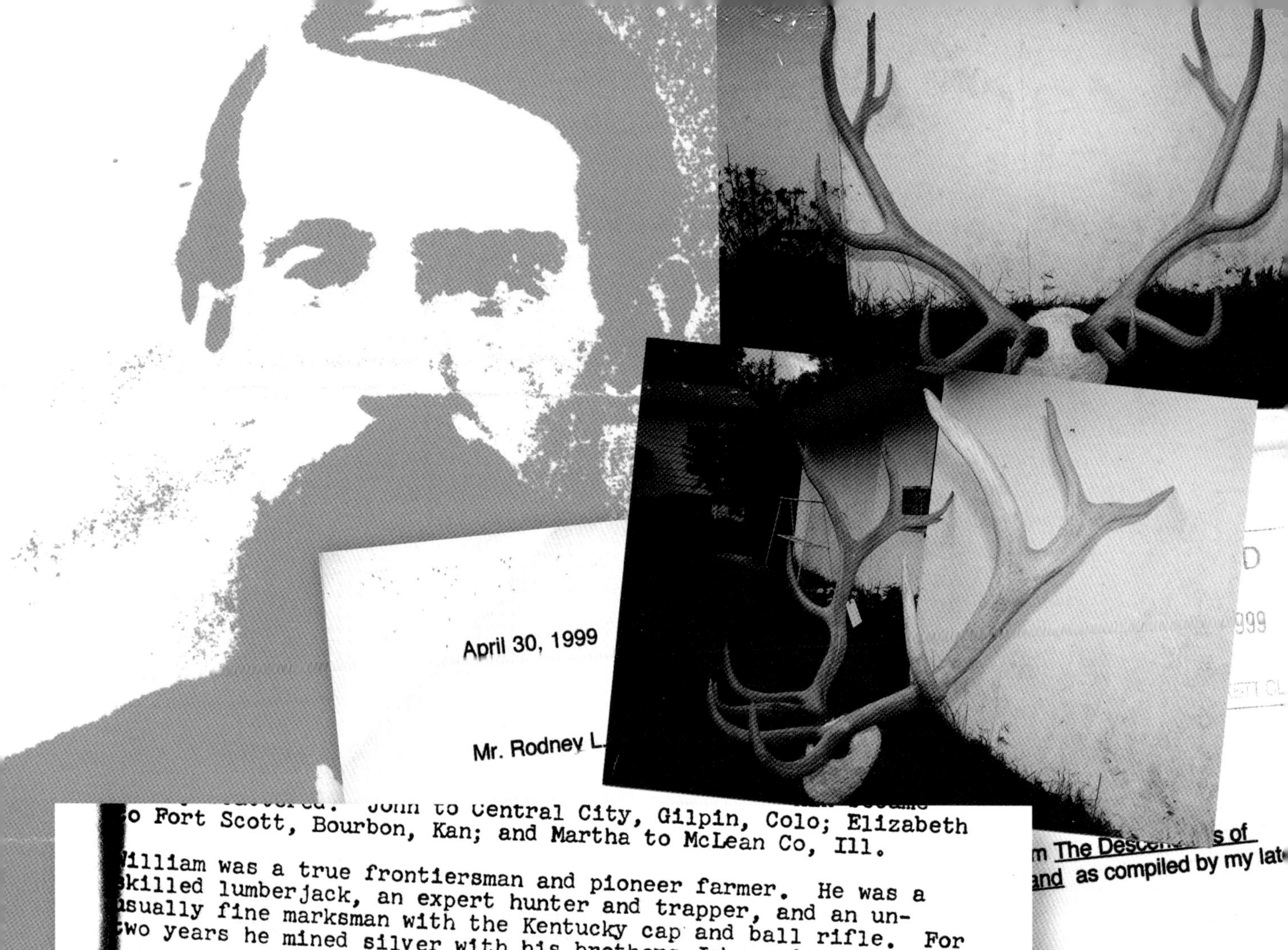

April 30, 1999
Mr. Rodney L.

...scattered. John to Central City, Gilpin, Colo; ... became ...o Fort Scott, Bourbon, Kan; and Martha to McLean Co, Ill.

William was a true frontiersman and pioneer farmer. He was a skilled lumberjack, an expert hunter and trapper, and an unusually fine marksman with the Kentucky cap and ball rifle. For two years he mined silver with his brothers John and Dan Butt in

Page 4

THE DESCENDANTS OF BENJAMIN AND ELLEN BOSLEY WHEELER (cont)

Gilpin Co, Colo. At the time of his death in 1908 he had accumulated a sizeable estate, about an half million dollars in 1985 money, including 240 acres in Webster Co, Mo and 156 acres in Clay Co, Minn, all clear. Pressed for the secret of his business success, William always replied with a smile: "Pay cash for what you buy." Throughout his lifetime he never used credit, nor did he or his family ever want for worldly goods. He did not accomplish this alone; Clementine was his loyal helpmate for 56 years. They were lifelong members of the Methodist Episcopal Church. William's thrift, foresight, and example in no small way contributed to the higher education and success of his children, grandchildren, and their descendants.

...m The Descen...s of ...and as compiled by my lat...

...ations, I was told many ye... ...ng kill in Colorado in or ab... ...r Wheeler, who at the time... **...orated by the fact that... ...lorado for two years...** ...een told to me by my late... ...ther (my father), Merritt W...

...W. Wheeler Jr. (my father)... ...ssion of Dr. Robert Whee... ...en given to him by his fat...

The Kentucky cap and ball rifle referred to on page 4, is still in my possessio... with its bullet mold, powder horn and other loading equipment. It was my fat... told me over the years that this was the rifle William C. Wheeler used to kill h...

I sincerely hope that the Boone and Crockett Club will in this case recognize... importance of the **"oral tradition"** as documentation is difficult in such cas...

I want thank you very much for measuring these horns. I wish that my fathe... alive to know of their significance.

...liam Carpenter...

SPECIAL TROPHIES

THE TEN OLDEST ELK ON RECORD

In the business of data and statistics, ten is a nice round number. Ironically, there happens to be ten elk in Boone and Crockett records taken on or before 1900, which also represents the oldest elk on record. So what's so significant about ten old elk heads? Plenty. There is a former World's Record (current No. 2 typical) in this list, as well as the current No. 3, No. 9, and No. 19 typical American elk of all-time. There is also a standout surrounded by bulls from Colorado and Wyoming — locations one would expect for elk — but a bull from Iowa? This bull may not rank as high, but stands as a reminder of what once was, and was lost. Following is a list of these ten elk ranked by the oldest.

Gilpin County, Colorado – 1850
384-1/8 points – 24th Award Program, 1999
Hunter: William C. Wheeler
Owner: James W. Wheeler
Current Rank: 295

Mt. Evans, Colorado – 1874
391-4/8 points – 10th Competition, 1961
Hunter: Unknown
Owner: Frank Brady
Current Rank: 134

Routt County, Colorado – 1879
Hunter: Henry Staats
Owner: Cabela's
410-5/8 points – 25th Awards Program, 2003
Current Rank: 19

Wyoming – 1886
418-7/8 points – 19th Awards Program, 1985
(appeared in 1932 and 1939 books, re-scored under new scoring system in 1985)
Hunter: J. G. Millais
Owner: Ray J. Hutchison
Current Rank: 9

Larimer County, Colorado – Prior to 1890
388-6/8 points – 20th Awards Program, 1988
Hunter: John Zimmerman
Owner: Fort Collins Museum
Current Rank: 176

Jackson Hole, Wyoming – Prior to 1890
376-7/8 points – 11th Competition, 1963
Hunter: H.M. Hanna
Owner: M.H. Haskell
Current Rank: 570

Big Horn Mountains, Wyoming – 1890
441-6/8 points – 4th Competition, 1950
Hunter: Unknown
Owner: Jackson Hole Museum
Current Rank: 3

Dark Canyon, Colorado – 1899
442-3/8 points – 10th Competition, 1961
Hunter: John Plute
Owner: Ed Rozman
Current Rank: 2

Colorado – 1899
362-4/8 points – 27th Awards Program, 2008
Hunter: Unknown
Owner: Double H Ranch
Current Rank: 911

Cherokee, Iowa – Prior to 1900
387-5/8 points – 21st Awards Program, 1992
Hunter: C.A. Stiles
Owner: Jim Haas
Current Rank: 202

from Canada ...
a General Store in Idaho Springs.
This head was among the fixtures
and hung over the Meat Market
untill 1954 when my Grandfather
retired. He leased the store and
it was remodeled, He was going
to throw the head away but I
take it and brought it to Denver.
... head was in poor condition ...
... to remove it from the
... was laced up the back
... hide and the "stuffing"
... out. After I removed
... and the plaster I found
... stuffed in the Eye
...

of the Denver Times, Territory
of Colorado, dated July 14, 1874.
My Grandfather did not know
who killed the animal, only that
it had been killed in the Mount
Evans Country which is only
a few miles from Idaho Springs Colo.
If I can be of ...

LEFT: Frank Brady entered this typical American elk that had been on display at his grandfather's store for decades. The bull was recognized with a Certificate of Merit at the 10th Competition.

BELOW: Henry Staats bull scoring 410-5/8 points was taken in 1879. However, it wasn't recognized in the Club's Records Program until 2003, when it was entered by new owner, the Cabela's sporting good retailer.

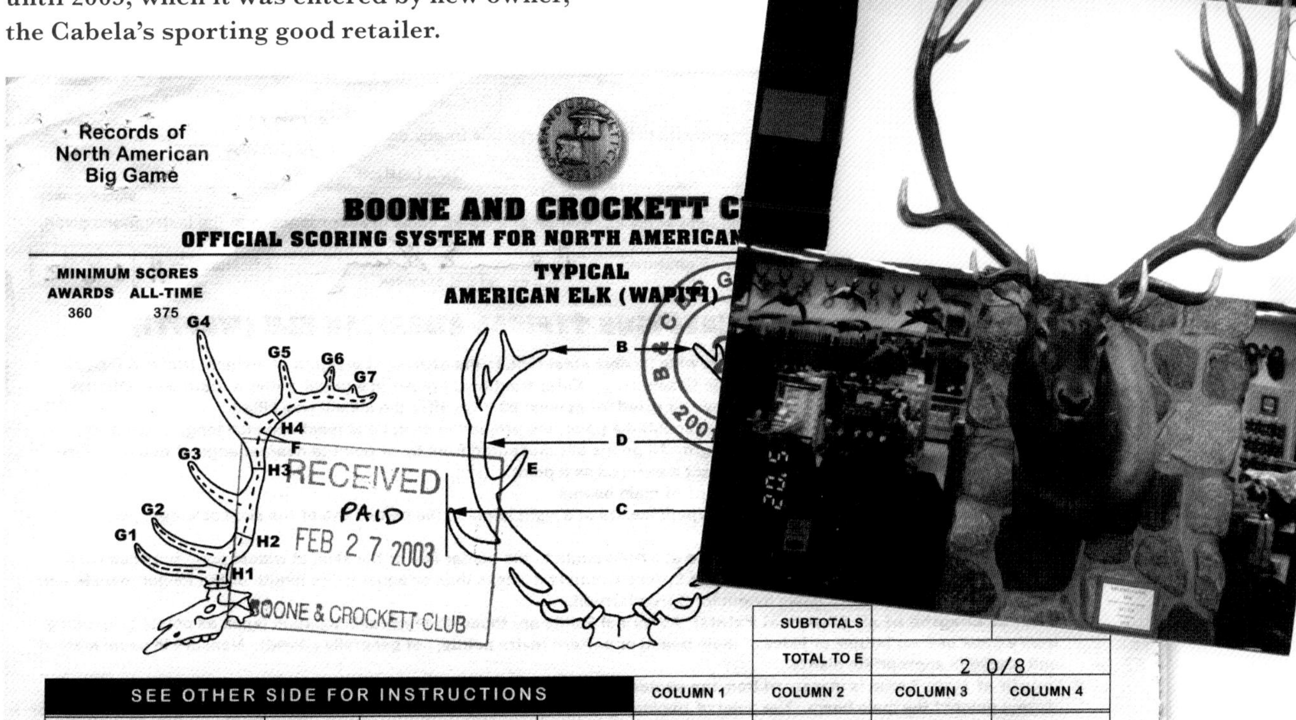

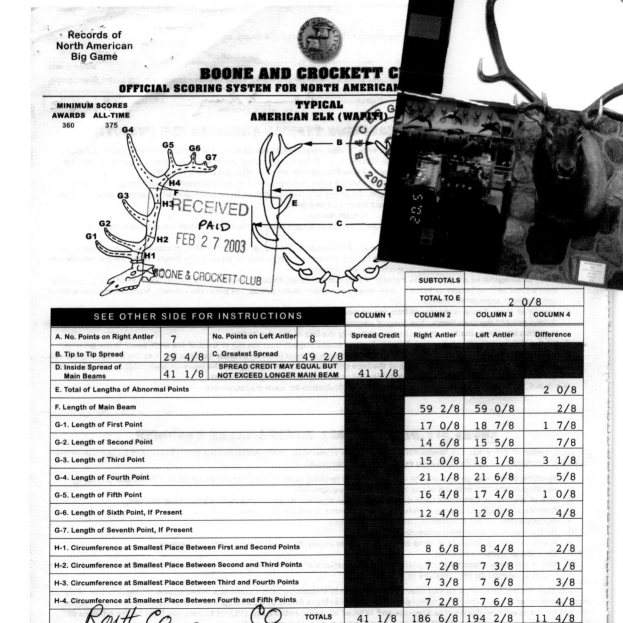

Records of North American Big Game

BOONE AND CROCKETT C

OFFICIAL SCORING SYSTEM FOR NORTH AMERICAN

MINIMUM SCORES
AWARDS 360 ALL-TIME 375

TYPICAL
AMERICAN ELK (WAPITI)

RECEIVED
PAID
FEB 27 2003
BOONE & CROCKETT CLUB

SEE OTHER SIDE FOR INSTRUCTIONS				COLUMN 1	COLUMN 2	COLUMN 3	COLUMN 4
					SUBTOTALS		
					TOTAL TO E	2 0/8	
A. No. Points on Right Antler	7	No. Points on Left Antler	8	Spread Credit	Right Antler	Left Antler	Difference
B. Tip to Tip Spread	29 4/8	C. Greatest Spread	49 2/8				
D. Inside Spread of Main Beams	41 1/8	SPREAD CREDIT MAY EQUAL BUT NOT EXCEED LONGER MAIN BEAM		41 1/8			
E. Total of Lengths of Abnormal Points							2 0/8
F. Length of Main Beam					59 2/8	59 0/8	2/8
G-1. Length of First Point					17 0/8	18 7/8	1 7/8
G-2. Length of Second Point					14 6/8	15 5/8	7/8
G-3. Length of Third Point					15 0/8	18 1/8	3 1/8
G-4. Length of Fourth Point					21 1/8	21 6/8	5/8
G-5. Length of Fifth Point					16 4/8	17 4/8	1 0/8
G-6. Length of Sixth Point, If Present					12 4/8	12 0/8	4/8
G-7. Length of Seventh Point, If Present							
H-1. Circumference at Smallest Place Between First and Second Points					8 6/8	8 4/8	2/8
H-2. Circumference at Smallest Place Between Second and Third Points					7 2/8	7 3/8	1/8
H-3. Circumference at Smallest Place Between Third and Fourth Points					7 3/8	7 6/8	3/8
H-4. Circumference at Smallest Place Between Fourth and Fifth Points					7 2/8	7 6/8	4/8
Routt Co., CO				TOTALS 41 1/8	186 6/8	194 2/8	11 4/8

ADD	Column 1	41 1/8	Exact Locality Where Killed: Red Mountain - Aspen, CO	
	Column 2	186 6/8	Date Killed: 1879	Hunter: Henry Staats

BELOW: This typical American elk was listed in the Club's 1932 and 1939 records books, but wasn't rescored under the new system until the 19th Awards Program in 1986. Well-known author and Boone and Crockett Club member J.G. Millais harvested the bull in Wyoming in 1886.

RIGHT: Colorado's Fort Collins Museum entered this interesting bull in the 20th Awards Program, nearly a century after it was harvested by John Zimmerman.

JAN 13 1986

BOONE & CROCKETT CLUB

Right	Left
	3 6/8
Total to E	3 6/8

NSTRUCTIONS	Column 1	Column 2	Column 3	Column 4
tler R. 6 L. 7	Spread Credit	Right Antler	Left Antler	Difference
40 3/8				
54 3/8				
ay equal but not ex- gth of longer antler	43 1/8			
. enter difference.				--
normal Points				3 6/8
		58	55	3
		19 6/8	19 6/9	---
		21 3/8	24 2/8	2 7/8
		25	20 6/8	4 2/8
Point		22 5/8	21 6/8	7/8
		16	17 4/8	1 4/8
f present		--	--	--
if present		--	--	--
t Place Points		10 5/8	11 3/8	6/8
t Place d Points		8 2/8	8	2/8
st Place h Points		8 2/8	8 6/8	4/8
Circumference ... st Place H-4. Between Fourth and Fifth Points		8 2/8	8 2/8	---
TOTALS owner Raymond J. Hutcheson	43 1/8	195 25/8	191 35/8	13 38/8

B&C BIG GAME AWARDS 19 1983 - 1985

ADD	Column 1	43 1/8	Exact locality where killed ~~Unknown~~ Wyoming
	Column 2	198 1/8	Date killed ~~prior1910~~ 1886 By whom killed ~~Unknown~~ J. G. Millais
	Column 3	195 3/8	Present owner G. ~~Kenneth Whitehead formerly owned by~~
	Total	436 5/8	Address ~~J. G.Millais and illustrated in his book~~ old House, Withnell Fold, Chorley, Lancashire
SUBTRACT Column 4		17 6/8	Guide's Name and Address Unknown England
FINAL SCORE		418 7/8	Remarks: (Mention any abnormalities or unique qualities) Has broken point, right G-5, repaired, measured to the break only. Photo of head from Millais book attached

Also attached, reference to an account of the head from

FORT COLLINS

FORT COLLINS MUSEUM

SPECIAL TROPHIES

THE TEN OLDEST ELK ON RECORD

April 11, 1988

Boone & Crockett Club
241 South Fraley Blvd.
Dumfries, VA. 20026

Gentlemen:

Enclosed please find an official score sheet and photographs for a set of American wapiti antlers that currently are in the collections of the Fort Collins Museum. Also enclosed is a check for the twenty-five dollar registration fee.

There is little historical information abou ... lers, however, we do have a photograph of the man who killed the ... with the antlers. If any of this information is useful to yo ... and I can send the information to you.

Please advise me of any further informat ... action we made need to take in having t ... records book.

Sincerely yours,

Karin B. Eberhart
Curator of Collectio

Enc. 4

REGISTERED
THOROUGHBREDS
QUARTER HORSES

MELVILLE H. HASKELL
4415 E. FT. LOWELL RD.
TUCSON, ARIZONA

March 8, 1962

Mrs. Grancel Fitz
5 Tudor City Place
New York 17, N. Y.

Dear Mrs. Fitz:

I am enclosing for possible inclusion in the Boone and Crockett Club record book the measurements of an elk head that has been in my posession for forty years. I have had several people tell me that they considered it good enough to be in the records - in fact I always understood as a boy that it was considered the record head at the time it was shot. However, although I have hunted all my life I have never been a trophy hunter and it is only recently that I have taken an interest in the records.

The elk was shot by my Grandfather, Howard Melville Hanna of Cleveland, Ohio, - probably in Jackson Hole, or somewhere between there and Cody, Wyoming, sometime in the 1880s or 1890s. I can remember as a boy listening to the old gemtleman tell about his experiences in the West and being fascinated by his stories of life with the Indians. He loved hunting and the outdoors and it is my understanding that he made a number of trips to Wyoming during the latter part of the 19th century - prior to the time when the country he went into had been explored by white men other than the old Mountain men and trappers. He would outfit in Cody and pack into the rockies with Indian packers - no other white man - and be gone for several months at a time.

I have one of his rifles - a Winchester M/1886 .45-90 - and have always supposed that this was the rifle he used but have no reason to believe that the elk may not have been killed on an earlier trip. I know he took one trip in the 90s with my Uncle, H. M. Hanna Jr., and that the latter collected a good, but smaller rack at that time. The old gentleman's house on Prospect Ave. was filled with trophies including buffalo, moose and sheep. I have no idea what became of the others.

LEFT: M.H. Haskell entered his grandfather's trophy elk in the Club's 11th Competition in the 1960s. H.M. Hanna had harvested the bull in 1890 near Jackson Hole, Wyoming.

RIGHT: The history about this bull is included in the letter below sent from Ross Sheridan, who serves on the board for the Double H Ranch in New York. When Sheridan removed the cape from the elk he discovered it was harvested in the 1800s by an unknown hunter. The bull was accepted in the Club's 27th Awards Program in 2008.

January 2, 2008

Boone and Crockett Club
250 Station Drive
Missoula, MT 59801

Re: Typical American Elk Trophy Entry

Dear Boone & Crocket Club:

Enclosed is a completed trophy entry for a typical American elk .

Contrary to what some may think the Double H Ranch is not a hunting ranch.
The mission of the Double H Ranch is to provide specialized camping and year-round support for children and their families dealing with life-threatening illnesses. Our purpose is to enrich their lives and provide camp experiences that are memorable, exciting, fun, empowering, physically safe and medically sound. All programs are FREE of charge and capture the magic of the Adirondacks.
The Ranch also provides the venue for weekends sponsored by a number of family based support programs. These weekends serve families coping with HIV/AIDS, breast cancer, the loss of a child, Von Willebrand's Disease, families where a parent has cancer and many more.

The elk mount was in the maintenance shop and previously owned by of one of the Ranch founders, Charley Wood, now deceased. After looking at the old mount for many years I decided to have it scored and re-mounted with a new skin. On Monday, 12/17/07 a Ranch employee and myself removed the cape from the mount and found misc stuffing inside consisting of grass, hay, wood slivers, plaster of paris and most interesting English & German newspapers with a **1899** date on the Colorado Springs paper. The mount even had the elk's natural jaw in the mount w/ teeth except the ivories were gone.
I feel it's safe to assume the animal was harvested prior to **1899** in CO. That is all the information I can provide for the elk rack.

Please contact me directly should you have any questions and forward the final B&C certificate to me at the address on the top of this letterhead.

Sincerely,

Arrowhead Agency

JIM & SUE HASS
ALL YOUR INSURANCE NEEDS

332 NORTH MAIN
PETERSON, IOWA 51047

TO WHOM IT MAY CONCERN:

The following information was derived from conversations with descendants of C.A. Stiles, the man most likely to have been the hunter of an elk now in the possession of Jim H. Hass, Peterson, Iowa.

C.A. Stiles, one of several children, was "orphaned" at an early age. His father went away to the Civil War and his mother died. Mr. Stiles was taken in by the E.B. Bailey family of McGregor, Iowa and later married a Bailey. The Baileys and the John Potter family came to northwest Iowa in 1869, settling in Silver Township. In reading the history of Cherokee County for that time period, we find several references to the fact that elk were inhabiting the area during this time and were often bagged by local hunters.

From this point we need to move to the present day and trace backwards. The elk antlers were purchased on the estate auction of Mr. Edgar Stiles, son of C.A. Stiles. Since immediate family members could only recall that the antlers, found in the basement at the time of the sale, had been there "forever", we turned to older relation. Mr. R.C. (Bud) Stiles, age 77, son of Nester Stiles, grandson of C.A. Stiles, and nephew of Edgar Stiles, remembers the elk antlers hanging in C.A.'s home in the library. He can recount stories of his grandfather and family friend, Mr. Potter, spending time together and hunting. Bud's sister, Margaret Stiles, could also recall stories of her grandfather, C.A. Stiles, killing an elk when he was a young man. Margaret Stiles, now deceased, was very active in establishing the Cherokee Archives. In visiting with a volunteer worker at the Archives, she recalled Margaret telling about the elk being killed and the fact that there was a picture of the antlers hanging in the C.A. Stiles' library, later the Edgar Stiles home, and ... Bud Stiles can also recall seeing

THE IOWA BULL

Daniel Boone found elk when he first pushed his way West into Kentucky. Evidence of elk has appeared in Wisconsin, Minnesota, and Michigan. Some are unsubstantiated stories, some are old racks tacked to the eaves of a barn and claimed to have come from "just up that draw" from an old farmer who knew the storekeeper, the cousin of an old trapper. This bull is in Boone and Crockett records and documentation proves it was taken in Iowa.

HISTORY OF CHEROKEE COUNTY 89

were stationed here to protect th
caused this to be erected. The
located near the brickyard is poi
in fact it is only a portion of th
enclosed a considerable area. I
mand the approach of an enemy
was on one angle and the second
to command every avenue of a
roofed, but a portion used as
closed.

"We had prairie fires every
near Sioux City and was drive
wind northeast, passing over th
continued eastward.

WILD GAME

"The wild game in those days was very plentiful. Besides the larger game, such as elk and deer, wild turkeys, prairie chickens, and a species of curlews as big as chickens with bills about eight inches long abounded. These curlews are now extinct. They had a peculiar whistle and were esteemed highly by the pioneers on account of their delicate flavor. Of water fowl there were myriads. Fat coons were slaughtered and considered very palatable by the settlers and aside from their meat the settlers derived a revenue from the sale of their skins. Brother John was the trapper of the family and derived a considerable revenue from the sale of pelts. On a knoll near the house on the present Micham farm, I remember John baited a trap with a skunk for bait and soon had the hides of eighteen foxes from this one place. Mink was very plentiful and one year John sold $100 worth of mink skins, all trapped within the present city limits.

HELPING THE NEW ARRIVALS

6: GRANCEL FITZ

BY THEODORE J. HOLSTEN, JR.

Although he was never a member of the Boone and Crockett Club, Grancel Fitz had a profound effect on Club activities as one of the fathers of its unique scoring system. A long-time advocate of an improved way to judge North American trophies, he wrote an extensive chapter on his views for the 1939 Boone and Crockett book, *North American Big Game*, the second book to rank big game trophies according to a system pioneered by Prentiss N. Gray.

Fitz pointed out that, for centuries, men have been interested in hunting trophies and records. In Europe, trophies were rated according to a jury system, with scoring designed for each specific species. Trophies were taken to exhibitions where they were measured and ranked. Under this system, penalizing nonsymmetry or freakishness is left up to the judges. Here in North America, such a jury system would be totally impractical.

Another system to be considered was that of Rowland Ward, which stood for a long time as the only standard reference record book. It, too, had limitations as many of the trophies–other than those of English sportsmen–were never sent to London for official measurement. To offset this, the Ward system designated a list of "owner's measurements," but these could hardly be trusted. Thus, we come to the need for a truly reliable North American measurement system, a concept already pioneered by Prentiss Gray but lying dormant after his untimely death in 1935.

Finally, in 1949, a special committee devised an equitable, objective measurement system for the big game of North America. Chaired by Samuel B. Webb, the committee included Fitz and as well as James L. Clark, who had developed a rival scoring system. The work of this committee evolved into the present Boone and Crockett system. Adopted in 1950, it became universally accepted as the standard for ranking North American big game.

Grancel Fitz, left, assists members of the Judges Panel sorting the trophies prior to verifying their scores.

The 1952 *Records of North American Big Game* book was the first to incorporate all previous and new entries under the newly adopted system. Grancel Fitz and his wife, Betty, are credited with tireless work in re-evaluating previous records. Fitz also contributed superb photographs and a chapter on scoring for the 1952 edition. For many years, Grancel and Betty Fitz were heavily involved in the North American Big Game Competitions; Fitz was three times a judge and twice was chairman of the Judges Panel.

Fitz had a passion for big game hunting. Contrary to popular notion, it was Fitz and not Jack O'Connor who originated the idea of a Grand Slam of mountain sheep. In an article he wrote in 1948 for *True Magazine*, titled "Grand Slam in Rams," Fitz explained how the idea came about. He was camped on Kusawa Lake in the southern Yukon Territory and seeking to bag a trophy Dall's ram. If he succeeded in securing a fine head, he would have the additional satisfaction of achieving something rare in big game hunting at that time: taking all four spe-

GRANCEL FITZ

(1894-1963) – SCORING SYSTEM PIONEER

cies of North American mountain sheep — the bighorn, desert, Stone's, and Dall's.

Fitz succeeded in his quest for a trophy Dall's ram and joined a group of only five other recorded hunters who had taken rams of all four species. Charles Sheldon did it at the turn of the century, closely followed by William Potter in 1910. Dr. Wilson DuComb became number three when he shot a desert ram in Sonora in the late 1930s. Several years later, Fitz's friend, Ernst von Lengerke, along with Jack O'Connor, independently and within a couple of weeks of each other, completed their Grand Slams in 1946. Two years later, Grancel Fitz became a member of this select group.

No other known individual picked up on the significance described in Fitz's *True Magazine* article until 1955, when Bob Housholder, a noted desert sheep hunter and guide, put out the word he was looking for people who had taken the four different rams as described by Fitz. Before long, he had a list of 20 names including that of Jack O'Connor, registered as member No. 1 of the newly formed Grand Slam Club. This organization became known as one of the most prestigious big game hunting club in the country.

Fitz is pictured above with a nice wapiti and his favorite hunting rifle, a .30-06. Note the inscription to Jack O'Connor. Fitz hunted throughout North America and was regularly accompanied by his wife Betty.

Grancel Fitz made 38 hunting trips for North American big game between 1926 and 1955. He became the first man to hunt all 25 classes of North American big game that could be legally taken. His book, *North American Head Hunting*, chronicles many of these adventures; several of his trophies still rank high in the cur-

New York Dinner

By RHEA TALLEY

of fresh air from
spaces blew into
spot in New York
talk was of 22
es for bear stew.
attention was a
useum of Natural
white-tailed deer
med the Texas
ou from Snow
ka, and assorted
oose, bighorn
ies were immor-
their heads, or
ntlers or, in the
ly bears, their

ards dinner of
Crockett Club,
amous hunters
l to be South-
one and Davy
b of big-game
91 awards for
nens of the
lled the walls

They'll go anywhere, to judge from their conversations at dinner. Mr. Fitz has hunted not only in Canada but in Mexico, and he was lamenting to Henderson Coquat, the Texan whose white-tailed deer set a new world's record, that he never had got a jaguar.

"Come down and visit me," said Mr. Coquat, who is a lanky, quiet type. "I'll take you hunting in Mexico and see that you get a jaguar." Mr. Fitz is going next week. Simple as that.

Antlers Decorate a Wall

A barrenground caribou, which won a third prize, reminded people that Uncle Sam sends men around, also. ...
of Madi...

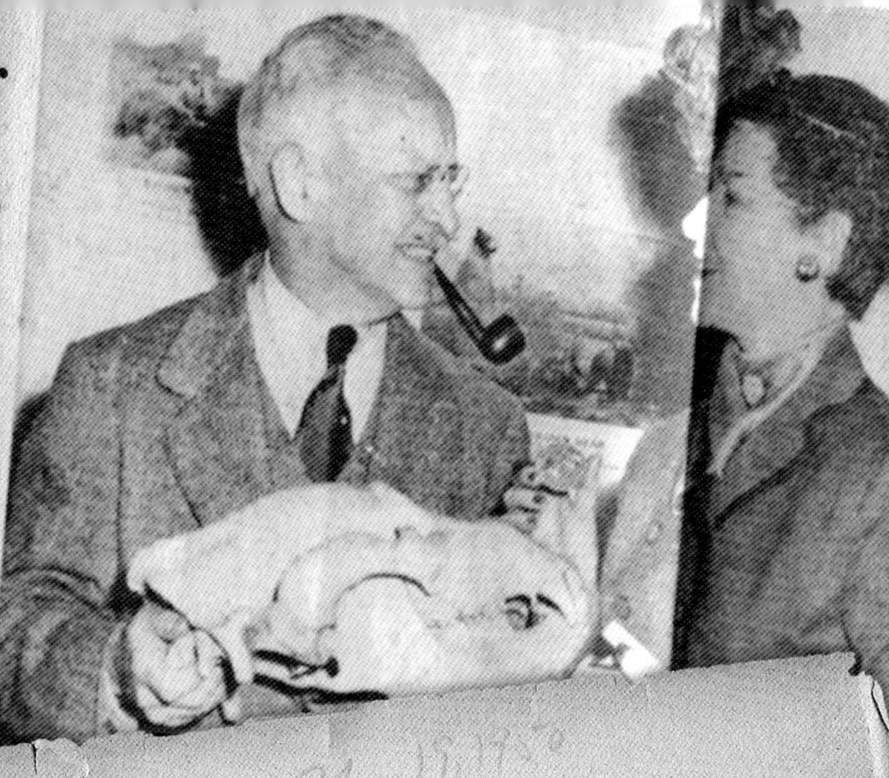

Apr. 1950

World-Telegram and Sun

29

SECOND SECTION

...acking the Big Cats

...ve Pulls ...ger in ...ht Spots

...hird of a Series
...ELOS W. LOVELACE,
Staff Writer.

trapped cougar had
a good hideaway.
by four dogs, the big
cat had holed up in a
t the base of an out-
ng of limestone in a
canyon.
as a mean cave, low, and
bad angles, as Grancil
New York advertising illus-
and famous big game hunt-
scovered when he and his
and a guide and the guide's
got to the spot. They found
f the dogs considerably torn.
ently the animal had dashed
essly into the dark cave after
snarling cougar.
... to crawl in

Mr. and Mrs. Grancil Fi... bagged three cougars on a r... ent trip to Utah. The big ca...

FILM
KODAK

rent trophy listings. When he secured his Dall's ram in the Yukon, it was at an estimated 500 yards, shot through the heart with a 180-grain silvertip bullet from his .30-06 rifle. All the game he shot during his hunting years was with one rifle, a factory .30-06 with just a few modifications. He cited familiarity with his weapon as his reason for his success and, on his many hunting trips, he never even bothered to take a spare rifle. Although different cartridges are usually prescribed for various sizes of big game, he felt that sticking with his .30-06 rifle gave him confidence, whether he was hunting an Alaskan brown bear or a Texas whitetail deer. He wrote, "*As I see it the answer is to have one rifle only – a .30-06 – and plenty of practice with it.*"

Fitz was also a highly successful artistic and commercial photographer for many years, serving as a former president of the Society of Photographic Illustrators. He won eight national awards from art directors groups and wrote and illustrated innumerable stories for national sporting magazines. His photography ranged from high fashion to a wide range of commercial subjects. Some of his most famous photographs included one titled *Gershwin's Hands* and another showing boys playing backyard baseball called *The Ball Game*. He crafted carefully staged photographic ads for Chevrolet, Imperial Whiskey, Dole Pineapple, and many other companies. A highly regarded advertisement titled *Cellophane* was one of these prints. Today, some of his original gelatin silver prints sell for thousands of dollars.

After suffering a heart attack while on a jaguar hunting trip in the Mato Grosso of Brazil, Fitz died in May 1963 at a hospital in New York. His book, *How to Measure and Score Big Game Trophies* (1963), had been in preparation and was published shortly afterward. Betty Fitz edited and published a revised and updated version in 1977. Why he never became a member of the Boone and Crockett Club is a mystery that grows dimmer with the passing years. His name at the Club headquarters in Missoula will live on through a memorial brick to Grancel and Betty Fitz donated by members of their family.

Fitz became the first man to harvest all 25 classes of North American big game that could be legally taken. Three of his North American big game animals are currently listed in the Club's records book including a woodland caribou from Newfoundland (334 points, ranked 28th), an Alaska brown bear from Deadman Bay (30-5/16 points, ranked 7th), and a grizzly bear from British Columbia (25-9/16 points, ranked 125th).

✓

Records of North American Big Game

46 WILLIAM STREET NEW YORK CITY

PRENTISS N. GRAY, EDITOR

2nd EDITION

ELK or WAPITI

SPECIES Elk

MEASUREMENTS

Length on outside curve **A** — Right 58 in. — Left 57 3/4 in.

Circumference midway between bez and trez **B** — Right 7 1/2 in. — Left "

Greatest spread **D** 52 in.

Number of Points on each horn:— Right 7 Points — Left 6 "

Exact locality where killed Montana

Date killed The year the N.P. Ry. built its first R.R. line thru Montana to the coast — prior to 1880

By whom killed Construction Crew

Owner Now owned by B.P.O. Elks No. 403 - Superior, Wis.

Address

Remarks: See letters under Superior, Wis of 6-27-34; 7-3-34; 7-10-34

See Photo file for other photo.

We hereby certify that we have measured the above described trophy on June 26th 1934, and that these measurements are correct and made in accordance with the directions overleaf.

B.P.O. Elks No. 403

By R. Stone Secy

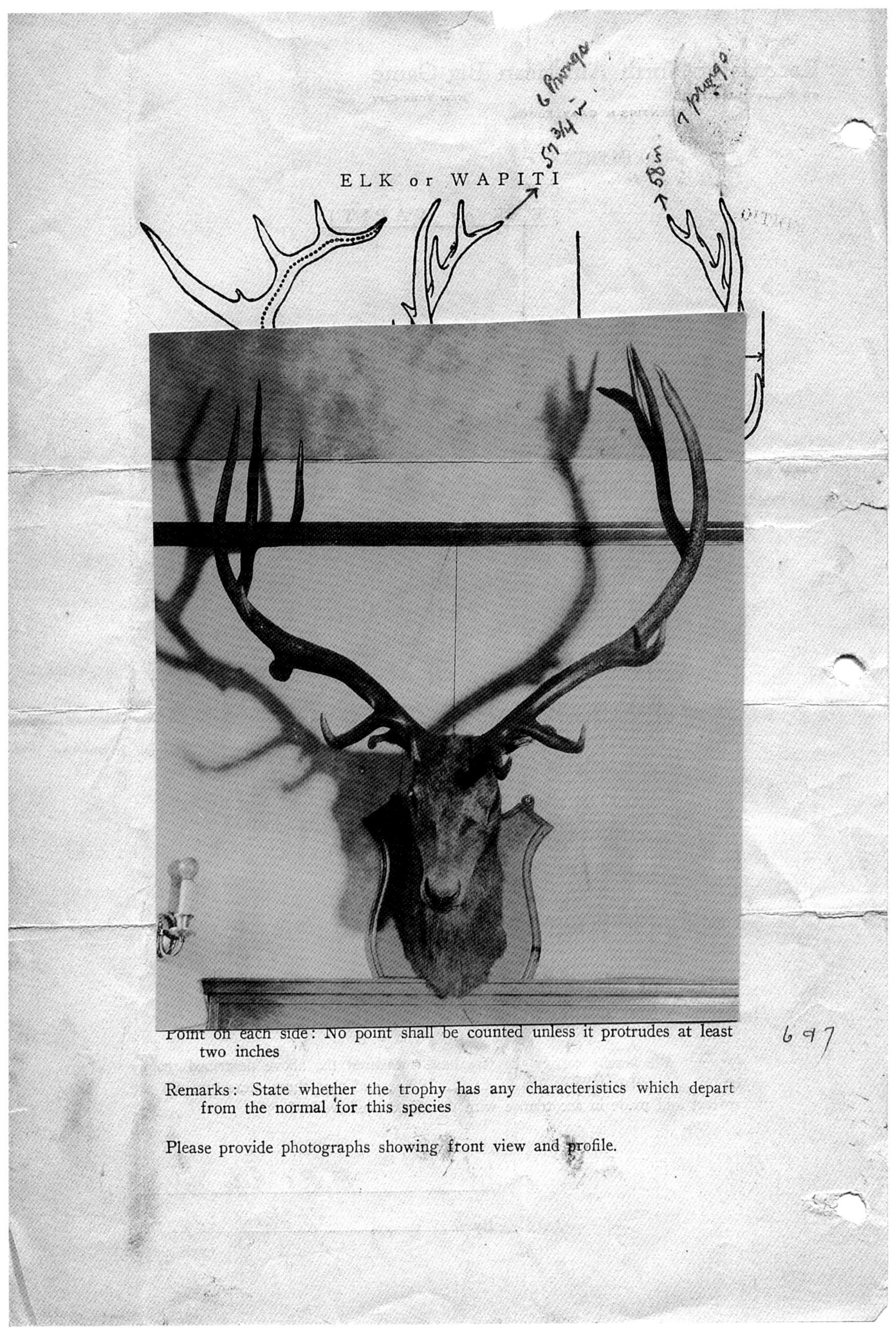

ELK or WAPITI

6 Prongs 57 3/4 in

7 prongs 58 in

Point on each side: No point shall be counted unless it protrudes at least two inches

Remarks: State whether the trophy has any characteristics which depart from the normal for this species

Please provide photographs showing front view and profile.

697

OFFICIAL

Official

Records of North American Big Game

183RD STREET AND SOUTHERN BOULEVARD BRONX, NEW YORK, N. Y.

PRENTISS N. GRAY, EDITOR

1st EDITION

2nd EDITION

WAPITI

SPECIES ....

MEASUREMENTS

Length on outside curve A 62½

Circumference midway between bez and trez B 8

Circumference of burr C ....

Greatest spread D 58½

Number of Points on each horn:— Right 7

Left 9

Exact locality where killed .... North Park Colorado

Date killed 1881

By whom killed .... A.F.T. Cooper

Owner .... Major R.F. Cooper

Address .... Cullamd Hall - Brailsford

Remarks: .... near Derby - England

....

We hereby certify that we have measured the above described trophy on .... 193 , and that these measurements are correct and made in accordance with the directions overleaf.

.... Rowland Ward Ltd

By .... Burlace

By P.N. Gray

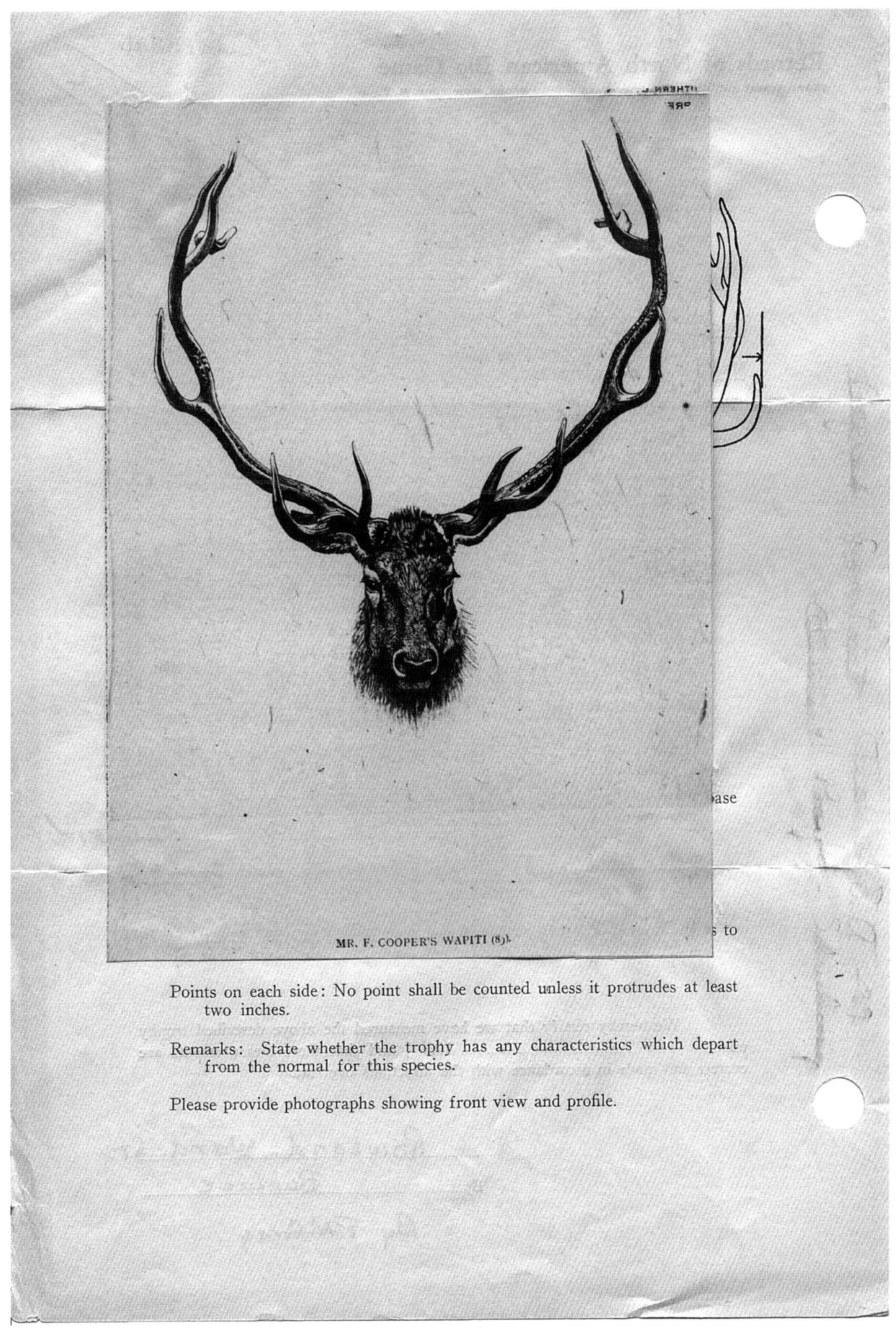

MR. F. COOPER'S WAPITI (8).

Points on each side: No point shall be counted unless it protrudes at least two inches.

Remarks: State whether the trophy has any characteristics which depart from the normal for this species.

Please provide photographs showing front view and profile.

Records of North American Big Game

183RD STREET AND SOUTHERN BOULEVARD BRONX, NEW YORK, N. Y.

PRENTISS N. GRAY, EDITOR

OFFICIAL

OFFICIAL

WAPITI

SPECIES C. canadensis canadensis.

MEASUREMENTS from Rowland Ward's "Records of Big Game"

Length on outside curve A 55½

Circumference midway between bez and trez B 7

Circumference of burr C 11½ – owners measurement.

Greatest spread D 45½

Number of Points on each horn:— Right 6

Left 6

Amount of horn material

Exact locality where killed South of the Yellowstone Park Wyoming.

Date killed Autumn 1901

By whom killed T. P. Kempson

Owner T. P. Kempson,

Address Densy Lodge, Sudbury, Derby.

Remarks: I saw nothing better than this head

T. P. K.

Profile photo in files

We hereby certify that we have measured the above described trophy on .... 1931, and that these measurements are correct and made in accordance with the directions overleaf.

....

By..............................

✓

OFFICIAL

Records of North American Big Game

183RD STREET AND SOUTHERN BOULEVARD BRONX, NEW YORK, N. Y.

PRENTISS N. GRAY, EDITOR

OFFICIAL

2nd EDITION

W A P I T I

SPECIES ....

MEASUREMENTS

Length on outside curve A ..... R 56 ..... L 54 1/2

Circumference midway between bez and trez B ..... R 8 ..... L 8 1/4

✓Circumference of burr C ....

Greatest spread D 53 1/2

Number of Points on each horn:— Right 7

Left 7

Exact locality where killed ..... Kendall, Sublette County Wyoming

Date killed ..... Nov. 1905

By whom killed ..... J. B. Budd

Owner ..... " " "

Address ..... Big Piney, Wyoming

Remarks: ....

Drop horns 12 in

We hereby certify that we have measured the above described trophy on ..... May 24 ..... 1934, and that these measurements are correct and made in accordance with the directions overleaf.

..... Prentiss N Gray

By..........

Method of Measuring

All measurements must be made with a steel tape.

A Length on outside curve: Measured along the main beam from the base of the burr to the tip of the most distant point on the main beam.

B Circumference midway between bez and trez.

C Circumference of burr.

D Greatest spread: Measurement between perpendiculars, at right angles to the center line of the skull.

Points on each side: No point shall be counted unless it protrudes at least two inches.

Remarks: State whether the trophy has any characteristics which depart from the normal for this species.

Please provide photographs showing front view and profile.

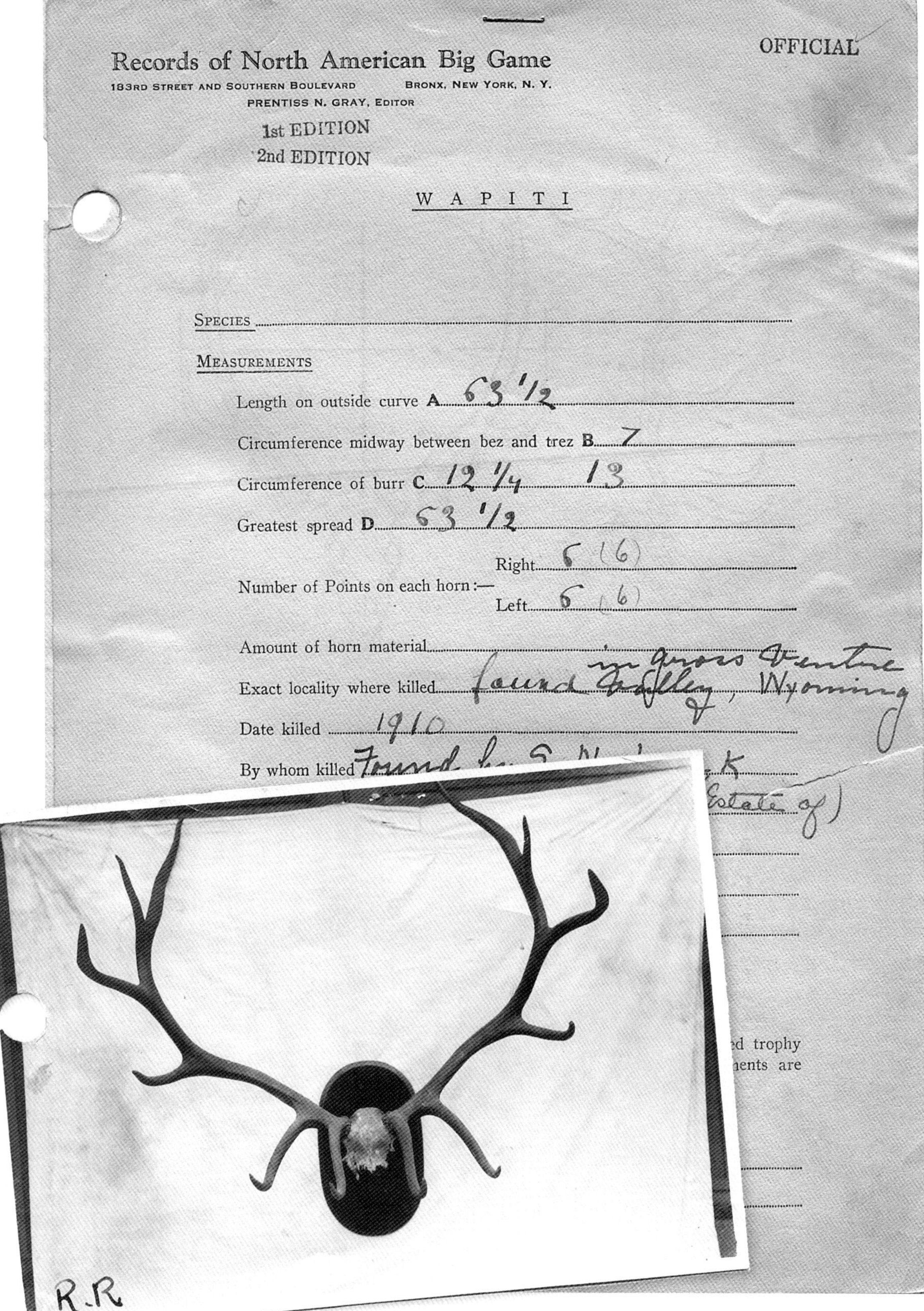

Records of North American Big Game
183RD STREET AND SOUTHERN BOULEVARD BRONX, NEW YORK, N. Y.
PRENTISS N. GRAY, EDITOR

OFFICIAL

1st EDITION
2nd EDITION

W A P I T I

SPECIES

MEASUREMENTS

Length on outside curve A 63 1/2

Circumference midway between bez and trez B 7

Circumference of burr C 12 1/4 13

Greatest spread D 63 1/2

Number of Points on each horn:— Right 6 (6) Left 6 (6)

Amount of horn material

Exact locality where killed found in Gross Ventre Valley, Wyoming

Date killed 1910

By whom killed Found by S. N. ... k

(Estate of)

...ed trophy
...ments are

R.R

R.R.

WAPITI

THE LEAK HEAD.

This head was picked up by S. N. Leak of Jackson, Wyoming (dead) in Gros Ventre Valley about 1909 or 1910. It was badly weathered. Appears to be record spread.

A 63 1/2 inches

B 7 inches

C 12 1/4 - 13 inches

D 63 1/2 inches

No. of Points - Right - 6 - Left - 6 - Total - 12

Widest inside 50 1/2 inches

See also Rowland Ward - page 32

I had the head ~~was~~ stained and filled and one point replaced. Most of the fore part of skull is missing.

Unmounted head - John C. Phillips, owner.

OFFICIAL

Records of North American Big Game

183RD STREET AND SOUTHERN BOULEVARD BRONX, NEW YORK, N. Y.

PRENTISS N. GRAY, EDITOR

1st EDITION
2nd EDITION

WAPITI

SPECIES C. canadensis canadensis

MEASUREMENTS from Rowland Ward's "Records of Big Game"

Length on outside curve A 61

Circumference midway between bez and trez B 8

Circumference of burr C 23 cent. } owners meas^t

Greatest spread D 32 9/8 83 cent.

We take it animals own right and left?

Number of Points on each horn:— Right 8 Left 7

Amount of horn material

Exact locality where killed Bighorn Mts, Wyoming

Date killed Summer 1911

By whom killed Prince Nicolas Ghika

Owner The late Prince Nicolas Ghika Princess Yvonne Ghika

Address Comanesti Bacau, Roumania

Remarks: my measurements are in centimetre

We hereby certify that we have measured the above described trophy on 1 August 1931 1931, and that these measurements are correct and made in accordance with the directions overleaf.

By Princess Yvonne Ghika.

W A P I T I

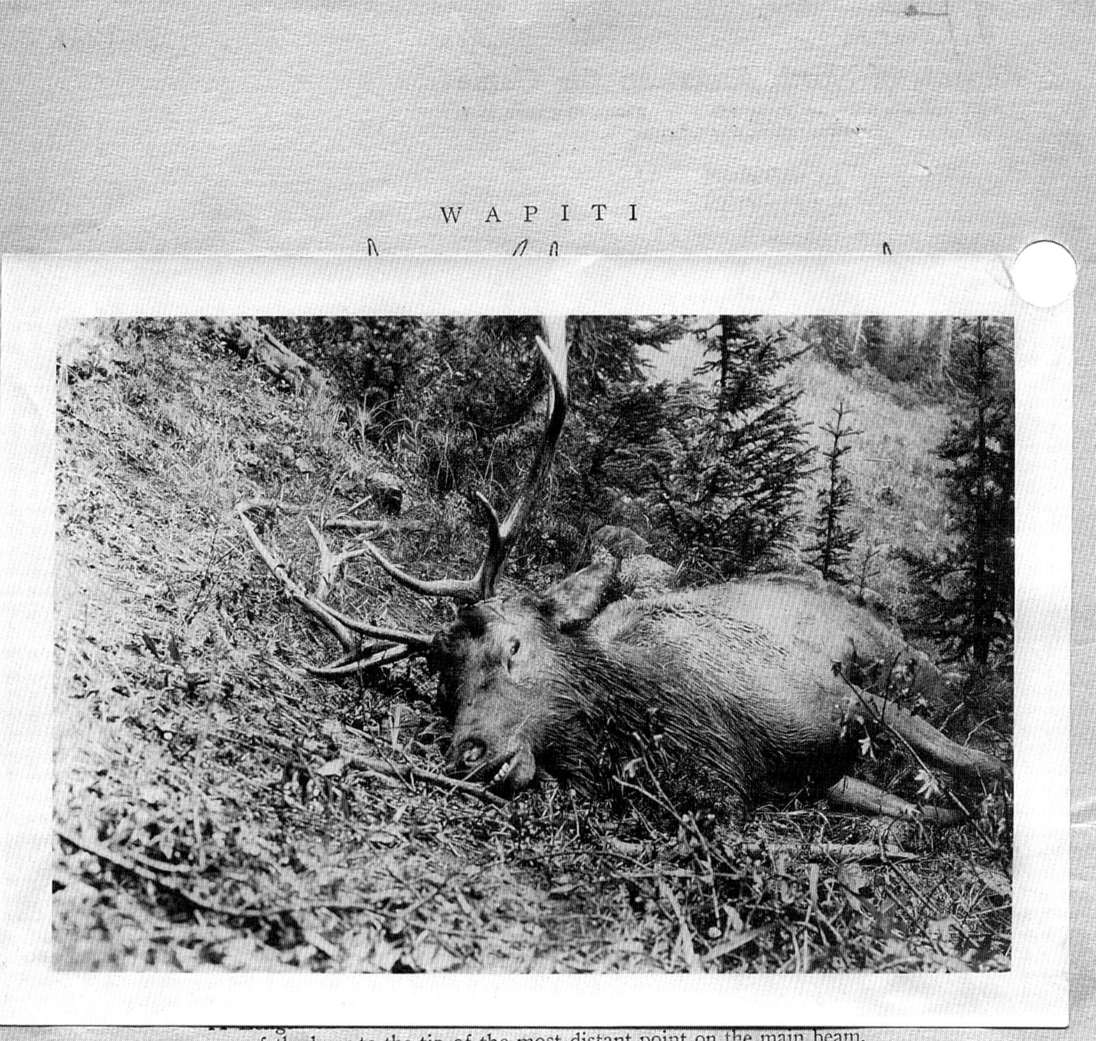

of the burr to the tip of the most distant point on the main beam.

B Circumference midway between bez and trez.

C Circumference of burr.

D Greatest spread: Measurement between perpendiculars, at right angles to the center line of the skull.

Points on each side: No point shall be counted unless is protrudes at least two inches.

Amount of horn material: Horns should be submerged separately in a tank of water to the base of the burr. The total water displaced by both horns (without skull) should be given in cubic centimeters.

Remarks: State whether the trophy has any characteristics which depart from the normal for this species.

Please provide photographs showing front view and profile.

OFFICIAL

Records of North American Big Game

183RD STREET AND SOUTHERN BOULEVARD BRONX, NEW YORK, N. Y.
PRENTISS N. GRAY, EDITOR

1st EDITION
2nd EDITION

WAPITI

SPECIES American Wapiti (Cervus C. Canadensis)

MEASUREMENTS

Length on outside curve A 55 3/4

Circumference midway between bez and trez B 7 1/2

Circumference of burr C

Greatest spread D 62 7/8

Number of Points on each horn:— Right 7 Left 7

Amount of horn material

Exact locality where killed ~~Southwest~~ Montana.

Date killed 1912

By whom killed Robert Swan

Owner National Collection of Heads & Horns

Address N.Y.C

Remarks:

Coll # 1172 Case Sec. 1 - # 7

We hereby certify that we have measured the above described trophy on June 6 1931, and that these measurements are correct and made in accordance with the directions overleaf.

M. S. Garretson

By

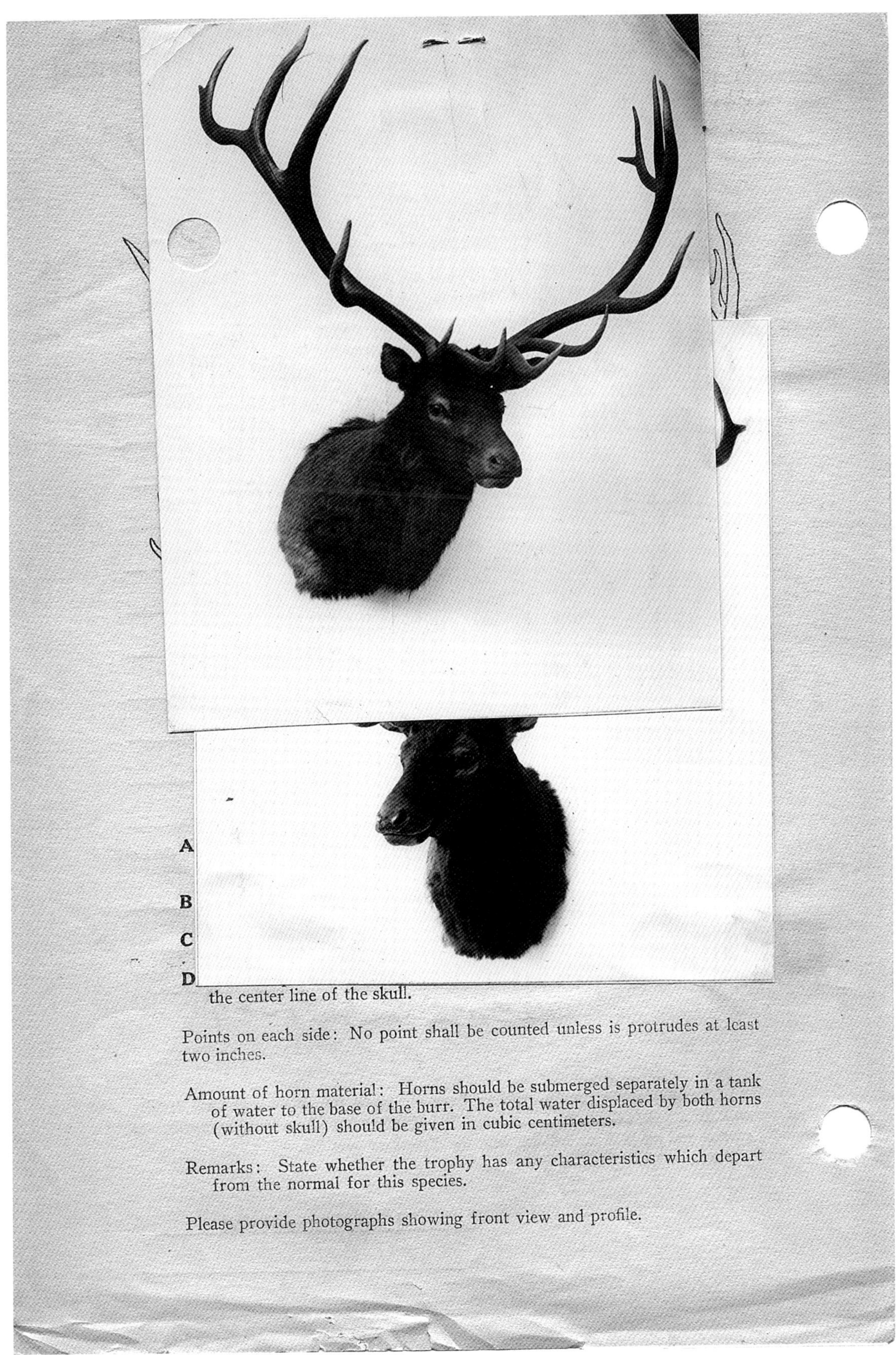

A

B

C

D

the center line of the skull.

Points on each side: No point shall be counted unless is protrudes at least two inches.

Amount of horn material: Horns should be submerged separately in a tank of water to the base of the burr. The total water displaced by both horns (without skull) should be given in cubic centimeters.

Remarks: State whether the trophy has any characteristics which depart from the normal for this species.

Please provide photographs showing front view and profile.

+

Records of North American Big Game

183RD STREET AND SOUTHERN BOULEVARD BRONX, NEW YORK, N. Y.

PRENTISS N. GRAY, EDITOR

2nd EDITION

W A P I T I

SPECIES ....

MEASUREMENTS

Length on outside curve **A** Right 56 Left 55

Circumference midway between bez and trez **B** $7\frac{1}{4}$

Circumference of burr **C** Right $14\frac{1}{2}$ Left 14

Greatest spread **D** 61 inches

Number of Points on each horn:— Right Eight
Left Nine

Exact locality where killed West Gallatin, Montana

Date killed Fall of 1915

By whom killed Henry Lambert, Sr.

Owner Henry Lambert, Sr.

Address R D #1 Livingston, Montana.

Remarks: ....

We hereby certify that we have measured the above described trophy on.......... 193 , and that these measurements are correct and made in accordance with the directions overleaf.

....

By..........

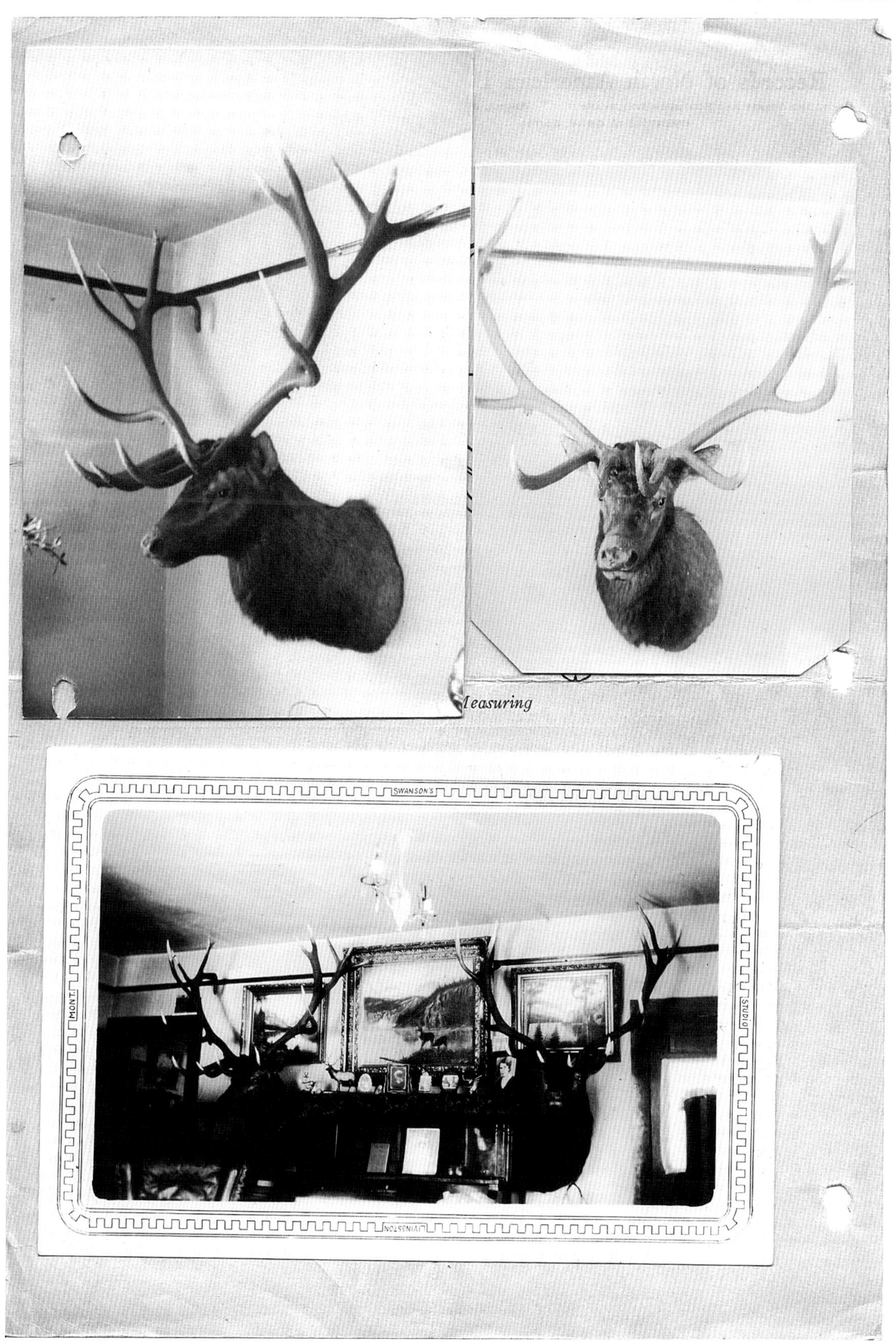
Measuring
SWANSON'S
MONT.
STUDIO
LIVINGSTON

Records of North American *Owners* Big Game

A PUBLICATION OF
THE BOONE AND CROCKETT CLUB
IN CARE OF
AMERICAN MUSEUM OF NATURAL HISTORY
COLUMBUS AVENUE AND 77TH STREET
NEW YORK, N. Y.

COMMITTEE
ALFRED ELY, CHAIRMAN
HAROLD E. ANTHONY
R. R. M. CARPENTER

UNDER THE AUSPICES OF THE NATIONAL MUSEUM OF HEADS AND HORNS OF THE NEW YORK ZOOLOGICAL SOCIETY

57 5/8

WAPITI

SPECIES

MEASUREMENTS	RIGHT	LEFT
Length on outside curve **A**	59½	56
Circumference between bez and trez **B**	7¾	7⅞
Circumference of burr **C**	12¼	12¼
Number of points on antler	6	6

Greatest spread **D** 51½

Exact locality where killed *Kittitas County, Washington*

Date killed *November, 1928*

By whom killed *S. Kaye*

Owner *E. T. Smelt*

Address *1808 State Street, Pullman, Washington*

Remarks: *One point on the left antler is broken off but is included in the six.*

Photographs: Front view.............. Profile..............
(Please place ∨ mark to indicate photographs furnished.)

We hereby certify that we have measured the above described trophy on *March 28* 193*7*, and that these measurements are correct and made in accordance with the directions overleaf.

Raymond Smelt

~~By~~ *E. T. Smelt*

3-28-37

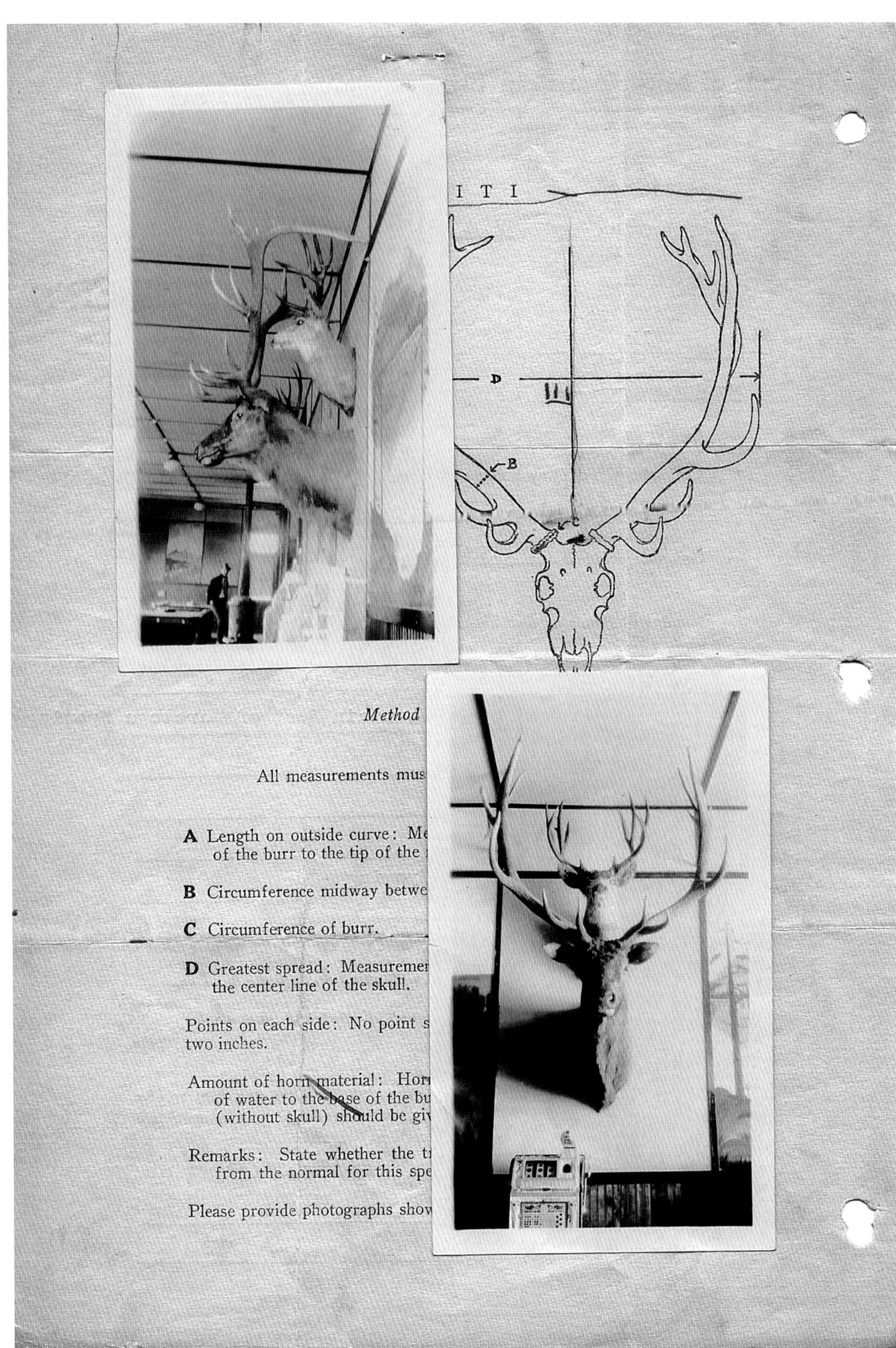
I T I
D
B
C
Method
All measurements mus
A Length on outside curve: Me
of the burr to the tip of the
B Circumference midway betwe
C Circumference of burr.
D Greatest spread: Measuremen
the center line of the skull.
Points on each side: No point s
two inches.
Amount of horn material: Hor
of water to the base of the bu
(without skull) should be gi
Remarks: State whether the t
from the normal for this spe
Please provide photographs show

Records of North American Big Game
183RD STREET AND SOUTHERN BOULEVARD BRONX, NEW YORK, N. Y.
PRENTISS N. GRAY, EDITOR

W A P I T I

OWNER'S

SPECIES Elk

MEASUREMENTS

Length on outside curve A. 60 inches

Circumference midway between bez and trez B. 8 inches

Circumference of burr C. 12.1/2 inches

Greatest spread D. 50 inches

Number of Points on each horn:— Right 8 Left 8

~~Amount of horn material~~

Exact locality where killed Bald Mountain East of Saratoga Wyoming

Date killed October 1930

By whom killed Sam Ivey

Owner Sam Ivey

Address Saratoga Wyoming

Remarks: These horns grew up and back instead of up and out, and the points match on each side.

We hereby certify that we have measured the above described trophy on Sept. 26th. 1931 193 , and that these measurements are correct and made in accordance with the directions overleaf.

Roy L. Griswold.

By J. A. Tichenor

Records of North American Big Game

Owners

55 3/8

A PUBLICATION OF
THE BOONE AND CROCKETT CLUB
IN CARE OF
AMERICAN MUSEUM OF NATURAL HISTORY
COLUMBUS AVENUE AND 77TH STREET
NEW YORK, N. Y.

COMMITTEE
ALFRED ELY, CHAIRMAN
HAROLD E. ANTHONY
R. R. M. CARPENTER

UNDER THE AUSPICES OF THE NATIONAL MUSEUM OF HEADS AND HORNS OF THE NEW YORK ZOOLOGICAL SOCIETY

WAPITI

SPECIES ....

MEASUREMENTS

	RIGHT	LEFT
Length on outside curve **A**	57 1/4 57 1/4	59 5/8 59 5/8
Circumference between bez and trez **B**	6 1/4 6 1/4	6 1/4 6 1/4
Circumference of burr **C**	9 7/8 9 7/8	10 1/8 10 1/8
Number of points on antler	6 6	7 7

Greatest spread **D** 47

Exact locality where killed Elk river Fernie District British Columbia

Date killed Oct 8th 1935

By whom killed Joe H Lorenz DDS

Owner Jos H Lorenz

Address 1214 Burlingame Ave Burlingame Calif.

Remarks: ....

Photographs: Front view ✓ Profile ✓
(Please place V mark to indicate photographs furnished.)

We hereby certify that we have measured the above described trophy on Jan 15th 1936, and that these measurements are correct and made in accordance with the directions overleaf.

By Joe H Lorenz DDS

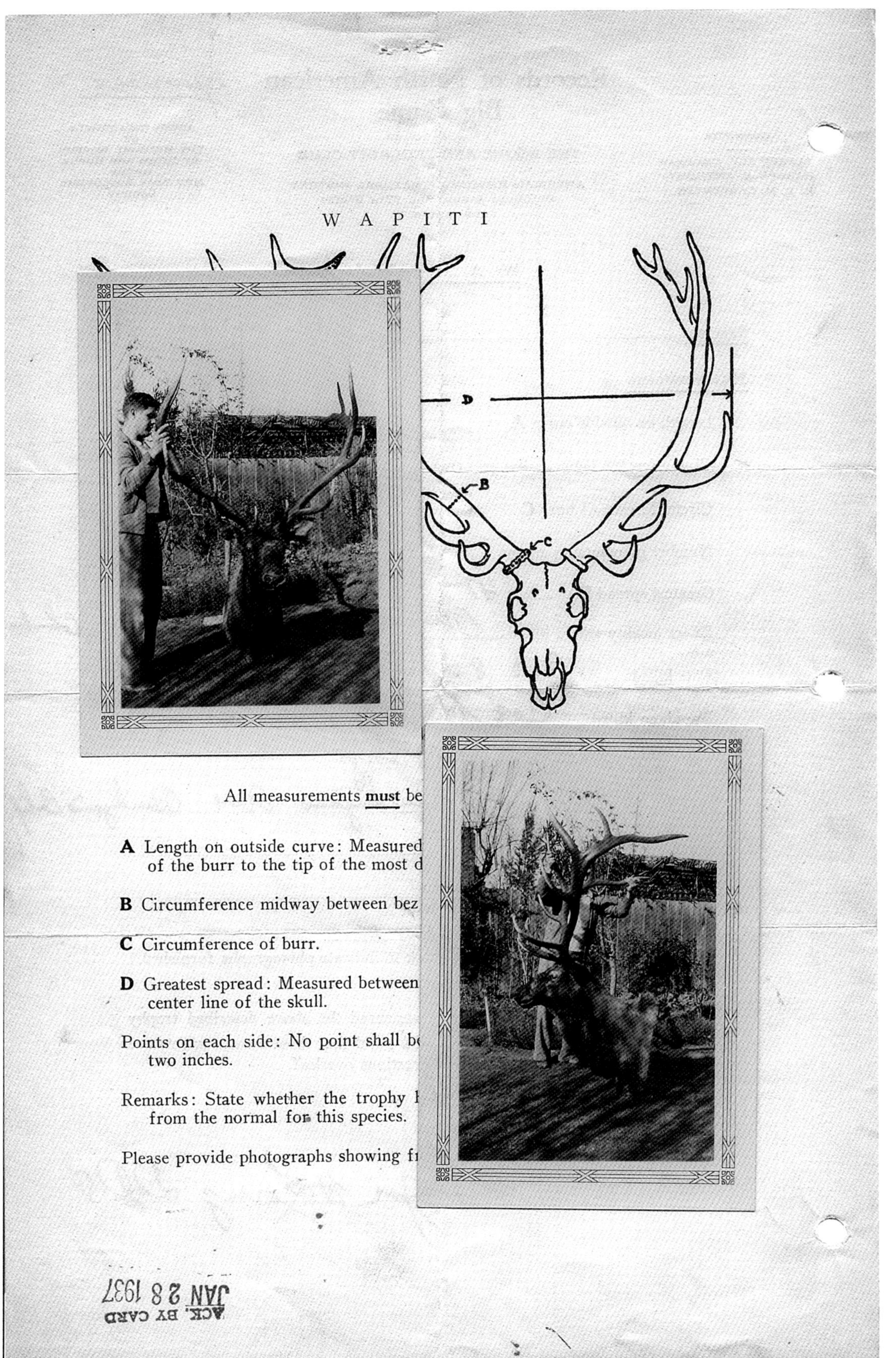
WAPITI

All measurements **must** be

A Length on outside curve: Measured of the burr to the tip of the most d

B Circumference midway between bez

C Circumference of burr.

D Greatest spread: Measured between center line of the skull.

Points on each side: No point shall be two inches.

Remarks: State whether the trophy from the normal for this species.

Please provide photographs showing f

ACK. BY CARD
JAN 28 1937

W A P I T I

A Leng ... he base of t ... n.

B Circu

C Circu

D Grea ... s to the cent

Points on each side: No point shall be counted unless it protrudes at least two inches.

Remarks: State whether the trophy has any characteristics which depart from the normal for this species.

Please provide photographs showing front view and profile.

Records of North American Big Game

A PUBLICATION OF
THE BOONE AND CROCKETT CLUB
IN CARE OF
AMERICAN MUSEUM OF NATURAL HISTORY
COLUMBUS AVENUE AND 77TH STREET
NEW YORK, N. Y.

COMMITTEE
ALFRED ELY, CHAIRMAN
HAROLD E. ANTHONY
R. R. M. CARPENTER

UNDER THE AUSPICES OF THE NATIONAL MUSEUM OF HEADS AND HORNS OF THE NEW YORK ZOOLOGICAL SOCIETY

2nd EDITION

WAPITI

SPECIES ....

MEASUREMENTS

	RIGHT	LEFT
Length on outside curve A	55½	56½"
Circumference between bez and trez B	7"	7"
Circumference of burr C	11"	11"
Number of points on antler	6	6

Greatest spread D 54½"

Exact locality where killed Jackson Hole, Wyoming

Date killed November - 1935.

By whom killed Dr. R. C. Luckey

Owner Dr. R. C. Luckey

Address Luckey Hospital, Wolf Lake, Ind.

Remarks: ....

Photographs: Front view ✓ ~~Profile~~ front oblique

(Please place V mark to indicate photographs furnished.)

We hereby certify that we have measured the above described trophy on January 14 1937, and that these measurements are correct and made in accordance with the directions overleaf.

Una Carr Luckey.

By Notary Public

Commission Expires Nov. 22. 1939

Records of North American Big Game

A PUBLICATION OF
THE BOONE AND CROCKETT CLUB
IN CARE OF
AMERICAN MUSEUM OF NATURAL HISTORY
COLUMBUS AVENUE AND 77TH STREET
NEW YORK, N. Y.

COMMITTEE
ALFRED ELY, CHAIRMAN
HAROLD E. ANTHONY
R. R. M. CARPENTER

UNDER THE AUSPICES OF
THE NATIONAL MUSEUM OF HEADS AND HORNS OF THE
NEW YORK ZOOLOGICAL SOCIETY

2nd EDITION

W A P I T I

SPECIES ....

MEASUREMENTS

	RIGHT	LEFT
Length on outside curve A	56	54
Circumference between bez and trez B	8¼	8¼
Circumference of burr C	12	12
Number of points on antler	8	7

Greatest spread D 41"

Exact locality where killed Elk Mt. Pecos Watershed - Mora Co. New Mexico

Date killed 10-27-1936

By whom killed C. C. Yoakam

Owner C. C. Yoakam

Address 2405 First Natl Bldg. Oklahoma City Okla

Remarks: Used 35 Remington - @ 292 paces

Photographs: Front view ✓ Profile ✓
(Please place ✓ mark to indicate photographs furnished.)

We hereby certify that we have measured the above described trophy on 5-2 1937, and that these measurements are correct and made in accordance with the directions overleaf.

C. C. Yoakam

By J. L. Carey

Jonas 12.3.36

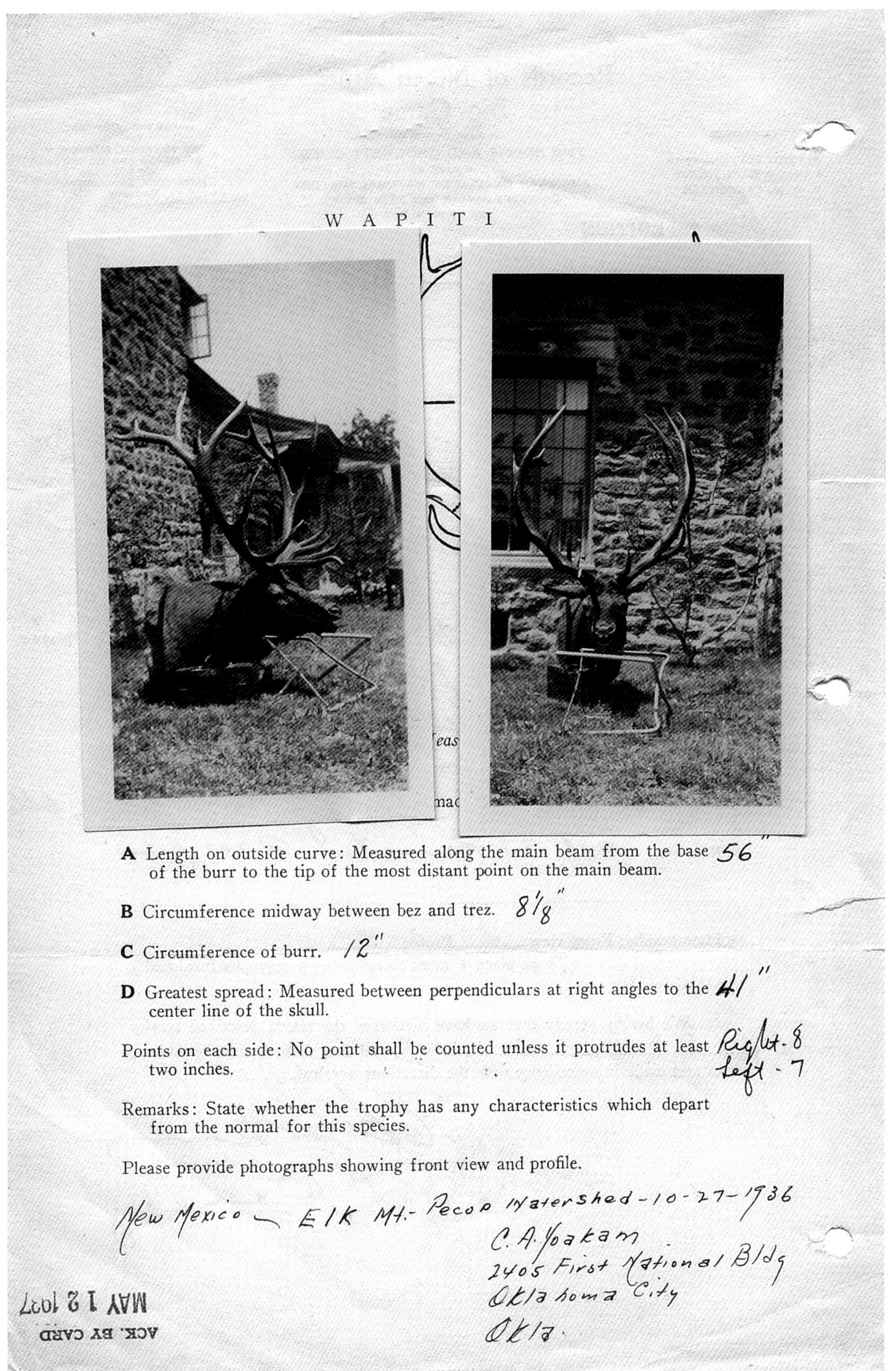

WAPITI

A Length on outside curve: Measured along the main beam from the base of the burr to the tip of the most distant point on the main beam. 56"

B Circumference midway between bez and trez. 8 1/8"

C Circumference of burr. 12"

D Greatest spread: Measured between perpendiculars at right angles to the center line of the skull. 41"

Points on each side: No point shall be counted unless it protrudes at least two inches. Right - 8 Left - 7

Remarks: State whether the trophy has any characteristics which depart from the normal for this species.

Please provide photographs showing front view and profile.

New Mexico — Elk Mt.- Pecos Watershed - 10-27-1936

C. A. Yoakam
2405 First National Bldg
Oklahoma City
Okla.

MAY 12 1937
ACK. BY CARD

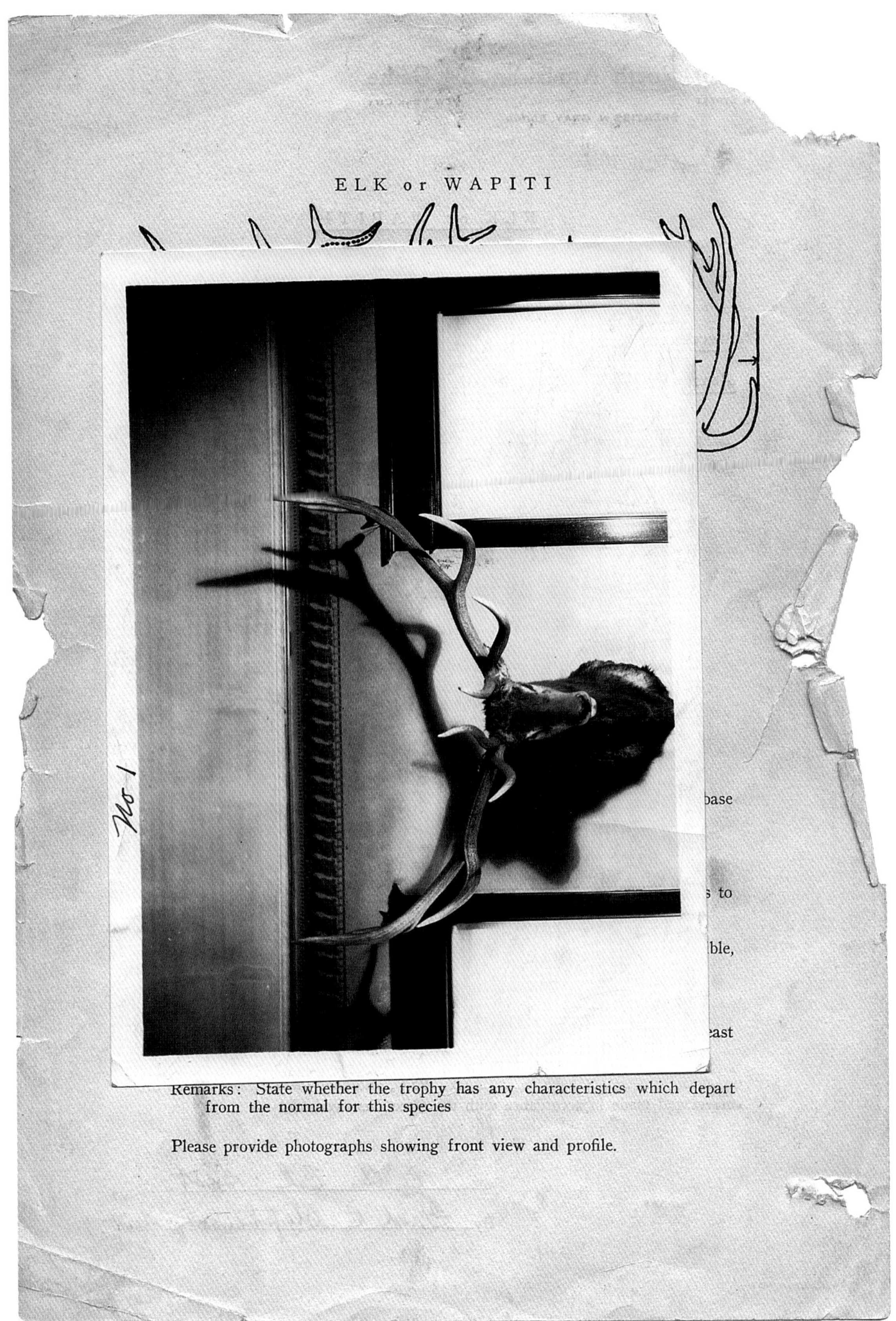

ELK or WAPITI

No 1

Remarks: State whether the trophy has any characteristics which depart from the normal for this species

Please provide photographs showing front view and profile.

...of North American Big Game

...M STREET NEW YORK CITY

PRENTISS N. GRAY, EDITOR

2nd EDITION

ELK or WAPITI

SPECIES #1

MEASUREMENTS

Length on outside curve A — Right 54 — Left 55

Circumference midway between bez and trez B — Right 7 1/4 — Left 7 1/4

Greatest spread D

Number of Points on each horn:— Right 6 — Left 6

Exact locality where killed

Date killed

By whom killed

Owner Burlington Lodge #84 BPO.E

Address Burlington, Iowa

Remarks: See 6-21-34 & 7-14-34

See Photo file for Profile Photo.

We hereby certify that we have measured the above described trophy on .... 193 , and that these measurements are correct and made in accordance with the directions overleaf.

E. A. El sect.

By Fred C. Stephenson ant.

Burlington
7-14-34

Records of North American Big Game — OFFICIAL

183RD STREET AND SOUTHERN BOULEVARD — BRONX, NEW YORK, N. Y.

PRENTISS N. GRAY, EDITOR

1st EDITION

2nd EDITION

WAPITI

Suspect that this is a duplication of the same mans trophy recorded as 61½" but no way of straightening out this confusion. N.S.A. Sept. 9 1938.

SPECIES Cervus canadensis

MEASUREMENTS

Length on outside curve A 62"

Circumference midway between bez and trez B 7 3/8"

Circumference of burr C

Greatest spread D ~~Inside~~ 50 7/8 ~~Outside~~

Number of Points on each horn:— Right 7

Left 7

Exact locality where killed Snake River Colorado

Date killed 1883

By whom killed LATE Ernest Farquhar

Owner Mrs Ernest Farquhar

Address 55 Eaton Square S.W.

Remarks: Measurements taken from Records of Big Game.

We hereby certify that we have measured the above described trophy on 1892 ~~193~~, and that these measurements are correct and made in accordance with the directions overleaf.

Rowland Ward Ltd

By J B Burlace

Records of North American Big Game

183RD STREET AND SOUTHERN BOULEVARD BRONX, NEW YORK, N. Y.

PRENTISS N. GRAY, EDITOR

~~not interesting~~

OFFICIAL

WAPITI

SPECIES C.canadensis canadensis

MEASUREMENTS from Rowland Ward's "Records of Big Game".

Length on outside curve A 55 5/8

Circumference midway between bez and trez B 7

Circumference of burr C 12 inches } owners' measurements

Greatest spread D ~~55 5/8~~ 47 5/8 inches (inside)

We take it animal's own right and left? Between main horns

Number of Points on each horn:— Right 6 Left 5

Amount of horn material (A massive head almost palmated)

Exact locality where killed Wyoming. (Shoshone Mountains)

Date killed September 3rd 1892

By whom killed Owner

Owner Lieut.-Col. Sir G. Dalrymple-White, Bart., M.P.

Address 95, Eaton Square, S.W.1.

Remarks: A curious and interesting mal-formed head. Has the appearance of having suffered from a fall whilst in the velvet. The hunter employed on this trip was the celebrated Tazewell Woody, Presᵗ Roosevelt's old hunter.

We hereby certify that we have measured the above described trophy on .... 193 , and that these measurements are correct and made in accordance with the directions overleaf.

....

By..

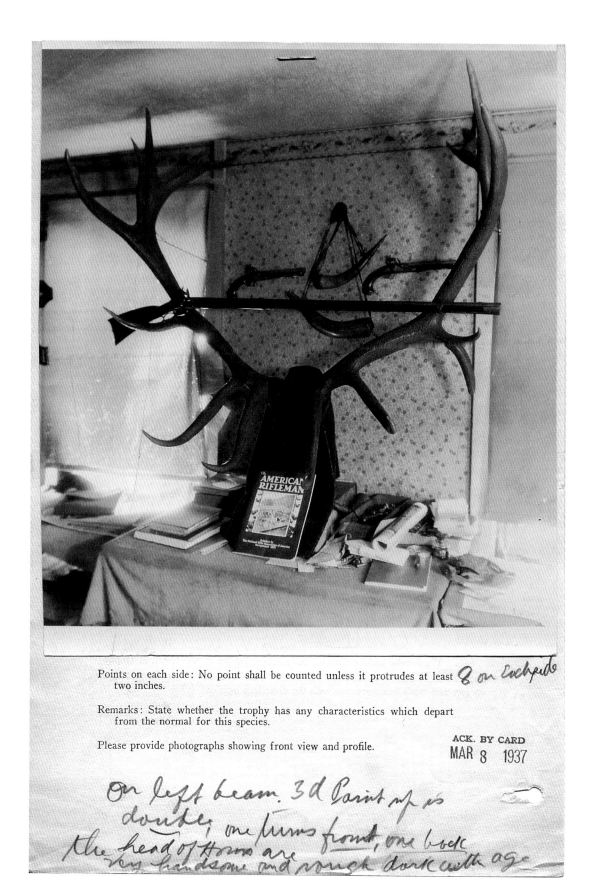

Points on each side: No point shall be counted unless it protrudes at least two inches. 8 on each side

Remarks: State whether the trophy has any characteristics which depart from the normal for this species.

Please provide photographs showing front view and profile.

ACK. BY CARD
MAR 8 1937

On left beam. 3d Point up is double, one turns front, one back
the head of Horns are very handsome and rough dark with age

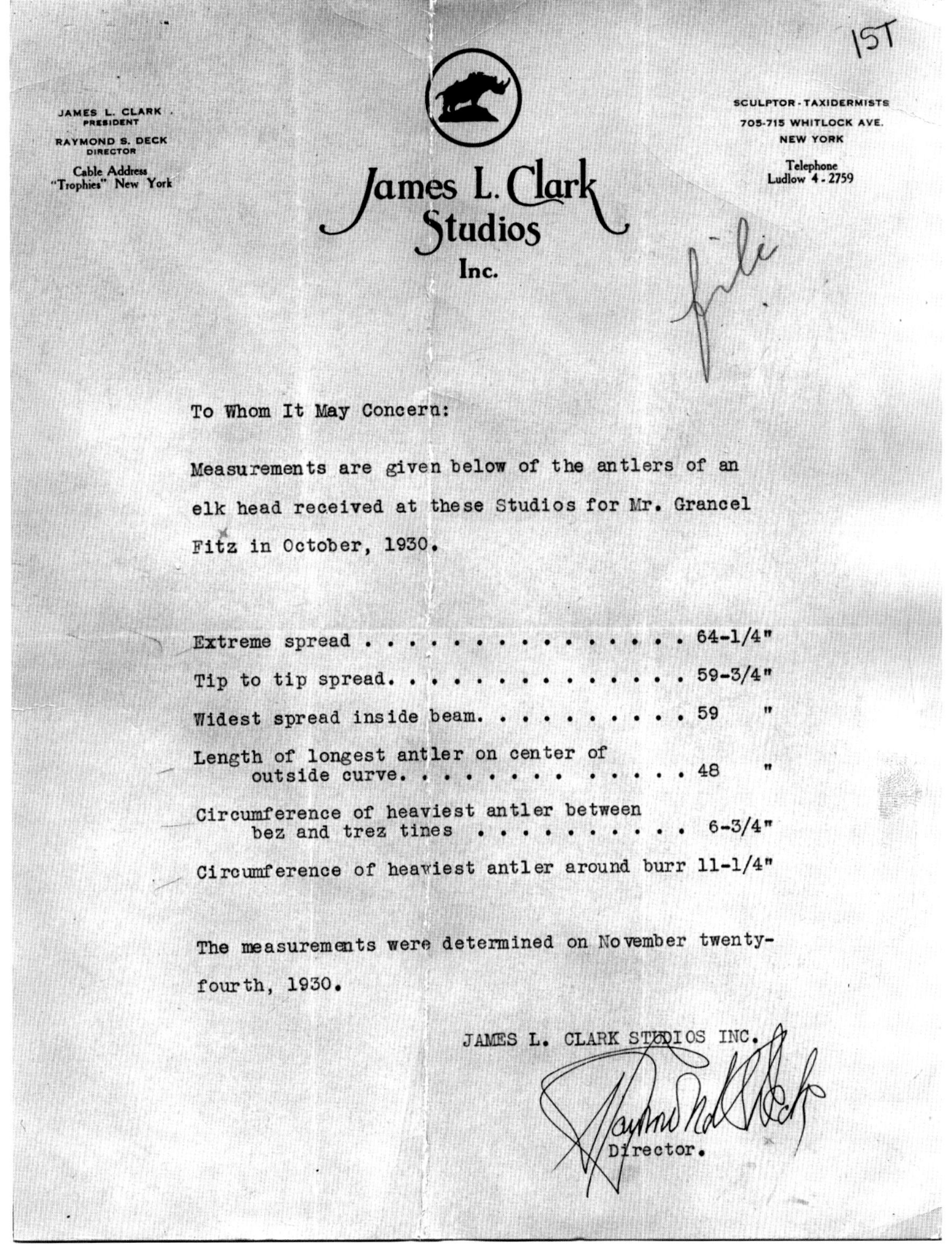

1ST

JAMES L. CLARK
PRESIDENT
RAYMOND S. DECK
DIRECTOR
Cable Address
"Trophies" New York

James L. Clark
Studios
Inc.

SCULPTOR - TAXIDERMISTS
705-715 WHITLOCK AVE.
NEW YORK
Telephone
Ludlow 4 - 2759

file

To Whom It May Concern:

Measurements are given below of the antlers of an elk head received at these Studios for Mr. Grancel Fitz in October, 1930.

Extreme spread . . . . 64-1/4"

Tip to tip spread. . . . . 59-3/4"

Widest spread inside beam. . . . . 59 "

Length of longest antler on center of
outside curve. . . . . 48 "

Circumference of heaviest antler between
bez and trez tines . . . . 6-3/4"

Circumference of heaviest antler around burr 11-1/4"

The measurements were determined on November twenty-fourth, 1930.

JAMES L. CLARK STUDIOS INC.

Raymond S. Deck

Director.

The various score charts and photos on the previous pages were donated to the Club's archives by the Fitz family. Most of them represent trophies that were included in the first two records books published by the Club before the advent of our current scoring system. Grancel Fitz and his wife, Betty, are credited with tireless work in re-evaluating these records.

Fitz's elk appeared as the introductory photograph to Harold E. Anthony's chapter, "The Wapiti – Description and Distribution" from the Club's 1939 edition of *North American Big Game.*

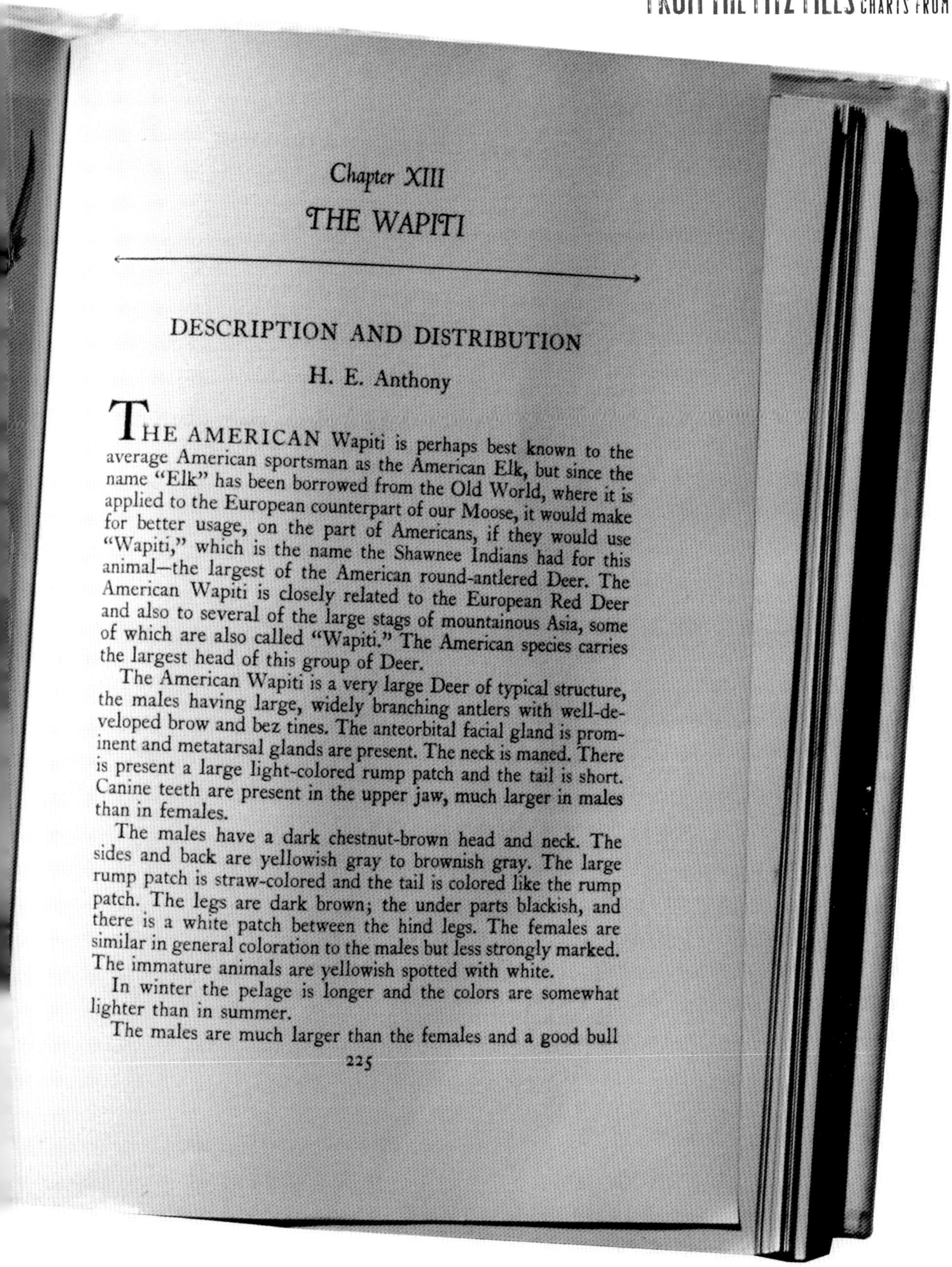

Chapter XIII
THE WAPITI

DESCRIPTION AND DISTRIBUTION

H. E. Anthony

THE AMERICAN Wapiti is perhaps best known to the average American sportsman as the American Elk, but since the name "Elk" has been borrowed from the Old World, where it is applied to the European counterpart of our Moose, it would make for better usage, on the part of Americans, if they would use "Wapiti," which is the name the Shawnee Indians had for this animal—the largest of the American round-antlered Deer. The American Wapiti is closely related to the European Red Deer and also to several of the large stags of mountainous Asia, some of which are also called "Wapiti." The American species carries the largest head of this group of Deer.

The American Wapiti is a very large Deer of typical structure, the males having large, widely branching antlers with well-developed brow and bez tines. The anteorbital facial gland is prominent and metatarsal glands are present. The neck is maned. There is present a large light-colored rump patch and the tail is short. Canine teeth are present in the upper jaw, much larger in males than in females.

The males have a dark chestnut-brown head and neck. The sides and back are yellowish gray to brownish gray. The large rump patch is straw-colored and the tail is colored like the rump patch. The legs are dark brown; the under parts blackish, and there is a white patch between the hind legs. The females are similar in general coloration to the males but less strongly marked. The immature animals are yellowish spotted with white.

In winter the pelage is longer and the colors are somewhat lighter than in summer.

The males are much larger than the females and a good bull

225

ACKNOWLEDGEMENTS

AN AMERICAN ELK RETROSPECTIVE

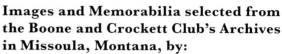

First, we would like to extend a special thank you to all of the past chairmen of the Boone and Crockett Club's Records Committee for their hard work and dedication:

Alfred Ely, Jr. *(deceased)*
Harold E. Anthony *(deceased)*
Samuel B. Webb *(deceased)*
Robert S. Waters *(deceased)*
Elmer M. Rusten *(deceased)*
Jack S. Parker
Philip L. Wright *(deceased)*
Walter H. White *(deceased)*
C. Randall Byers *(deceased)*
Eldon L. "Buck" Buckner – Current

Images and Memorabilia selected from the Boone and Crockett Club's Archives in Missoula, Montana, by:

Julie T. Houk
Karlie Slayer
Justin Spring

Editorial Contributors:

Keith Balfourd
Eldon L. "Buck" Buckner
Richard T. Hale
Theodore J. Holsten
Julie T. Houk
Howard P. Monsour, Jr.
Jack Reneau
Justin Spring

Proofreading by: Jule Banville, Missoula, Montana

Records Archive Filing Ace:
Wendy Nickelson

An American Elk Retrospective was designed and produced by Julie T. Houk, Director of Publications, with the assistance of Karlie Slayer, Assistant Designer, for the Boone and Crockett Club using Baskerville and Roadkill typefaces.

Printed in the USA by Lifetouch, Inc. through Four Colour Print Group

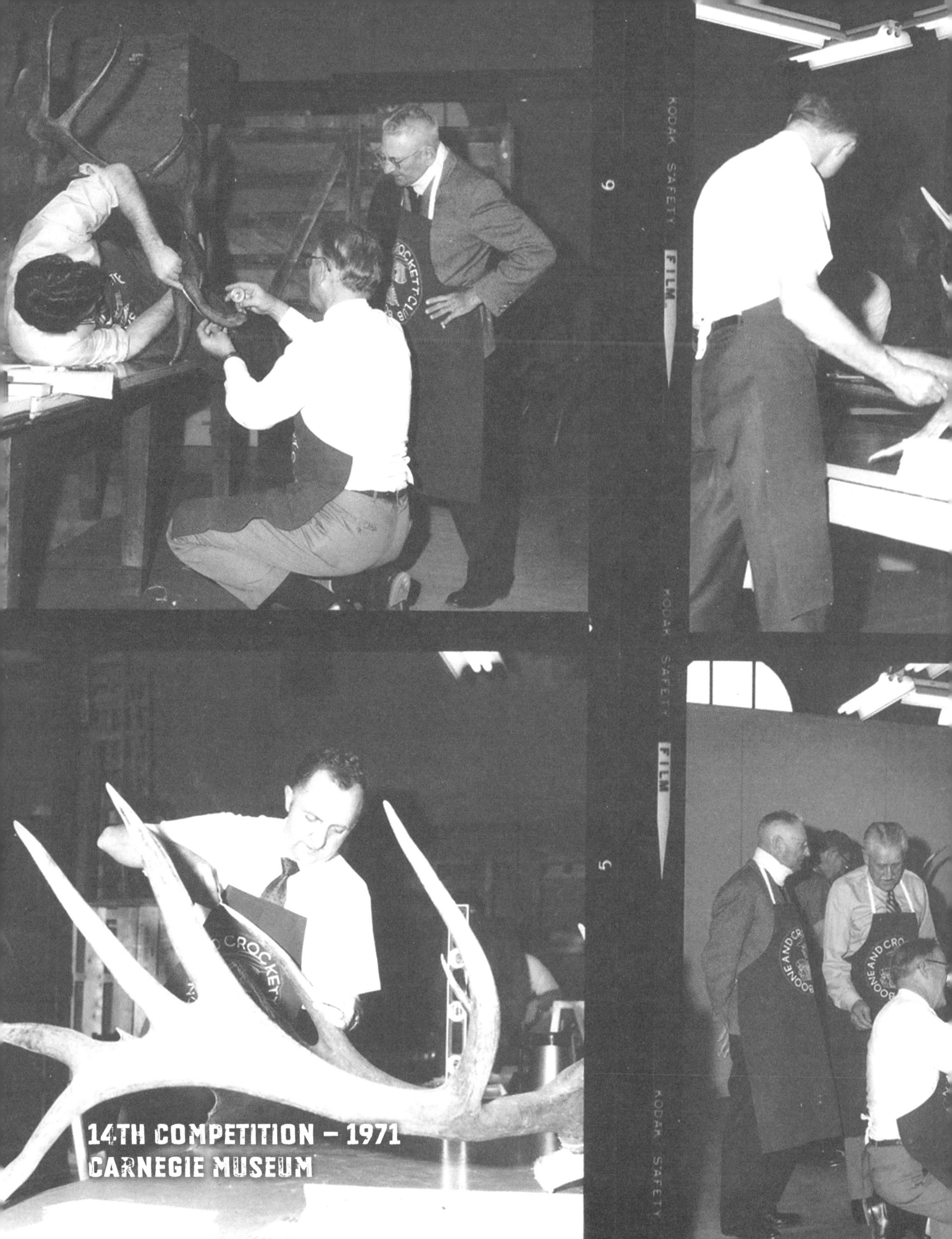

14TH COMPETITION – 1971
CARNEGIE MUSEUM